Conflicting Political Ideas in Liberal Democracies

Terence H. Qualter

Nelson Canada

© Nelson Canada,
a division of Thomson Canada Limited

Published in 1990 by
Nelson Canada,
A Division of Thomson Canada Limited
1120 Birchmount Road
Scarborough, Ontario
M1K 5G4

Originally published in 1986 by Methuen Publications.

Canadian Cataloguing in Publication Data

Qualter, Terence H., 1925-
 Conflicting political ideas in liberal democracies

Includes bibliographical references and index.
ISBN 0-17-603495-1

1. Democracy. 2. Political science. I. Title.

JC423.Q34 1989   320.5'1   C89-090676-9

Printed and bound in Canada

1 2 3 4 5 CA 93 92 91 90

Contents

Preface

The central assumption of this book is that some awareness of the philosophic or ideological foundations of any society is necessary for an understanding of its institutions and mechanics. Judgments about the effectiveness or propriety of any organized activity, be it the foreign policy of a national government, or the academic priorities of a university, are based on expectations about what the organization can or should do. In the political world people pass conflicting judgments because their expectations are based on widely different perceptions of the nature of society and of its purposes. Even excluding the options of Soviet communism, fascism, military dictatorship, apartheid, theocratic absolutism, or hereditary autocracy, and focussing solely on the familiar territory of the liberal democracies, one still finds a wide diversity of political values based on conflicting interpretations of the world. People disagree in their support or opposition to different political parties or in their approval or disapproval of government policies on such matters as taxation, defence, capital punishment, social welfare, education, or the sale of alcohol, because they do not all share the same understanding of either the nature of the state or the objectives of its activities. Their perceptions of the meaning of liberty, their different views on the nature and origin of rights, or the value they place on equality lead them to different solutions to the problems of unemployment, religious or racial tolerance, urban renewal, or the mechanics of international trade. They disagree about the competence or willingness of parties or bureaucracies to solve critical issues, because above all, they disagree about the nature of the issues themselves.

The world of politics does not have an objective reality of its own, impartially available to all. Instead it exists as a set of perceptions in the minds of participants and observers. How one views the nature or the purpose of the state has a profound impact on what one expects it to do or refrain from doing. Some see naturally egoistic individuals competing in a social organization whose major purpose is to bring order to their acquisitive instincts. For others, the state is an organic unity in which naturally social beings work together to realize their full human potential. For some, liberty exists when the state does not interfere in the freedom of the marketplace, all other liberties being derived from economic liberty. For others, liberty has a more varied, positive connotation and is being threatened by many, so political and social liberty for all may require restraining the economic liberty of some. An appreciation of the diversity and origin of views on these and other related issues is essential if we are to understand why some demand of government what others are bitterly against.

My goal here is to introduce in an outline, specifically designed for the student as yet unfamiliar with the complexity of the questions, some of the major ideological issues that divide opinions within the ranks of the liberal democracies. The focus is deliberately limited to the liberal democracies, especially the Canadian version. Alternative views of the world are set aside, not because they are unimportant, nor from any narrow spirit of chauvinism, but because this text is presented simply as the first step in a longer study of politics. It is argued that before engaging in an analysis of other ideologies, or other systems, one needs a firm grasp of one's own ideological principles. Before we can examine or evaluate others, we need to understand ourselves. The object of the book, therefore, is some clarification of the diversity of the political world views that are part of our own liberal democratic tradition.

While the broad territory of liberal democracy may encompass many perceptions and understandings of what to do and how to do it, most of us as individuals, living much of the time surrounded by people who think like us, easily imagine that our version of reality *is* reality, so those who dispute with us must be either misguided fools or wicked evildoers. It helps, therefore, to know where one's world view originated, for none of the ideas held by any of us today has existed from all eternity nor did they spring spontaneously into existence when we were born. The book is directed particularly to students in their introductory years who wish some clearer insight into the nature of those issues which divide or unite them. It is hoped that it might make any later, more detailed, examination of the political system much more productive. The success or failure of parties, governments, or bureaucracies become more intelligible to those who have some idea about what they were supposed to be doing, and for what reason.

The following chapters deal with different conceptions of the nature and purpose of the state; the nature and origin of rights; the specific right of freedom of expression and its limitations; the complicated and interwoven questions of liberty and equality; the bounds to the moral authority of majorities; the right to resist the law versus the obligation to obey it; and the right of property, with the restrictions which have or should be imposed on the exercise of that right. All these lead to a clearer exposition of the assumptions and goals of the three major ideologies that co-exist within the broader ideology of liberal democracy: liberalism, conservatism, and democratic socialism. A final question to be asked is that if liberal democracy can accommodate so many diverse threads, what are the unifying factors? No exclusive dichotomies exist, but it is possible to establish criteria enabling one to say, "These nations come closest to the ideals of liberal democracy, while these are furthest from them." In the more liberal democratic societies where dissent and disagreement are broadly tolerated, people may properly disagree about a wider variety of issues or understandings of life without losing the rights of citizenship, or suffering any great social or political penalty. In the less democratic societies, the range of legitimate disagreements is narrowly defined. Most non-democratic regimes impose close ideological conformity. The liberal democracies can agree to disagree about many more things, although not about all things, and so must develop institutions that can accept a diversity of opinion.

Books do not normally spring spontaneously into existence. This one was a long time germinating. Its themes provided the subject matter of introductory lectures offered on and off over a period of many years. The ideas have gradually been refined in response to the reactions and interests of hundreds of students. Although not aware of it at the time, those students were all part authors of this text. I thank them for their contributions. More specifically I would like to express my very great appreciation of two colleagues, Richard Nutbrown and Sandra Burt, who read the draft of the present text and offered detailed criticisms. They are not to be held responsible for the fact that I sometimes chose to ignore their suggestions.

CHAPTER ONE

Politics and Political Science

The need for politics arises from the conflict of human desires and from different understandings of the world. If everybody agreed, there would be no need for government or politics, for all would simply go ahead and do whatever it was they wanted to do. But this is not the situation around us. Even with the best will in the world we disagree not only about what should be done but also about ways of doing those things. On any issue of consequence, people will honestly and sincerely hold different opinions. One should not expect to find, in any random gathering of people, a unanimous opinion on any issue: capital punishment, the right of public servants to strike, the sale of government owned corporations, the proper status of the French language in Ontario, the times and places where one should legally be able to buy beer, and so on. On none of these things are we agreed, and the people who disagree with our position are not necessarily, for that reason, fools or rogues.

In a dictatorship such diversity of opinion is intolerable. Where dictators demand conformity, dissent must be suppressed. Criticism of the "official" line is suspect—it may even be treasonable. But a liberal democracy,[1] such as Canada, accepts the fact and propriety of a certain level of disagreement. It is even given official status by recognizing and giving formal respect — with a special salary — to a Leader of the Opposition. Opposition, at least within broadly defined limits, is a legitimate, honourable activity. Legitimacy of dissent is an important characteristic of liberal democracy.

Given the fact of a diversity of opinion, how are decisions to be reached? For, on any disputed question, no matter how long it is discussed, at some point debate must cease and a decision be taken. Differences could be settled by each side attacking physically those who are in opposition. It would be possible to resolve, say, the capital punishment debate by letting supporters and opponents have it out with guns and bombs. Or one could turn to a "strong arm," a dictator empowered to bludgeon into silence all challenges to the official line. All of us are, I suppose, occasionally attracted to this idea of the strong leader who will put a halt to "squabbling," who will "get things done" and "act for the common good" by silencing "disturbers of public order," "disruptive radicals," and indeed, dissenters in general. But before turning to this option, reflect that *you* might not be the dictator or it might be *your* ideas that are held to be disruptive squabbling and "getting things done" might involve discounting *your* qualms and objections.

An alternative way of resolving disagreement is through political action. This involves the acceptance of controversy while allowing for the expression of alternative points of view. Politics provides institutionalized or legitimized procedures for resolving disputes about what to do, and when and how to do it. *Institutionalized* and *legitimized* are key words in the vocabulary of political science. In the simplest sense, quite adequate for the present purpose, institutionalized procedures are those that have been broadly agreed upon in advance as appropriate procedures. They are the understood rules, either written or existing by long-standing convention, by which we have agreed to be governed. In Canada, for example, an election is an institutionalized procedure for selecting a government. Most accept this as proper, with even those upset or disappointed by the results of a particular election still acknowledging that the elected party has a right to govern and to have its laws obeyed. We would be outraged if a government defeated at the polls refused to give up office. On the other hand, at least in a liberal democracy, a coup d'état is a non-institutionalized way of changing a government, so although we might obey such a government out of fear, we might feel no moral obligation to it. There would be no sense of "rightness" about its actions.

Legitimate behaviour is socially sanctioned behaviour, or behaviour that is accepted by the community at large as right and proper, undertaken by those acknowledged to have the right to undertake it. Legitimate rule does not necessarily mean democratic rule. Other rulers have acquired legitimacy by establishing to the satisfaction of the ruled that they are the true inheritors of kingly power, or are specially divinely blessed, or possess some other unique attribute that qualifies them to govern. Whatever the composition of its government, any regime must establish its legitimacy by gaining some level of at least tacit support, if it is to rule by anything other than brute force. In our era, some of the formalities of democratic machinery are a principal legitimizing agency. Democracy itself is a relatively novel idea, unwelcome in most territories through most of history, with its practice still untried in much of the world. However, since the middle of the nineteenth century the rhetoric of democracy has commanded enormous respect, so much so that modern dictators go through fanciful charades with all the formalities of elections (without the possibility of defeating approved candidates) to demonstrate that they are democratic.

Liberal democracy accepts the propriety of resolving issues through advocacy by conflicting interests. Those who argue that "we should rise above politics, to work together for the common good" are, frankly, talking nonsense. Politics offers a way of deciding what the common good is. We have politics because, on many important issues, there is no consensus on the common good. There is, for example, the matter of capital punishment. It would be hard to find an agreed common good between those who see capital punishment as basic retributive justice and deterrent action for the good of society; and the abolitionists, who view capital punishment as itself another form of murder, ineffective as a deterrent. Or, as another example, does the common good require that social services be cut in order to reduce the burden of taxation or that taxes be raised in order to provide economic security for all? J.D.B. Miller addressed this situation:

> A common concern will sometimes be found in society at large, and sometimes not. More often, it will not be there. That is to say, societies of a developed character, which contain a wide variety of competing and differential interests, will only now and then show sufficient agreement to enable us to say that a common concern exists throughout the society.[2]

Commonly we will find in practice that those who argue for forgetting about politics in the interests of the common good are really saying, "I know what I think, and I don't want to have to consider any one else's opinion." On many local councils, school boards, and club executives, you will hear it said, "Let's keep politics out of this." This view reveals a profound misunderstanding of the nature of a liberal democratic society, which in essence is based on the propriety of politics. Political activity to resolve conflict is at the foundation of our way of life, without which we would not be a liberal democracy.

The tasks of government and politics, therefore, are to make choices among alternative courses of action. The goal is to reach a workable understanding, to reach consensus; but when no further agreement is possible, the goal is to make decisions. What is decided may not necessarily be what *everyone* wants — that in most cases being impossible — nor even what anybody in particular wants; but at least the solutions must not be totally unacceptable to too many people, too often. It may seem odd, but a strong case could be made for the proposition that a good liberal democratic government probably has *everybody* slightly upset with it most of the time. If any one segment of society — employers, workers, farmers, importers, oil companies, civil servants, or whoever — is completely satisfied with the government, if government policy gives one segment everything it wants, you can be sure that some other group is getting an unfair deal. If *all* are to get something of what they want or are entitled to, no one group can expect to get everything it wants.

Politics deals with disagreements and their reconciliation, with gathering effective support for some proposals rather than others. From this perspective, the first obligation of the politician is to be aware of how options are restricted, often limited to a choice among several undesirable courses of action. Idealists, dreamers, and neophytes in politics, or even barroom and clubhouse politicians, often declare that given power they could solve the problems of the world. Experienced politicians, on the other hand, acknowledge the limiting power of forces beyond their control, accepting the futility of demanding from any system more than it can give. They accept that, as they live in a world of nation states, they cannot act in total disregard for the reactions of other nations. They understand, for example, that if they wish to continue selling exports, they cannot cut off all imports. Above all, in domestic politics, they know that because governments depend upon the support of electors, they cannot adopt policies that will offend too deeply, for too long, too many of those electors. The political world is an exceedingly complicated place where those who offer simple solutions to complex problems can do an enormous amount of harm. The leader who would change the world, even slightly, must first accept the fact of the world as it is. Politics is thus concerned with arriving at *workable* solutions about what to do and how to get it done.

It is government's responsibility to find balances, compromises, or harmony between the competing and irreconcilable demands made upon it. In liberal democratic politics compromise is often a sign, not of weakness, but of maturity, a recognition that no one has all the answers to anything nor all the rights. Of course, on some issues, especially those which arouse deep moral conviction, no compromise is possible. In these cases those with responsibility must make the best judgment they can, living with their decision and its consequences until changing circumstances lead them to think it is time to change. In a democratic society governments must govern; they must make choices, often difficult, that may offend and anger some people.

This is politics. It is concerned with decision-making and, by extension, with the institutions, practices, and events that affect decisions: the rise and fall of political parties, the mechanics of the election system, the influence of public opinion on policy, the amount of control the elected representatives have or should have over the permanent bureaucracy, the protection of civil rights, and so on.

THE STUDY OF POLITICS

For many, politics means arguing about such things as the advantages or causes of higher or lower interest rates, the priority of solving inflation before unemployment, the allocation of resources to new highways rather than higher education, the direction of foreign policy, and so on. But while this may be politics, it is not political science.

Political science, at least in one of its aspects, is directed to the scientific, objective analysis of politics.

> So far as I can judge, "political science" is still the name which carries meaning to the general public. . . . The word science here indicates simply that there exists an academic tradition of the study of politics, a discipline communicated from teacher to pupil, by speech and writing, for some 2,500 years now. It does not mean that this discipline claims to be a "natural science," or that it could be improved by copying the methods of physics and chemistry more exactly.[3]

Political science is concerned less with the political debate as such, than with the origin and resolution of the varying positions. It attempts to explain the support for conflicting arguments and attends to the machinery, processes, and pressures for resolving political disputes. Political scientists attempt to describe and explain political phenomena and to develop theories that will explain them in a more complete and generalized way.

The study of politics as outlined above has, as one objective, the development of an empirical science of politics, that is to say, the development of ideas and explanations based on observations and hypotheses that can be tested in the "real world." One of the stated goals of this empirical political science is to be "value free." This means that political scientists should attempt to set aside values, or judgments of right and wrong, so that they can focus their attention on how the political system actually does work, without being concerned with how it ought to work or the quality of the ends to which it might be directed. There are some who are sceptical about the degree to which the empiricists are able to stand apart from their value orientations. It might be contended, for example, that even the selection of a topic for empirical observation involves a value judgment as to the significance of that topic. This is, however, not the place to deal with the controversy. Such an account of political science still leaves unanswered a great many questions about how to proceed with the description and what sort of theories offer the most meaningful explanation. There is a vast literature on the methods of political analysis.[4] This, however, is another topic beyond our present scope. The student proceeding further in political science will have many opportunities to study contending schools of political science.

NICCOLO MACHIAVELLI

Born in Florence May 3, 1469; died in Florence June 22, 1527.

Machiavelli was deeply involved in Florentine politics, so when the Republic fell and the Medici were returned to power (1512) Machiavelli was dismissed from office, never to be fully employed again. As one who lived and breathed politics, when excluded from its practice Machiavelli spent the rest of his life writing about politics, power, and the state. He was, above all, the exponent of the realities of power politics and the secular national state. But he was not, as he is popularly portrayed, an advocate of evil and deceit. He was, indeed, a passionate patriot and nationalist. His principal works were The Prince *(1513),* The Discourses on the First Ten Books of Titus Livius *(written between 1512 and 1516), and* The History of Florence *(published 1532).*

For further reading see:
Burnham, James. The Machiavellians. New York: John Day, 1943.
Butterfield, Herbert. The Statecraft of Machiavelli. London: G. Bell, 1940.
Strauss, Leo. Thoughts on Machiavelli. Glencoe: Free Press, 1958.
Anglo, Sydney. Machiavelli: A Dissection. London: Gollancz, 1969.

But while a detailed examination and evaluation of empirical observation and theory belong to another time and place, it is crucial to the understanding of the purpose and method of this book to delve a little further into the implications of this separation of facts and values. The concept of such a separation is not a twentieth-century invention. Indeed, the most famous exponent of the "realist" approach to politics was the Renaissance politician and diplomat Niccolo Machiavelli (1469–1527). In setting aside moral questions, Machiavelli and those guided by him did not consider themselves immoral. They were amoral — believing it to be possible to separate the study of politics from the study of morality. Machiavelli did not *ignore* questions of ideals nor deny their importance. He was a passionate believer in the cause of a unified Italian republic, a patriot who believed the survival of the nation state to be an overriding imperative. He did, however, believe that *study* of political means could be separated from the assertion of political goals. The wise student of politics would be concerned only with understanding the world as it is, without passing judgments on how it might or ought to be.[5] He stated his case clearly:

> But my intention being to write something of use to those who understand, it appears to me more proper to go to the real truth of the matter than to its imagination; and many have imagined republics and principalities which have never been seen or known to exist in reality; for how we live is so far removed from how we ought to live, that he who abandons what is done for what ought to be done, will rather learn to bring about his own ruin than his preservation.[6]

One useful and revealing illustration of Machiavelli's approach to politics is indicated by his assessment of the political role of religion. On the question of the importance of religion, most people would take one of two very different positions:

(1)   There is a God who is interested in human affairs. Religion, of some specific form or another, provides an appropriate or approved way of communicating with God. Religion generally, or at least some "true" religion, ought to be encouraged and supported in the society if the final goal of all people, eternal salvation, is to be reached.

(2)   The contrary point of view is that, as there is no God, all religions are by definition false. Religion is, at best, a harmless superstition; at worst, the instrument by which the few, for whatever reason, exploit the credulity of the faithful. Society would be better off if it freed itself from the constraints of religious belief and the power of the churches.

Machiavelli's approach, however, was different. He seemed indifferent to the truth or validity of any particular religion. Nevertheless, he argued that religion should be preserved and encouraged because a religious faith is *useful*. Belief in God helps keep a people law-abiding not only out of fear of the law but also as a matter of conscience. Also, a people united in one religion tend also to be united in other matters. Therefore, religious faith, even if it is simply superstition, should be upheld because of its useful consequences. This is how he expressed it:

> It is therefore the duty of princes and heads of republics to uphold the foundations of the religion of their countries, for then it is easy to keep their people religious, and consequently well conducted and united. And therefore everything that tends to favor religion (even though it were believed to be false) should be received and availed of to strengthen it; and this should be done the more, the wiser the rulers are, and the better they understand the natural course of things.[7]

Machiavelli went on to an attack on the Christian religion not on grounds of doctrinal truths, which he thought to be irrelevant, but because the Christian virtues of humility, charity, love, forgiveness, etc., were unsuited to the building of the strong, united Italy he wanted. He favoured the gods of ancient Rome, again, not out of any concern for theological truth but because the old gods offered more practical virtues.

BENITO MUSSOLINI

Born July 29, 1883; died April 28, 1945.

Italian dictator and founder of Italian fascism. Led the march on Rome (October 28, 1922) that overthrew the government and established the fascist regime in Italy. He directed the invasion and capture of Ethiopia in 1935–36. He aided Franco in the Spanish civil war (1936–39) and established friendly relations with Hitler's Nazi Germany, entering the Second World War in alliance with Germany. After the allied invasion of Italy in 1943 Mussolini was deposed. He was rescued by the Germans and held under their protection but was finally assassinated by partisans in 1945.

The same view of the practical utility of a faith, even a false faith, was expressed by the Italian dictator Benito Mussolini in a speech in Naples in 1922:

> We have created our myth. The myth is a faith, it is passion. It is not necessary that it shall be a reality. It is a reality by the fact that it is a goad, a hope, a faith, that it is courage.[8]

POLITICS AND POLITICAL SCIENCE / 9

The basis of this Machiavellian view of political ideas is that people need a faith, so by all means give them one. It doesn't have to be true in any objective sense for people to believe it and fight in defence of it. The fact of believing in it makes it true to its believers. People will work better when they have a cause to believe in. So give them a cause but design it to lead to the desired political goals. Ideas like democracy, or national self-determination, cease to have any force or validity in themselves. They become simply slogans or myths through which the powerful recruit the weak in the furtherance of their own ambitions. To the Machiavellians, this was not cynicism, but down to earth realism.

Machiavelli's general message is that, at least in matters of politics, we must accept humanity as it really is, with all its warts and blemishes. We must deal with real people in the real world, rather than with people as we imagine they might be or ought to be. Machiavelli was not, of course, an empirical political scientist. Far from being a neutral observer, he was a committed advocate of a strong Italian nation state. However, in his recognition that the world of real politics was not the world as imagined by philosophers and theologians, he separated the world as it is from the world as it ought to be. The modern tradition of an objective political science accepts this division. But in attempting a theoretical explanation of political phenomena, it brings to bear sophisticated techniques of survey research and the specialized knowledge provided by behavioural psychology, sociology, and other disciplines, all of which were unknown to Machiavelli.

If Machiavelli's view of politics was correct, we could not profitably study political values as ends in themselves. We could look at values or ideals as historical curiosities, as things people have believed in from time to time, or we could attempt to explain how different peoples came to hold certain beliefs and the consequences of their faith in those beliefs. But we could not examine values as having an intrinsic merit of their own, as real objectives of human endeavour. Moral assessments would have little independent explanatory power.

POLITICS AS "WHY?"

While some aspects of the study of politics are profitably separated from the study of values, those values remain an inherent part of the political world. Although we might be able to distinguish the "is" from the "ought" for purposes of study, they are both part of the world of political action. The decision-making process is affected everywhere by the values of those who make the decisions and those who are affected by them:

The political actions of every individual in the political system, at whatever level, are only comprehensible within some value framework. Individuals are prepared to fight for causes, often realistically hopeless causes, or to undergo savage ill-treatment and torture in the belief that some political values are superior to others.[9]

There is, thus, another level in the study of politics, reaching directly to the value judgments behind the decision-making machinery; going beyond what is done, and how it is done, to ask why it is done and why in that way. One must ask what assumptions about people and their society would lead one to argue for, or against, say, the public ownership of natural resources? Or, what views of the purpose of the state lead some to advocate, or oppose, universal, free, and compulsory education? Political science at this level returns the questions of right and wrong, and good and bad, to the forefront of discussion.

Any political system will reflect the concepts of right and wrong and the aspirations or fears of those who direct it, and of those who, from time to time, determine its particular format. It is argued here that we cannot therefore meaningfully judge the efficiency of a system without some understanding of the ends that guide it. There are therefore two kinds of questions. One kind relates to the skill with which a regime achieves the goals it has set for itself. The other kind relates to the quality of the goals themselves: their moral worth or internal rationality.

Many are at first puzzled by the raising of these issues. Having been raised to one set of assumptions, absorbed without question, it does not at first occur to some that their personal moral judgments are not immutable, eternal, self-evident facts, but simply time and space based faiths. It is not easy to accept that no matter how intensely or sincerely you believe whatever it is you do believe, if you were born in another time or another place within another society, you would probably just as sincerely and intensely believe other things. This is not intended to imply that all faiths are equally valid nor that all are free to believe anything they wish. Faiths that have "survival value," that serve societies well over a long period of time, reveal a discoverable and explainable rationality and logical consistency. They tend to be objectively defensible and shared by others with similar backgrounds. So, while questions about the working of the system are important, interesting, and worthy of attention, they are not the most useful starting point for an understanding of a political system. A study of the machinery of politics in any society becomes more meaningful if it is set within the context of the goals that the society and its members have set for themselves. One should not be content to just ask how a system works; one should also ask what the users of the system think it is intended to do. The study of ends is not something distinct from the study of "practical" politics but is part of the knowledge necessary to assess the effectiveness of the practical politics.

There are, of course, many versions of what the ends of political activity ought to be. And given what has already been said about the legitimacy of dissent in a liberal democracy, it would be both improper and futile to proclaim any one interpretation as the final solution. The following pages offer a few possible explanations of political life as it is in a liberal democracy like Canada. The object is not a survey of Western political thought but an examination of those elements that make us what we are, with their origins and their diversity. It is not an exhaustive listing but it does illustrate the most important message of this book: Even within the limits of a liberal democratic society there are several different understandings of the fundamental meaning and purpose of life, and these basic understandings will guide and explain the varied responses individuals make to specific situations. We each deal with the "real world" in terms of our very subjective perceptions of what this world is and ought to be.

One can begin by asserting that perhaps there is no transcendental purpose — no grand design, no ultimate meaning or end of life beyond continued existence. Consider what Professor Michael Oakeshott said in his inaugural lecture at the London School of Economics in 1951:

> In political activity, then, men sail a boundless and bottomless sea; there is neither harbour for shelter nor floor for anchorage, neither starting-place, nor appointed destination. The enterprise is to keep afloat on an even keel; the sea is both friend and enemy; and the seamanship consists in using the resources of a traditional manner of behaviour in order to make a friend of every hostile occasion.[10]

This appears to be a depressing philosophy, suggesting that we have come from nowhere and are going nowhere. It implies that the only point of life is to keep on living and to make the most of whatever long and short term opportunities circumstances allow us. There is no meaning to what we do. There is no final end or goal to be achieved beyond that which we impose on the world. We are largely guided, but not totally controlled, by our traditional way of doing things. And political philosophies, rather than being blueprints or maps helping us to our destination, are more appropriately considered as rationalizations of what we have been doing. By this view, philosophies are guides to the past not blueprints for the future. They have no independent causal existence, although they may be extremely important in explaining ourselves to ourselves. This is, perhaps, Oakeshott's major point. We find understanding of ourselves only through an aware-ness of our own political traditions and beliefs. We can explain ourselves, our world, and what we expect of the future only in terms of our accumu-lated traditions, including our beliefs and philosophies of life. In a sense we make a self-fulfilling prophecy — by believing in a goal or purpose, we make that goal a reality. And, of course, this is part of Oakeshott's argu-ment: our vision of the future reflects our image of the past, a projection of our entire experience. Oakeshott's views are most unsettling to those who want the certainty of some objective meaning to life or some universal external authority providing a reason for existence beyond the mere fact of living. Many need the confidence that there is real explanatory power, real causal force, in the things they believe in. They need a "truth" more universal, more authoritative, than mere tradition and belief. But, while there is widespread belief that life must have some "real" meaning and end, there is less agreement on the nature of that end.

MICHAEL OAKESHOTT

Born December 11, 1901.

Professor Oakeshott was Professor of Political Science at the London School of Economics from 1951 to 1969 and is currently Professor Emeritus at the University of London. He is the author of several books on political philosophy, including Social and Political Doctrines of Contemporary Europe *(1939),* Hobbes' Leviathan *(1946), and* Rationalism in Politics and Other Essays *(1962).*

TELEOLOGICAL THEORIES

One approach is through *teleological* explanations. Teleology is a consider-ation of those doctrines or studies of final causes that assume some notion of design or purpose in nature. A teleologist explains the essence of things in terms of their ultimate purpose or final end. Teleologists evaluate the present in terms of their concept of the future. Drawing back to Oakeshott's imagery, they focus on the destination, which explains the purpose of the journey.

In our society the most familiar teleology is the Christian explanation of human existence. Christianity views the whole of creation in terms of God's grand design for the salvation of the human race. We are what we are because of our eternal destiny. In the simplest terms, Christians believe that they are created in God's image, with the physical universe created for their use and enjoyment and as a manifestation of the power and glory of God. For more than a thousand years of European history, from the Christian conversion of the Roman Empire until the dawning of the new age of scientific rationalism, few disputed the proposition that church and state had a joint responsibility to work together for the spiritual and material well-being of all. There may have been bitter arguments about where the powers of king or bishop began and ended. Ambitious and cynical rulers might often have exploited the simple faith of the many for their own selfish ends. But the overriding principle remained clear: The state was to be a Christian state, promoting and protecting Christian living, and the church was to support the state by stressing the moral obligation to obey the laws.[11] In accordance with this doctrine medieval Christians assigned to the state a much more positive moral role than would be acceptable to nineteenth-century individualists. In contrast to the autonomous individualism of nineteenth-century industrial society, the early Christian church recognized as the good society that which actively promoted the moral development of its people. In a truly Christian community each individual bore a share of the responsibility for the collective good of all.

Those who today turn to this Christian teleological world view that humanity has an ultimate purpose, realized in an afterlife, will be inclined to express their political values in moral and spiritual terms. They are likely to be concerned with the quality of their society's moral standards. In modern Canada they will tend to see as salient issues such matters as the spread of pornography, the breakdown of marriage, excessive materialism, and the general societal conditions that lead to these things. In accepting that one of the responsibilities of the state is the moral well-being of its members, they will tend to be unhappy about leaving such questions to the free play of the marketplace and will reject the values of a "permissive society." Where, as in the contemporary United States, a "new right" urging greater free enterprise in the economy is allied with a conservative, fundamentalist Christianity, there is a strong belief that the state ought to actively intervene to promote Christian values everywhere except in the economic marketplace.

A note of caution: Nothing here is intended to imply that only Christians are concerned with moral dimensions of political issues nor that all who call themselves Christians live according to the standards outlined above. But we should expect that the Christian whose faith is more than an exercise in public relations will express Christian concerns in political behaviour. These will be indicated both in the matters regarded as important and in the ways in which such broader issues as the economy, education, and national defence are approached. The Christian teleologist should expect the state to conduct itself in a manner consistent with the ultimate purpose of human existence, which is eternal salvation.

THE UTILITARIANS

A more mundane explanation of the purpose of political life was offered by a group of nineteenth-century English political and social philosophers known as the utilitarians. For a number of reasons, which go beyond the limits of this present text, the utilitarians rejected metaphysical abstractions, declaring themselves unmoved by theological concerns. They asserted instead that the major explanation and the sole purpose of all human activity, individual and social, was "the greatest happiness of the greatest number." The primary exponent of utilitarianism was Jeremy Bentham (1748–1832), an eccentric genius who dominated English political theory both during his own lifetime and for several decades afterward. We shall come back to him from time to time in the chapters that follow. For the moment, it is enough to write a few words about his understanding of the purpose of political life.

Although in modern political thinking, especially in North America, right-wing conservatives espouse ideas partly adapted from Benthamism, Bentham in his own day was considered a dangerous radical seeking to "liberate" the new capitalist middle classes from the restrictions of a dying feudal order. This introduces one of the continuing themes of this text, which is to explain how the revival of early nineteenth-century radical liberalism has come, in some places, to be considered conservatism. The "new conservatism" of the present generation is neither new nor conservative. It is an old liberalism revived.

In one of his most important works, *The Principles of Morals and Legislation*, published in 1789 but written some years earlier, Bentham set out most clearly the guiding principle of his whole system:

Nature has placed mankind under the governance of two sovereign masters, *pain*, and *pleasure*. It is for them alone to point out what we ought to do, as well as to determine what we shall do. On the one hand the standard of right and wrong, on the other the chain of causes and effects, are fastened to their throne. They govern us in all we do, in all we say, in all we think:

every effort we can make to throw off our subjection, will serve but to demonstrate and confirm it. In words a man may pretend to abjure their empire:
but in reality he may remain subject to it all the while. The *principle of utility*
recognizes this subjection, and assumes it for the foundation of that system,
the object of which is to rear the fabric of felicity by the hands of reason and
of law.[12]

This uneasily brought together both a psychological theory and a moral
theory. The psychological theory proposed that the overriding, determining motive of human behaviour was the desire to maximize pleasure and
minimize pain. All human behaviour could be explained in terms of the
counter thrusts of pleasure and pain. Bentham's primitive psychology considered people rather as pieces of clockwork machinery, with an external
stimulus or event being processed by a fairly automatic pleasure-pain mechanism, producing a predictable response. From this psychological theory
Bentham developed a moral theory. The standard for measuring the worth
of human actions, social and individual, was their usefulness, or utility
(hence utilitarianism), in maximizing human happiness. Those things that
increased happiness were by definition good, and those things that decreased
it were, also by definition, bad. One of the unresolved problems of
Bentham's scheme was how there could be merit or virtue in doing something one was psychologically impelled to do anyway. There was also the
conflict between the pursuit of individual happiness and the social goal
of the greatest happiness of the greatest number.

As pleasure is the ultimate measure, pleasures themselves cannot be
evaluated by any other standard. Where one pleasure is as good as another,
comparisons can be made only in quantitative terms. That which gives
the greater pleasure is morally more worthy than that which gives the lesser
pleasure. To Bentham, the sole standard for judging the desirability or worth
of any social action or piece of legislation was not some abstract moral or
philosophical principle, but its anticipated utility in promoting the greatest happiness of the greatest number.

The technical name for the philosophical principle that attempts to
relate right and wrong, or good and bad, with pleasure and pain is called
"hedonism." There is a problem with the concept of hedonism that is
caused by semantic confusion between happiness and pleasure, both of
which are used to define hedonism. In the English language, the word
pleasure carries the connotation of sensual, physical, or materialistic satis-
factions; whereas the idea of happiness can invoke as well more spiritual,
intellectual, or aesthetic concepts. The Benthamites used both words, but
it was principally happiness they had in mind. Hedonism, an old concept

going back to the days of ancient Greece, was developed by Bentham with new strengths and new implications as a guide to public policy.

Bentham, of course, did not live isolated from his age. Because he was developing the concepts of utilitarianism, the great Scottish economist Adam Smith (1723–1790) was a major new intellectual force. Smith, the first theoretical economist, articulated the basic doctrines justifying free enterprise. We will come back to him in later chapters. Bentham incorporated Smith's economic theories in the particular application of his utilitarian creed. Bentham came to believe that the maximum human happiness would be reached through the minimum government interference in economic affairs. The free play of the marketplace was defended not as an abstract principle of rights but as that policy having the greatest utility in promoting happiness. This association of philosophic utilitarianism and economic capitalism was largely a historical accident. At another time or in other circumstances, Bentham might well have reached different conclusions. Nevertheless, the association is vital, for from the combination of the two ideas emerged the ideology of capitalism, the dominant mode of thought of the last century and a half.

Utilitarianism has generally, although not universally, been a materialistic philosophy, measuring success in terms of possessions and wealth. Few today would seriously admit to being labelled utilitarians, for as a psychological-moral theory it is thoroughly discredited. But many of the assumptions of individualistic hedonism remain part of the lifestyle of the modern generation. Those who see the purpose of life in some fulfilment of the individual, as individual, free from moral commitment to the community at large, are in a sense inheritors of a philosophy of egoistic hedonism, although they are far from Bentham's own application of hedonism. From such a point of view individuals stand alone, tending not to recognize obligations to others. As individualists they feel they must achieve whatever they are capable of achieving by their own efforts, without the help of others and, most certainly, without the help of the state. Their virtues are independence, personal liberty, and self-reliance. Joint social action for some common purpose, whether organized formally through the state or by voluntary co-operation of other individuals, has a much lower appeal.

HISTORICISM

Many who learned a little history at school approached the subject as nothing more than a chronicling of past events; a collection of dates of kingships, wars, and explorations. History was an exercise in memorizing who did what, when. It seldom occurred to ask why the particular events read about were the ones chosen for the record or how one might decide which events were important, having far-reaching consequences, and which were the reflections of larger changes elsewhere. For some philosophers of history, however, history involves more than an arbitrary record. To these "historicists" history does not just happen but is governed by laws almost as precise as those of physics and chemistry, following a logical pattern of development. The historicist's task is to discover that pattern, to determine its grand design, leading to an understanding of the universal laws of historical change.

Looking at history as the unfolding of some huge scheme inevitably diminishes the status of the individual. Great individuals do not make history; they are simply the figures thrown up by history itself—individuals perceptive or lucky enough to be pushed to the front, appearing to lead events over which they have little control. Napoleon and Hitler become the creatures of history, not its creators. Those who explain the purpose of political life in terms of the privileged destiny of their own nation or race will often be historicists who see this destiny as the unfolding of historical laws. To believe that history is on your side gives added confidence and assurance of victory, and of course, confidence in victory goes a long way to making victory a reality. Further, if history follows a determined pattern, it would appear plausible that the future can be predicted and, to a small extent, manipulated. History can thus be a tool for understanding and influencing social change. The study of the past reveals the way to change the future.

Few historicist theories are totally rigid; most allow that while the general pattern is determined and predictable, this applies only to the great sweep of historical development. Within this broad pattern there is room for individual intervention. Human activity can slow the process here and speed it up there, affecting minor details somewhere else. The most influential historicist has been Karl Marx (1818–1883). His historicism explains a great deal of his enormous influence. Marx was not content just to preach revolution nor to defend the cause of the working classes against oppression. Most of his life was spent as an economic historian assembling elaborate arguments to demonstrate that history was on the side of the proletariat, so victory was ultimately theirs. Just as the multiclass, hierarchical structure of feudalism had led necessarily and inevitably to the birth of capitalism, equally inevitably capitalism would, of itself, produce the conditions for its own defeat and the triumph of socialism. This is the meaning of one of the most quoted phrases from The Communist Manifesto (1848): "What the bourgeoisie therefore produces, above all, are its own grave-diggers. Its fall and the victory of the proletariat are equally inevitable."[13] But while the laws of history guaranteed the eventual victory of the proletariat, success would not come without effort. Marx proposed a qualified historicism that allowed, even demanded, considerable human intervention to advance or obstruct the course of history. Individuals can act to change things, but only within the limits of history itself:

> Men make their own history, but they do not make it just as they please; they do not make it under circumstances chosen by themselves, but under circumstances directly found, given, and transmitted from the past. The tradition of all the dead generations weighs like a nightmare on the brain of the living. And just when they seem engaged in revolutionising themselves and things, in creating something entirely new, precisely in such epochs of revolutionary crisis they anxiously conjure up spirits of the past to their service and borrow from them names, battle slogans and costumes in order to present the new scene of world history in this time-honoured disguise and this borrowed language.[14]

Historical change does not proceed smoothly or automatically. It would not be expected that the ruling class of a capitalist society would quietly acquiesce in its own demise. Its resistance could frustrate the moment of truth for generations. It was thus the task of the revolutionary party to ensure that success came sooner, rather than later. There was, therefore, still a role for greatness for leaders, parties, and revolutionaries in the Marxist system. While victory was assured, the old order could survive for a long time, obstructing the course of history but powerless to stop it forever. The revolutionaries' task was to hasten the moment, to pluck the fruit while it was ripe. The war would be won; history guaranteed that, but human energies would determine when, how, and where the battles would be fought and how many separate battles would have to be won or lost before final victory.

Historicist arguments in general, especially as propounded in the nineteenth century, tend to be optimistic; that is, they tend to view historical development as progress. History not only changes, it moves "upwards" to some higher more advanced form. History, despite popular slogans, never repeats itself. It moves ever on to new forms or until some final fulfilment of its own logic. To the historicists, history was neither random, arbitrary, whimsical, nor circular. It continued to unfold in a progressive development to higher stages. Marx's pattern was the unfolding of an increasingly polarized class struggle until the eventual disappearance of that struggle in a classless society. All historical change, therefore, even allowing for minor setbacks and reverses, was progressive.

Historicist theories raise the problem of determinism — the extent to which human actions are the product of some individual act of "will" or are merely the automatic or determined responses to external stimuli. Historicism, even at its most flexible, by imposing on human history some notion of predestination, reduces the range of human control. Similar problems of determinism are raised by modern psychology, which tends to explain behaviour as predictable, measurable responses to stimuli. In its extreme form, determinism reduces us all to the role of puppets on the stage of history taking part in a play of which no one knows the full plot and where actors come and go playing out their role in an endless drama.

For my own part I am prepared to accept in my behaviour reflexive action, inherent drives, conditioned responses, habitual attitudes, and so on; but I can still insist that these explanations cover only part of my behaviour, leaving still considerable room for my own independent, freely initiated self-will — including my own self-willed decision to write this book, just as it is your self-willed decision to read it. But only part of human behaviour is completely self-willed. Much more is governed by forces beyond control and largely outside conscious awareness. Those who imagine that they are completely free of the influence of dogmas and creeds, that they look at the world impartially and objectively, and that they are capable of seeing things "as they really are," simply fail to appreciate the extent to which we are all creatures of a historical environment. This is part of what Professor Oakeshott was suggesting. Our perception of the world around us and our understandings of right and wrong are slowly acquired and absorbed from innumerable sources influencing us from the earliest moments of childhood. The number of things we can know by direct personal experience is extremely limited. For the most part, what we think we know about the world is mediated knowledge brought to us through the experiences and reports of others. We deal largely with a second-hand world, interpreted in the light of our own psychological make-up, our experiences, and the limitations of our environment. For each the supposed real world is simply a perception of that world, a knowledge, not of reality itself, but of words and pictures about reality.

The importance of all this is indicated when we begin to make judgments about the world, to assert right and wrong, good and bad. Our judgments, based on our perceptions, will differ because our perceptions differ. There are various ways of looking at the world, some of them described above. Each version, and any others that might be put forward, arises from a complex interplay of many variables: individual rational investigation, psychological drives that impinge on our being in various ways, the traditions and expectations of our society and group, levels of education and information, and so on. From all these will emerge a set of assumptions about the world that will guide, but not totally control, the responses we individually make to external events. But this does not give equal authority to every arbitrary, idiosyncratic world view. Not all moral evaluations are equally valid nor is one point of view necessarily as good as another. To serve as an adequate guide to social life, assumptions need to have some logical internal consistency. They must be capable of rational defence, and they cannot, without evidence, willfully ignore the generally accepted information about the universe. For example, I cannot be expected to be taken seriously if I assert that the world is flat and that the existence of Australia is a fiction concocted by a round-earth theory conspiracy.

In the chapters that follow I attempt to be objective, that is to say, I attempt to explain, as fairly and as accurately as I can, what various positions, propositions, and theories are. But because I find some explanations more valid, more morally defensible, than others, I cannot be neutral. In most cases, my preferences will be apparent to the reader. At the same time I try to make it clear that my value preferences are only that — value preferences arising out of certain perceptions of the nature of the universe and the role of humanity in that universe. I am therefore setting out below, as a kind of author's testament, my own philosophic assumptions, because the responses I make to the external world, and therefore to the several questions raised in the following chapters, will be based on those assumptions. They probably affect even the selection of questions considered worthy of raising. In brief they are:

(1)   The entire universe is rational, governed by a fixed system of laws. That is to say, it is not an arbitrary universe, nor a random one, nor one that is interfered with by the whim of the gods. Things in a rational universe do not just happen. They are predictable responses to observable laws.

(2)   These laws are knowable to the human mind. That is to say, the laws that govern the physical universe are such that they can be discovered by human intellectual effort, although they are not necessarily accurately known now by any particular person. This raises a question of very great importance about the conflict between the two major sources of our modern civilization: on the one hand, there is the Greek tradition, which is the starting point of much of our intellectual life and which stresses a rational, mathematically ordered knowable universe, and on the other hand, there is the Judaic-Christian tradition, which envisions a universe that, in its entirety, is known only by God. This God will reveal certain truths,

some part of the universal knowledge, to be accepted as acts of faith. The Greeks, with their enormous confidence in their own capacity to understand the universe, put very little trust in faith as a source of truth, while Christians, especially the fundamentalist Christians, distrust the evidence of science when it appears to lead to conclusions contrary to revelation. The concept of a knowable scientific universe does not preclude the existence of a God. It asserts no more than that the empirical observation of public data is the appropriate source of knowledge about the material universe.

(3) Human life within this rational, scientific universe is, *within limits,* controllable by individual free will. It is important to stress "within limits," for we must always recognize the existence of circumstances beyond our control that limit the options open to us. Our existence is neither completely determined, nor completely free-willed.

(4) Life has a meaning and purpose, and that purpose is, in some sense, an improvement of the human condition — some raising of the intellectual, spiritual, and material quality of human life, and of *all* human life, as members of an organic community.

That is my declaration of faith, as it will govern many of the statements made in the chapters that follow. For your own use, you should now attempt a similar exercise. What kind of assumptions do you make about the nature of the universe, the meaning and purpose of existence, and the role of humanity in the general scheme of things? At this stage it need not be a very detailed statement, but you ought to have some idea of what you believe, and see how what you believe affects the judgments you make about other aspects of social life.

CHAPTER TWO

The Concept of the State

With the exception of a few islands or uninhabited territories, the whole world is today divided into states. One cannot easily leave one state without coming under the jurisdiction of another. It is a near universal form of political organization and the principal forum within which political activity takes place. (Such international organizations as the United Nations deal with relations between states.) But what exactly is to be made of the state? What sort of thing is it, and how or why does it dominate our lives?

It is useful to begin with a formal definition. It must be emphasized that this is not *the* definition of the state. There are possibly as many definitions as there are people attempting to define it, although most definitions will include the same essential elements. The problem is not made any easier by the fact that the word *state*, along with such related terms as *nation*, *politics*, *government*, and so on, are part of popular speech. People use them daily in a more or less intelligible manner without feeling any need for unambiguous terminology. But for the purposes of the present discussion, where something more precise is needed, the following definition is as useful as any:

> The state is an association, which, acting through law as promulgated by a government endowed to this end with coercive power, maintains within a community territorially demarcated the universal external conditions of social order.[1]

Let us deal with each of these elements:

(1) The state is an association, that is, a more or less permanent, organized collection of people. Associations may be large or small, formed for

very limited, or near universal, purposes, but implicit is the notion of some identifiable membership. A crowd at a beach is not an association, although most there will be members of several associations — their families, as the most basic of associations, clubs, churches, political parties, and, above all, the ruling association in any territory, the state. The state is the one involuntary association. One may decline or resign membership of a church, a union, or a service club, although perhaps not always without penalty. One cannot refuse membership of one state without becoming a member of another.

(2)   The second major characteristic of the state is that it has definable boundaries. Borders may be disputed, and some states may lay claim to the territories of others, but by and large we can determine where each state begins and ends. Without recognizable territorial boundaries, there is no state. Such structured, but otherwise very different, associations as the Catholic Church or the Palestine Liberation Organization, lacking definable territories of their own, are not states. Both elements must be there. Thus, while the land and lakes of Canada establish its geographic entity, it is as an association within that territory that it becomes a state.

(3)   Within its territory, the state is *sovereign*; that is, it is the legally unlimited lawmaker and enforcer, responsible for the preservation of public order. The legal aspects of sovereignty, as the word is used today, owe much to John Austin (1790–1859), who defined it in terms of the political fact of habitual obedience given by a people to some identifiable authority not itself in the habit of obedience to any superior.[2]

It is true that in the complex world of today few states are in a position to practise completely the full extent of their sovereignty. But the fact that a small state might find it politically, economically, or militarily expedient not to pass laws, nor to take actions, that might offend some larger, more powerful state, does not mean that the smaller territory is not sovereign. Even the largest superpowers must consider the impact of their activities on others, both friend and foe, and do, or refrain from doing, some things contrary to their first inclinations. The crucial point is that the state's own government is the sole *legal* instrument for the expression of the state's purpose. If some facet of the territory's political control is formally in the hands of another government, as in the case of a colony, then it is not sovereign, and hence not a state. From this approach, the United Kingdom, Canada, France, and so on, are states. The Falkland Islands, Scotland, and Ontario are not. The fact that a state is governed by its own laws does not, of itself, mean that the people need to have had any part in choosing those laws, nor does it imply that they approve of the laws or are happy with them, nor that everyone always obeys them. All that the definition means is that if, within a given territory, all the laws applying to that territory can be made by its own government without formal reference to an external government, that territory is a state. A military dictatorship under the thumb of corrupt and ruthless generals is as much a state as a liberal democracy. A state, in short, governs itself by whatever system it determines or inherits from the past. The state is thus an association of people who, within a given territory, are governed by their own laws.

There is a certain semantic confusion here. The United States is a state, but by this definition, the states of New York, Ohio, etc., are not. The Canadian term *province* would be much more appropriate. However, this is a matter of linguistic convention, having its roots deep in American history, and does not really affect the argument. The word *state* normally refers to a sovereign political association. In federal systems, such as Canada and the United States, sovereignty may be shared between a central government and some number of constituent units, but the complexities of this question are beyond the present concern.

(4) The state, as defined above, possesses supreme coercive powers, that is, powers of force and punishment originating in itself. The state is a unique association, claiming an exclusive right to define the conditions under which other associations may exist or operate. It is the state that determines what municipalities, police forces, corporations, trade unions, churches, universities, and so on, may legally do, or not do. The legal coercive powers of other associations, such as the powers of a university to impose fines for overdue library books, are derived from the state and extend only so far as the state, from time to time, permits or requires.

(5) Finally, the state expresses its will through a government. But the government is not the state. The state is, more or less, a permanent association embracing many other associations. The government is that body of people temporarily charged with acting in the name of the state, formulating and executing its laws. In the liberal democracies, governments may smoothly change without affecting the continuity of the state. One can also be loyal to the state while at the same time opposed to its government. Many governments have been deposed by those most anxious to preserve the state.

NATIONS AND STATES

Although it is not always an entirely accurate description, we speak today of a world of nation states. The nation, which involves the idea of a people sharing a common ethnic, religious, or historical tradition, does not lend itself to formal definition. It is a matter of belief. As Jacques Maritain expressed it, a nation is

> a human community based on the fact of birth and lineage, yet with all the moral connotations of those terms: birth to the life of reason and the activities of civilization, lineage in familiar traditions, social and juridical formation, cultural heritage, common conceptions and manners, historical recollections, sufferings, claims, hopes, prejudices, and resentments. . . .
>
> A nation is a community of people who become aware of themselves as history has made them, who treasure their own past, and who love themselves as they know or imagine themselves to be, with a kind of inevitable introversion.[3]

People become a nation when they believe themselves to be one, perceiving themselves as having an identity that both unites them, and sets them apart from other peoples.

The idea that a nation and a state ought to occupy the same territory is relatively modern. The first states in Europe were "city-states," single cities, perhaps with surrounding villages and farmlands, as completely self-governing political units. In the ancient world, the Greeks recognized themselves as a people with a common cultural tradition and a common language, which separated them from the "barbarians." But while there was a Greek "nation", there was no unified Greek state. Instead, there were the city states: Athens, Sparta, Corinth, and so on, independent and often at war with each other. The one nation was divided into many states. Later, under the rule of Rome, the state became larger than the nation, embracing the whole empire. The object of the Empire was one state embracing all nations, eventually constituting a world state under one emperor, one law, and, after the fourth century, one church. Later still, with the collapse of the Empire, political units became no more than fiefdoms ruled by minor kings and princes, who perhaps offered lip-service to some remote emperor, and whose territories were expanded or exchanged by marriage contract or conquest. It is only since about the sixteenth century that nationalism, the struggle to unify each nation in the territory of its own state, became a dominating political force. So that, while not all nations are states, the nation-state is now the model, or norm, to which most nations aspire. Our own era witnesses the constant striving of peoples who conceive of themselves as being separate nations to gain their political independence from what they regard as alien, oppressive states. France, Germany, Japan, and Thailand are nation states. The Basques, the Sikhs, the Kurds, and many others, would like to be. Most subject nations have a yearning for their own statehood. The peculiar character of the United States and

Canada is that, with only small aboriginal populations, they have attempted to mould a new spirit of nation among peoples of very diverse cultural origins.

PURPOSES OF THE STATE

A legalistic concept of the state, such as discussed above, helps toward an understanding of what a state is. But it does not tell us much about what a state can or should do. The state is an association. But what kind of association? What is the proper relationship between this association and its members, either as individuals or members of other associations? Here a different perspective is called for. The task now is to go beyond legal criteria to discover how varied and subjective are our perceptions of what a state is or ought to be.

The way in which individuals respond to specific social questions is greatly influenced by their understanding of the nature and purpose of the world in general. These world views are not necessarily right or wrong. They are largely individual interpretations of the world — a product of individual personality structures, the environment (including such things as ethnic background, religion, occupation, social class, and the circumstances of the age and place in which one lives) and, most important, how, where, and from whom individual judgments of right and wrong and appropriate and inappropriate behaviour were learned. These things together contribute to what is called an "attitude set," a composition of roughly related and consistent value judgments. And while, in all its details, an individual's attitude set is unique, people with similar backgrounds and experiences will find many shared attitudes. The attitude set is the main determinant of how people react to perceptions of the real world. For we do not all see the world in the same way. What we see is very much influenced by what we expect to see. And seeing different things, we respond in different ways by making different judgments about the world. From their different perceptions, people understand the world differently and in ways that colour almost all their other political evaluations.

Within the liberal democratic tradition, one of the most critical distinctions is made between individualistic and organic conceptions of the state. These two views are at the root of a great many of the other issues that divide us. The individualistic view is that the state is merely a meeting place, or an organization of independent individuals: an artificial creation of autonomous beings in which the individual is the primary unit. From the organic view, the relation of state and individual is analogous to that of a body and its cells. The body is composed of cells and would be meaningless without them. The cells in turn have no purposeful existence outside the body of which they are part. The state, the body, is the primary political entity. In discussing these views the object is not to decide which is correct. These are subjective perceptions, but a great many other things depend upon them. Those who think of the state in individualistic terms will respond to other political issues, such as the future of the welfare state, differently from those who think in organic terms.

THE INDIVIDUALISTIC STATE

In the Western democracies for the past two centuries the most widely shared image has been that of the individualistic state. Graphically, one can imagine this state as a bucket of marbles. The individuals, or the marbles, are all much the same size and more or less equal in quality. They are hard, independent, and unrelated to each other. Some are on top of the bucket; some are stuck at the bottom. But there is no natural hierarchy. There are no permanent barriers or strata between levels. With a little churning there would be a changing of positions, with some marbles rising and some falling, but it would still be an unorganized bucket of marbles. The bucket is no more than a container to keep them together in some kind of union. It is distinct from them, and they would continue to exist as marbles even if the bucket disappeared. If one stretches the imagination to think of the marbles as building their own bucket and finding their own level within it by their own individual efforts, we have a simplified version of the individualistic interpretation of the state. Individual and state are separate things, united simply by convention and convenience and the desire to provide some kind of order to the lives of atomistic individuals.

This individualistic view of the world developed as a reaction to a hierarchically structured feudal society, under which political and economic power were largely controlled by a hereditary land-owning aristocracy, by the Church (also a powerful landowner), and by the guilds (which were not the predecessors of the trade unions, but organizations of master craftsmen whose main objective was to keep the cost of their services up by restricting entry to their trades and controlling the conditions of their work).

This traditional pattern of life unduly constrained the new forces of commercial capitalism that began to flourish in the revived cities of the late Middle Ages.[4] The new class of urban capitalists, whose power was based on money, did not fit easily into a society based on land and prescriptive authority. Its strengths were founded on risk capital investment, innovation, experimentation, and ambition. To break out of the strangle-hold of castle, church, and guild, new concepts of the relation of individ-ual to society were therefore needed. As capitalism developed, European political philosophy began to approach people, not as members of tradi-tional communities with duties and rights set by birth, but as individuals responsible for their own destiny and making their own success or failure by their own efforts.

A new perception of humanity emerged: "liberal man" or "bourgeois man," who supposedly possessed a relatively fixed human nature. Conse-quently, if society was to function efficiently, its institutions had to be shaped to accommodate the realities of human nature. Although the empha-sis varies, most liberal writers accept egoism as a major characteristic of the human personality. Individuals are selfish, concerned primarily with themselves and their own well-being. Human beings are not naturally social or co-operative, although they can learn to *behave* in a social manner, or to co-operate with others, once it is discovered that such behaviour is rewarded. Individuals discovered that they best served their own advantage by work-ing for the advantage of the whole society. This is a crucial point. Egoism does not necessarily lead to anti-social behaviour. Egoists have no stake in the well-being of others and do not care what becomes of them nor whether they are happy. But egoists also want certain things for themselves: a vari-ety of material goods they cannot produce by their own unaided efforts, some sense of security in their possessions, some amusement or entertain-ment, or whatever else. In short, I must work with you not out of any spirit of community but because only in co-operation can I achieve the greatest satisfaction of my own selfish desires. It is a rational egoism.

Human nature is also competitive. All individuals, it is believed, are deeply motivated to succeed and advance their condition — not in con-junction with others, as part of a general rise in standards, but relative to others. There is, it is said, a universal desire to get to the top, or to win. "Liberal man" is also deemed to be acquisitive, wanting to acquire things and to multiply personal possessions. It is crucial to this individualistic view of humanity that the desire for private property is an innate attribute of human nature, and that, therefore, socialist ideals of property in common must fail because they are contrary to human nature.

THE SOCIAL CONTRACT

The problem of early liberal philosophy was to explain how selfish, com-petitive, acquisitive individuals formed societies. The favourite device was called the *social contract*. The basic proposition was that "natural" autonomous individuals contracted among themselves to set up a society, exchanging some or all of their rights as individuals for collective protection and security. The contract took several forms. One version was offered by John Locke (1632–1704), who will be discussed more fully in chapter nine. The contract he proposed would establish a formal organization to regulate and control the mutual affairs of the contractors, to define and enforce the other agreements made among themselves, and to use the organized force of the society, that is, of all its members acting together, to protect the property of each. To do this, a government would have to be set up, but because such a government is established from a society that individuals have themselves made, the powers of government would be limited to those defined for it by its creators. Since the authority of government is limited by the terms of the social contract, there is no obligation to obey it beyond those terms.

It is not suggested that there has ever been a real "historical" social contract. We know of no circumstances in which a number of primitives have sat down together and consciously decided to create a society. There is no record of any such thing and no pretence that there ever was. The social contract was a fiction invented largely in the seventeenth century,[5] with even those who invented it knowing it as a fiction. Seeking to explain what society ought to be like, the social contractors began by imagining what life would be like if there was no society and people lived, instead, in a "state of nature" never seen in the real world. They could then speculate on what kind of society such natural beings might establish to achieve what kind of purpose. And as there were no historical realities, the only constraints in this exercise were the bounds of each theorist's own imagination or objectives.

The starting point of a social contract theory is thus a "state of nature," an imaginary pre-social condition in which individuals have certain advantages, or certain rights, accruing to them as individuals, which they would want to preserve, and certain disadvantages, which they would want to correct. Society is thus seen as nothing more than an artificial construction set up to preserve the advantages of the state of nature and eliminate the disadvantages. The principal implication is that society is not a natural environment, but the creation of autonomous individuals, established for limited purposes. Society, state, and government become subordinate to the interests of the individuals who established them. The consequence of the social contract is to see society as a loose association of more or less equal individuals, creating for themselves some structure of law and order, and some acceptable procedures for the exchange of goods and services.

Government is justified solely in terms of the benefits it will bestow upon individuals who are unfortunately not able to do everything for themselves.

If we were perfectly rational, we might not need government. But as we are far from perfect, some fabric of law becomes necessary to enforce co-operation on those who do not offer it of their own free will. Because the most aggressive, most hostile, most competitive, or strongest individuals might be able to advance themselves without any respect for others, it is in the best interest of those others to use the state and its laws to prevent the strongest few from getting away with too much to the disadvantage of all. This view of individual and society recognizes that, while each individual could gain a certain personal advantage from exclusively selfish behaviour, all gain even more from co-operative behaviour, especially as related to the protection of property. The state is thus seen as a kind of grand police officer, forcing upon the recalcitrant few the behaviour accepted voluntarily by the rational many.

THOMAS HOBBES

Born April 5, 1588; died December 4, 1679.

Although Hobbes was first interested in the classics, he soon developed an interest in mathematics and science, and later in philosophy. He travelled widely in Europe, during which time he became acquainted with many notable thinkers, including, especially, the Italian astronomer Galileo (1564–1642). His major political work was Leviathan *(1651), an immensely influential and controversial work.* Leviathan *was primarily written in defence of royal absolutism, but after the defeat of the Stuarts it could also be read as a defence of any regime in power, being thus of little comfort to those seeking a restoration of power. Hobbes based his political system on an imaginative attempt to create an associational psychology with an almost mechanistic explanation of cause and effect.*

For further reading see:

Hobbes, Thomas. Leviathan. *Oxford: Blackwell, 1946. Introduction by Michael Oakeshott.*

Goldsmith, M.M. Hobbes's Science of Politics. *New York: Columbia University Press, 1966.*

Macpherson, C.B. The Political Theory of Possessive Individualism: Hobbes to Locke. *Oxford: The Clarendon Press, 1962.*

Strauss, Leo. The Political Philosophy of Hobbes. *Oxford: Clarendon Press, 1936.*

Leydon, W. von. Hobbes and Locke: The Politics of Freedom and Obligation. London: Macmillan, 1981.

One of the first great social contract theorists, who explained how rationality rescued humanity from the hostile environment of the state of nature and brought it into society, was Thomas Hobbes (1588–1679). Hobbes had a remarkably long and active life. He was born in the last years of the Elizabethan era, living through the reigns of the first Stuarts (James I and Charles I), the English civil war and the Commonwealth under Cromwell, and on into the Restoration under Charles II. His life bears the imprint of this violent era for his major preoccupation was the creation of a society of order and stability. Hobbes's state of nature was a condition of pure, competitive, selfish individualism, unchecked by any external control, which he described as "the war of everyman against everyman." Each was the enemy of all the rest, solely responsible for the preservation of life and possessions. In describing individuals as motivated by an overwhelming desire for power, he said, "In the first place, I put for a generall inclination of all mankind, a perpetuall and restless desire of Power after power, that ceaseth only in Death."[6] But as no individual could be permanently on the alert nor stronger than any possible combination of enemies, there could be no security, even for the strongest. In such perpetual conflict there could be no accumulation of possessions and no advance of civilization. Here is the state of nature in Hobbes's own words:

> In such condition, there is no place for Industry; because the fruit thereof is uncertain: and consequently no Culture of the Earth, no Navigation, nor use of the commodities that may be imported by Sea; no commodious Building; no Instruments of moving, and removing such things as require much force; no Knowledge of the face of the Earth; no account of Time; no Arts; no Letters; no Society; and which is worst of all, continuall feare and danger of violent Death; and the life of man, solitary, poore, nasty, brutish, and short.[7]

The saving grace that rescued humanity from "the war of everyman against everyman" and turned it into the ordered, peaceful existence Hobbes so passionately desired, was reason; the capacity to see that boundless personal ambition could not be satisfied in the insecure warring conditions of the state of nature. People would come together to create a government powerful enough to enforce social co-operation through fear of the law, for it was only fear that could compel obedience. Government existed solely to preserve law and order, but government remained the sole judge of what steps were necessary to achieve this. Nevertheless, although the government was set up as a law enforcer with almost unlimited power, it remained a human institution, taking its authority solely from those who created it. The state has no natural constitution or hierarchy and no innate authority beyond that conferred by its members.

THE MODERN INDIVIDUALISTIC STATE

These explanations of the origins and purpose of social organization and of the natural characteristics of humans have flourished in Western political thinking for the past three hundred years, being especially influential in North America. A romanticized version of the expanding western frontier could be portrayed by some as a reliving of Locke's state of nature, creating a myth of the virtues of rugged individualism. At the heart of the Lockean social contract, there is a concept that still lives in American thought today — the idea that people created their own government for their own needs, with that government beholden and subordinate to the people.

These general perceptions of the relation of state and individual can be translated into more specific responses to actual political issues. Those who see the state as the limited-purpose creation of individuals who are by an unchangeable human nature egoistic, competitive, and acquisitive will, in political questions, tend to place low value on public action and high value on the satisfaction of individual desires. There will be a strong sentiment that the greatest good lies in the accumulation of material possessions. Consumerism, as a lifestyle, is a fairly natural corollary of egoistic acquisitiveness. Further, if the state is created by individuals, it will exist for the good of independent individuals, not of some anonymous general public.

Determined, self-reliant individualists tend to be unhappy with the paternalism of modern Western societies. They are generally unsympathetic to government-sponsored welfare systems, prepaid state medical schemes, subsidized housing and education, and so on, arguing that people have an obligation to provide these things for themselves. It is difficult to convince individualists of the virtues of public spending on such things as parks and libraries. There will be pressures to keep public expenditure at the lowest possible level — even at the cost of bumpier streets, understaffed hospitals, or infrequent public transport. They dispute the notion that it is the business of society to save people from themselves. Their moral well-being, they will argue, is their own business; it is not the responsibility of society to care for their souls. Nor is it the business of the state to protect them from their own self-chosen folly. If free individuals want to take the risk of splattering themselves over their own windshields, that is their affair. Attempting by law to compel them to wear seat belts is an unwarranted interference with the rights of individuals.

This is a principle that goes beyond money. Individualists are unhappy with government action, simply because it is *government* action, and arguments about greater or lesser efficiency or cost do not really have decisive impact. Thus, one of the classic defenders of liberalism, John Stuart Mill (1806–1873), included in his catalogue of objections to direct government intervention in the economy his belief that "every increase of the functions devolving on the government is an increase of its power, both in the form of authority, and still more, in the indirect form of influence."[8] Mill was convinced that any expansion of government influence, no matter how benign or well-intentioned, involved some threat to political freedom. In his opinion, any increase in government activity, even the most justifiable, had at least some harmful side effects on the character of a society and its members:

> Even if the government could comprehend within itself, in each department, all the most eminent intellectual capacity and active talent of the nation, it would not be the less desirable that the conduct of a large portion of the affairs of society should be left in the hands of the persons immediately interested in them. The business of life is an essential part of the practical education of a people; without which, book and school instruction, though most necessary and salutary, does not suffice to qualify them for conduct, and for the adaptation of means to ends.[9]

Note that Mill does not say that governments should do nothing. Indeed, he went a good deal further than most of his contemporaries in describing the things governments ought to do. All that he implies here is that, by and large, it is better if people do things for themselves, if for no other reason than to foster self-reliance, independence, and the development of individual capacities. If it is necessary to add to the powers of government or to increase government intervention in society, such intervention should be approached cautiously, keeping alert to the dangers.

Pre-individualistic thinking was dominated by the concept of class, meaning a fairly permanent, durable, inherited social ranking. The medieval world had been sustained by a rigid class structure, accepted as natural and permanent, and in accordance with God's will. By contrast, the liberal approach accepts that although there are enormous inequalities, especially economic inequalities, in society, these differences cannot be attributed to any permanent class structure. Rather they are seen as a consequence of individual qualities: talent, ambition, energy, luck, and so on. Even the division of society into the bourgeoisie, or capital-owning class, and the proletariat, or wage-earning class, as is stressed in socialist thought, is not perceived as the same kind of permanent division as that which separated an aristocracy from the common people. The proletariat are forever being told that with thrift and hard work they, too, can become capitalists. In the United States, the Horatio Alger rags to riches myth is still a powerful force. Although sociologists may be able to establish that the great majority of Canadians and Americans will remain all their lives at roughly the economic and social level to which they were born, and their children will probably follow them at that level — in other words, in objective socio/economic terms, we do have a class structure — there is a very low consciousness of class in North American society. In the liberal ideology, most continue to believe that their individual place in the social structure is determined largely by their own efforts, although perhaps partly by luck.[10]

It must be emphasized that liberalism and conservatism are here being considered as philosophic concepts, not as party identifiers. Therefore, talk of the dominance of liberal individualism does not mean the supremacy of any Liberal party, anywhere. The dominance of liberalism means the pervasiveness of a certain view of individual and society, and no particular political party holds a monopoly on such world views nor are all those who are ideologically liberals, members of Liberal parties. Indeed, most of those today who boast of their new conservatism, the Margaret Thatchers and Ronald Reagans of the world, who take up an anti-welfare state, pro-business "conservatism," and who castigate "liberals" as pinko sympathizers, are themselves the purest examples of an earlier nineteenth-century liberalism, before its later moderation. Today's conservatives are yesterday's radicals.

THE ORGANIC SOCIETY

Some version of liberal individualism, at least as a faith, permeates the life of our society. But while it is the foremost pattern of thought — the ruling faith of the majority — it is not the faith of everyone. Within the liberal democracies there are other ways of viewing individual and society. In particular, there is an older and newer version than liberalism, going back, in fact, to the beginnings of Western political philosophy in Athens in the fifth century B.C., and later monopolizing the political ideas of the Middle Ages and revived, with quite different implications, in the socialist and collectivist creeds of the modern age. This is the organic view of life, shared by pre-liberal traditional conservatives and modern democratic socialists.

In its simplest form, the organic view of the world rejects isolated individualism. It proposes, instead, that there is no meaningful existence in any pre-social state of nature. It is believed that people find their natural fulfilment only *within* society. Instead of looking on society as some artificial constraint individuals create for themselves, they look on society as the natural and proper setting for all human activity, the setting in which human beings find their true humanity. Individual and society become fused in a harmonious whole. Society, perceived as much more than a collection of autonomous individuals, has a life and a purpose of its own, which is separate from, though dependent upon, the life of its members.

A crude analogy may be drawn with a biological organism (hence the term, *organic theory*). An organism is composed of a multitude of cells, which are themselves separate living entities capable even in certain favourable circumstances of surviving outside the body. But the organism has, in addition, an independent life of its own, with an identifiable unity beyond that of the cells composing it. The cell, in turn, is essentially part of something else, attaining its full significance only when performing a role appropriate to its place in that larger body. Cells are all functionally differentiated — skin cells, nerve cells, and so on — in a mutually interdependent relationship. A body has no meaning apart from the cells through which it lives. But it is more than just a collection of unrelated cells, for the body provides an organizing principle through which the cells find the meaning of their existence in their specialized contribution to the whole organism. This is the analogy through which the organic view of the state is explained, but as with all analogies, one must be cautious about carrying it too far and of demanding of it closer parallels than it can provide.

The simplest graphic depiction of the organic state is in the form of a pyramid, although we need to imagine it with a living, organic existence. The pyramid is a set of building blocks, in fairly strictly defined layers, constituting a unity and recognizable as a whole identifiable thing, before its individual parts can be seen. Unlike the marbles of the individualistic model, the parts, the blocks of the pyramid, need no container, for they are container and part in one. The bucket and the marbles were distinct things, with each marble separate from its fellow. But the pyramid and its blocks are one. There is no pyramid at all without the blocks, and until they are assembled into a pyramid, the blocks are just a heap of stones. The point to be emphasized here is that a random collection of autonomous cells does not make a body. Cells constitute a body only when each performs a particular function in a complex pattern of functions. An organism is a "relationship of functional parts."

An organic view of the world, of course, puts the state in quite a different relationship from that envisaged by individualists. The body, as a whole, being greater than the sum of its parts, is more important than its parts and much more important than any individual cell. Each cell is explained largely in terms of its contribution to the body as a whole. Such a world view focusses not on the individual but on the society, seeing it as the natural environment in which individuals find the true meaning and purpose of their existence.

When carried to the extreme an organic view of society leads to the complete subjection of individuals to the state as an end in itself. The argument appears so appealingly simple. If the individual has no meaning in life except as a contributing member to the good of the state, and if the state is a new person with a life and purpose of its own, larger than the sum of the individuals who make it up, then the state is obviously, necessarily, superior to these individuals; and they are subordinate to the state. The state is conceived as a kind of collective superman with absolute rights and authority over all its members. From such a point of view, all the interests of the individual could be sacrificed to the ends of the state. The state would need no justification for its own actions other than its own will — expressed, of course, through the will of its leader. The individual finds a purpose in life only in the total subordination of personal desire to the collective will of the community. This is the kind of rationalization behind the excesses of the fascist regimes of Germany and Italy in the 1930s and 1940s. Organic theories can thus become an excuse for the glorification of the state, personifying that glory in its king or fuhrer. In this setting, any criticism of the fuhrer becomes a criticism of the state itself, which is a matter of treason and therefore something to be punished severely. Here the rights of the individual are all too easily dismissed as irrelevant or as wicked obstructions of the national will.

More moderate, and more widely shared, versions of an organic society recognize the limits of the analogy. The cells that constitute a biological organism have no independent consciousness or will. The blood cell, unaware of the fact that it is a blood cell, has no choice about the role it is to perform. It cannot decide that it is tired of being a blood cell and strive to achieve its ambition to be a brain cell. The arrangement of cells of the biological organism is programmed by a genetic code, independent of any decision-making by the cells themselves. In its less extreme social applications, the organic analogy makes no such demands. There is nothing in most versions that requires that each individual can have only one function. There is nothing essential to suggest that individuals can have no independent choice in selecting their own function, nor does it preclude the idea that they might choose to change their function. Here one may imagine individuals choosing their own role in life, with the kind of body that emerges being dependent on the outcome of those choices. Individuals are thus not necessarily confined to the functions they were born to. All that is suggested is that, at any given time, each individual has, or ought to have, a specific role, status, or function, and that the performance of that role is more than just the external action of an otherwise complete individual. My role in life, by the organic view, is part of me. In a sense I am what I am because of what I do and because of what others do around me. My complete self is a functioning person in a total society.

This draws attention to the concept of the interdependence of parts, which is an essential component of an organic view of the world. Just as the cell exists as part of the body, contributing to its life and health, unable to exist at all without other cells performing their functions, so the citizen finds the meaning of life in the one social body and in relations with its other parts. In an organic society, individuals do not live in isolation, but are dependent upon, and responsible to, each other. Each can enjoy a healthy development and satisfy individual needs, only through the development of all. Co-operation is accepted as the natural, spontaneous behaviour of mutually interdependent beings, working for the good life of the organism that binds them together. Organic theories have sometimes been used for the glorification of the state and its leaders. However, more moderate interpretations recognize that, although the organism draws its independent life from the activity of its members performing dependent roles to create the well-being of the whole, the organism itself more importantly exists for the good of its parts.

Ultimately it is true of any society that when the claims of the individual threaten the health or the security of the whole, the claims of the individual will be subordinated to the good of the whole. Even in the most liberal individualistic society, it is recognized that sometimes the rights, the freedom, or the property of some individuals must be sacrificed for the common good. The home-owner whose house is dynamited to stop the spread of a fire, the farmer whose cattle are slaughtered to control a disease, the person whose land is taken over for defence, all illustrate the principle that even when individual rights have the highest respect, they are never absolute and cannot be exercised if they constitute too great a threat to the rights or safety of others. The ultimate subordination of the individual to the common good is thus not really an issue. The question is, what *kind* of justification must the state provide before demanding such a sacrifice. In the democratic version of organic society individuals recognize obligation to the society not as an end in itself but because it is the instrument for the good of the individual members. Individuals are finally subordinate to the society but only to that society which sets as its goals the greatest possible good of its members. If state and individual share a common interest, each in the health of the other, and if, as is proposed in the organic concept of the state, the individual is incomplete apart from the state, individual and state cannot be set in two separate worlds. Tensions between state and individual must be kept to a minimum.

Historically, this model found its nearest approach to reality in the Middle Ages, when society was structured in a more or less rigid hierarchy of social and economic classes, all contributing to a social "whole." It was during this period, as part of the developing ideas of corporate unity,[11] that there emerged the crucial political distinction between the office and officeholder. The top of the pyramid was occupied by the king, who had great privileges and great powers, but also great responsibilities. However, the privileges and responsibilities belonged to the king as officeholder, not the king as person, because it was the unity, the continuing living whole thing, that mattered and not the passing, mortal individual. When the king abused the privileges of office or failed to fulfill his duties, his subjects could resist, and in extreme cases depose, him out of loyalty to that office.

THE MORAL PURPOSE OF THE STATE

An understanding of the character of the organic state leads into a teleological analysis, that is to say, an attempt to explain the nature of something in terms of its purpose. There are two fundamental teleological propositions relating to organic theories of the state:
1.   The state does, or should, have its own purpose, and
2.   That purpose is an ethical one.
In place of the individualistic view of the state as the neutral container of individual human aspirations, the idea is put forward that the state itself has a moral role to play and that it is part of human life. The state, as an organic whole, has an active concern for the moral and physical well-being of all its members.

This is a notion found repeated through history. In the Greek world, in the fourth century B.C., the city state was identified with the community and the entire collective life of its citizens. The greater part of the *Republic* of Plato (428–348 B.C.) was concerned with the nature of the just state as the necessary environment for the just individual. And Aristotle (384–322 B.C.) asserted that while states come into existence for the sake of life alone, they continue to exist for the sake of the good, that is, the moral life.

States are first established to satisfy the diverse needs and talents of individuals and to take advantage of the division of labour. But their larger purpose is to provide an environment in which individuals can realize their full potentiality as moral beings. The Greek conception of the role of the state can be summarized in a phrase as "an ethical association for the attainment of virtue."[12] It thus extends its role beyond that of a legal institution or simply a guardian of private property, to that of a moral agency. By education, by example, by its laws and institutions, and by its physical setting, the state was to promote the highest possible moral and intellectual development of its citizens.

ARISTOTLE

Born in Macedonia 384 B.C.; died 322 B.C. in Chalcis.

Aristotle went to Athens at the age of 18 to study under Plato and remained until Plato's death in 347 B.C. He was for a time tutor to the young Prince Alexander of Macedon, later remembered as Alexander the Great. In 335 B.C., Aristotle established his own school in Athens, the Lyceum, teaching there until just before his death when the political turmoil following the death of Alexander forced him into exile. Aristotle possessed probably the greatest intellect of all times. No other person has ever been able to cover so many fields of knowledge. On logic, ethics, politics, metaphysics, psychology, physics, zoology, embryology, poetry, and the techniques of public speaking, he wrote important far-reaching works that guided and influenced all subsequent Western thought. For the most part he worked without the guidance of any predecessor. The central threads of Aristotle's political doctrines are (1) the concept of the state as an organic community existing to promote the conditions for the fullest moral development of all its citizens, and (2) the supremacy of the rule of law over the rule of men.

For further reading see:

Aristotle. Politics. Translated with Introduction by Ernest Barker. Oxford: Oxford University Press, 1946.

Bambrough, R. New Essays on Plato and Aristotle. New York: Humanities Press, 1965.

Barker, Ernest. The Political Thought of Plato and Aristotle. New York: Dover, 1959.

Sixteen hundred years later, in the thirteenth century, the great medieval scholar St. Thomas Aquinas (1226–1274) restated Aristotle's views on the moral purpose of the state. Like Aristotle, Aquinas took for granted that the state had a moral function as the promoter of the "good life." But a certain amount of caution is necessary in drawing modern conclusions from this. F.C. Copleston acknowledged that it would be anachronistic to present Aquinas as a participant in the controversies of the nineteenth century:

> But we can say that the policy of laisser-faire would not be compatible with his view of the purpose and function of political society and government. The task of the State is actively to produce the conditions under which a full human life can be lived.[13]

Note that for Thomas the state could not sit back passively and watch the behaviour of individuals, nor act simply as a referee to their competitive efforts. Rather, the state must consciously intervene to produce those conditions of life that raise human beings above the level of the animals. The state has a moral responsibility to be concerned with how people live and how they earn their daily bread.

SAINT THOMAS AQUINAS

Born near Aquino, Italy, c.1225; died in Italy 1274.

One of the greatest medieval theologians and philosophers. He became a member of the Dominican Order in 1244 and taught at the universities of Cologne and Paris. He was the founder of the system known as Thomism, which is still the official philosophy of the Roman Catholic Church. His most famous work in philosophy and theology was the massive Summa Theologica, written between 1267 and 1273. Thomas is largely responsible for reintegrating Aristotle's philosophy into the Western philosophic tradition.

For further reading see:

Copleston, F.C. Aquinas. Harmondsworth: Penguin Books, 1955.

d'Entrèves, A.P., ed. Thomas Aquinas: Selected Political Writings. Oxford: Blackwell, 1948.

Gilson, Etienne. The Philosophy of St. Thomas Aquinas. Cambridge: W. Heffer, 1924.

Maritain, Jacques. St. Thomas Aquinas. New York: Meridan, 1958.

Another six hundred or so years later, at the end of the nineteenth century, the English political philosopher T.H. Green (1836–1882) departed from the mainstream of English liberal individualism in a restatement of Aristotle. This is how Green expressed the moral function of the state:

> The real function of government [is] to maintain conditions of life in which morality shall be possible, and morality consist[s] in the disinterested performance of self-imposed duties.[14]

Green's modifications of traditional liberalism will appear several times in the chapters that follow. At this stage it is enough to make two points:

1. Although his ideas on the function of the state appeared radical in the late nineteenth century and aroused the hostility of laissez-faire liberals, they were not in fact something just invented. Green was returning to an older conception of individual and state that had dominated political thought for some two thousand years until it was replaced in the seventeenth century.

2. Green does not say that the state should use the law to force people to be moral, which he would argue is impossible. It is essential to Green's philosophy that moral behaviour is an action of the free will. It is, however, the task of the state to produce the conditions under which people can choose for themselves to be moral.

That is what is meant by the disinterested performance of self-imposed duties — disinterested, meaning unbiased or not influenced by self-interest, not uninterested. We impose duties on ourselves and perform them, not because we must, but because we choose to do so. In Green's philosophy it is the task of the state to ensure that we have the opportunity and the means to make moral choices. To use one of Green's famous phrases, it is the task of the state "to remove the obstacles" to our development as full, morally responsible human beings.

To Green's mind, society itself could be the principal impediment to the realization of this full human morality, making impossible a life of dignity, of self-respect, or of personal integrity. The major obstacles included a grinding debasing poverty, ignorance, and a barren, sterile physical environment. The dehumanizing conditions of dirty, noisy, unsafe factories and overcrowded, mean slum housing denied the possibility of a full human life to the great masses of the industrial cities. It was therefore the responsibility of the state to concern itself with these matters and exert itself to remedy such intolerable conditions. Such ideas, of course, provide much of the background to the establishment of what later came to be called the welfare state, but that is a theme to be more fully explored later.

These abstract concepts can be applied to the real world of practical politics. In the first place, believers in a general philosophy of a social unity larger than the sum of its component individual entities will tend to have a greater sympathy for both the fact and value of other unities. There will tend to be a greater willingness to accept an enormous variety of human associations having a unity and purpose larger than that of their individual members. Such a vision of society, with its emphasis on auxiliary associations, more easily accepts the legitimacy of such things as labour unions or professional or occupational associations as the instruments of social purpose. It is perfectly consistent that those who believe in the common bond of humanity will be more inclined to put their trust in co-operative endeavour to articulate and promote shared interests than those who see the human race as made up of egoistic, competitive individuals. Political activity is seen as more appropriately conducted between organizations than by the efforts of aggressive individuals.

From this it follows that one might also expect a much greater willingness to use social action to solve social problems; a turning to the power of the state, rather than individual initiative, for purposes of reform or development. Those who think in terms of an organic state are generally more inclined to trust the ultimate goodwill of that state. Hence, there is a greater inclination to turn to collective action for help — to expect the state to assume a major share of the responsibility for educating children, for looking after the poor, the aged, or the unemployed, for stimulating the economy here, and protecting industries there, for active participation in international trade, for constructing highways, for imposing building codes in our cities, for warning us of the dangers of smoking, and generally trying to protect each of us from the consequences of our own weaknesses and follies. In short, for doing all the things modern governments tend to do.

Part of our modern political dilemma and one of the sources of the confusions and suspicions about politics in the popular mind has its roots here. For the past three hundred years the leading political ideology has been that of sturdy, self-reliant individualism. The rhetoric of many in our society is uncompromisingly that of competitive individualism. Yet governments over the past eighty years or so, and especially since the Second World War, have come to do many things that seem more appropriate to an organic view of the world. And they have done those things, not as a matter of imposing an alien philosophy on a reluctant people, but because those same people, as voters, have demanded that governments do them. Again there is the paradox in the honour paid, even by determined individualists, to heroes whose behaviour violates the principles of egoistic individualism. The actions of Sydney Carton, the hero of Charles Dickens's

The Tale of Two Cities, for example, were by liberal standards foolish, irrational, and contrary to human nature.

Many who decry the welfare state in principle still demand that the state accept responsibility for their own concerns. Students who can be very vociferous against governments spending money helping the unemployed, still protest against any attempts to reduce the government subsidy on university fees. The 1980s reaction, the retreat into a newer conservatism (which, as already pointed out, is really a retreat to old-fashioned liberalism), is a break with decades of Western political activity. This is a paradox that will be explored in the chapters to follow, but in the meantime one might reflect on the problem.

A strong current running through all organic theories is the notion of brotherhood, the idea that I am, indeed, "my brother's keeper." This is the organic rationalization of the welfare state. It is not something done as a mere expedience or simply as a response to specific electoral demands. It is something that is the shared responsibility of all members of a unified community. There is a natural correlation between the principle of a welfare state and an organic view of the world, for such a view accepts the responsibility of each member of society to contribute, as a matter of rightness, to the well-being of all. Just as a united family accepts, without question, responsibility for caring for its aged or sick relatives, so the united family of a society will care for all its members without being concerned with repayment or justification, but simply because those unable to help themselves are still members of the family.

The notion of duty thus plays a prominent role in organic theories. Where the individualist stressed *rights* against the society, the organic approach stresses *duties* to the society. Hence, organic theories naturally carry with them a high sense of self-imposed social obligation, whether it be the duty consequent upon the privileges of rank and status, which formed the background of the older feudal aristocratic order, the same notion of service that is still a strong current in some elements of contemporary toryism; or whether it be the notion of universal fellowship, which motivates many socialists. There are, as shall be shown later, some strong conceptual and philosophic common grounds that make it relatively easy for socialists and tories to understand each other. They do not agree with each other, but simply understand what the other side is talking about.

So we are faced with two fundamentally different views of the relationship of individual and society. One starts from an individual with an independent natural life who joins with other equally autonomous individuals to create a state for very limited and specific purposes of organization and security—to harmonize a naturally competitive and selfish human nature. The other starts from the point of view that society is the natural setting of human beings, providing the sole environment in which individuals can fully realize their humanity. Individual and society have a common purpose. Neither of these is the objective, *correct* view. If we all think of ourselves as individuals, our society is an individualistic one. If we think of ourselves as members of an organic community, we live in an organic society. But from these first assumptions many other values and attitudes can be derived, and they are assumptions to which we must constantly return. It will be discovered that those who share assumptions about the nature of society will also share many other political values.

In Canada today both concepts command wide support, a fact that explains not only why we do not all agree among ourselves on specific policy questions but also why sometimes even a basic understanding of what the other person is talking about seems to be lacking. Because both concepts of the nature of society have co-existed over a long period, most combine elements of each in their personal world views. Few people maintain an unqualified individualistic or organic approach to life, although there will be an inclination to give greater weight to one over the other. You should examine your own attitudes to see which vision of society, organic or individualistic, comes closest to your own understanding of the world.

CHAPTER THREE

The Nature of Rights

In a liberal democratic society, our rights, or what we believe to be our rights, are of the greatest importance, as they are crucial to our self-identity. We are anxious to assert our rights, feeling deeply aggrieved when they are trampled upon or ignored. We believe we have many rights: the right of free speech; the right of property; the right not to wear a seat-belt; the right to grow a beard; and the right to worship in a manner of our own choosing, or not to worship at all.

But what exactly are rights? The concept, as we have come to understand it, carries the connotation of something fundamental, sometimes guaranteed by law or custom, and not to be arbitrarily denied. We must ask how can such a notion of *right* be distinguished from mere claims for things desired, even those things which might, or might not, have some merit in them? In Canada and the United States, for example, there is an ongoing debate about the private ownership and possession of firearms. The advocates of stricter gun control claim to assert the controls out of respect for the the good of society, the reduction of homicide, safety, security, the primacy of life, and so on. On the other hand, the opponents, the gun owners, tend to couch their argument as an assertion that controls violate their *right* to own firearms. This is a proposition that needs to be very carefully examined. In the United States there is at least a constitutional text (Article II of the Bill of Rights) that might be interpreted as granting such a right. But in Canada the gun groups, although greatly influenced by the Americans, have no such constitutional support. In the Canadian situation, therefore, it would be hard to establish where such a right might come from. It is certainly not a universal right. In very few states do private citizens make any such claim to be armed and the law rarely acknowledges such a right. Furthermore, the ownership of firearms, or any other more or less modern invention, can scarcely be an eternal right, unless we have evidence of some up-to-date statement on the point from God. Now, there might be very good, valid arguments for the private ownership of guns. But should not such arguments be made on their own merits, based on the proven or assumed consequences of carrying guns, rather than being expressed in terms of fundamental rights?

In short, how do we decide which of the several things we want, or feel entitled to, are rights? Are my rights the same as your rights? What happens when my rights conflict with your rights? If I am guaranteed a right of free speech, why am I not also guaranteed a right of employment, a minimum income, or a happy marriage?

These are critical issues that can all eventually be related back to two rather basic questions: What is a right? and Where do rights come from? Are my rights things that I possess by virtue of some absolute law of God, or nature, or reason, or simply the fact of my existence as a human being? Or are they something I acquire only as a consequence of living in a particular society at a particular time and, therefore, are relative to that society or time?

ANTIGONE

A useful starting point for an exploration of these questions is a scene from the play *Antigone*, by Sophocles (c.495–406 B.C.). The play, first performed in Athens around 450 B.C., is one of the great dramas of all time and it still has enormous power to arouse deep emotions. It is one of the earliest presentations of the conflict between the official proclaimed law — the positive law — and the belief in a higher law, a law of conscience, or, as it is called, a *natural law*, which takes precedence over the positive law. This natural law comes in time to be held up as the source of natural rights. Believers in a natural law argue that the positive law can never morally repeal the obligations imposed by that natural law. They present the proposition that when the positive law commands one to act contrary to one's conscience, as a reflection of God's law, or the natural law, one is obliged to disobey the positive law.

SOPHOCLES

Born c. 495 B.C.; died 406 B.C.
One of the three great tragic poets of Greece (the others being Aeschylus and Euripides). Of the more than one hundred plays he wrote only seven, including Antigone, *have survived intact.*

Antigone assumes that the audience will be familiar with certain events that supposedly took place before the opening scenes. Very briefly, the preliminary story is as follows: After the death of King Oedipus, his son Polynices should have inherited the throne of Thebes. But Polynices was deposed by his younger brother, Eteocles, and driven from the city. Seeking revenge, Polynices raised a force to attack Thebes. In the ensuing battle, in which Polynices' army was defeated, Polynices and Eteocles killed each other in personal combat. The throne of Thebes then went to their uncle Creon. Creon's problem as king was to restore law and order to a troubled city. As both brothers would still have many friends and supporters in Thebes, the city might well destroy itself in factional conflict. But Eteocles had died defending his city, while Polynices had attacked it with a foreign army. Creon therefore ordered that Eteocles be buried with full military and religious honour as a hero, while Polynices' body was to be left to rot in the sun. This was something more than an insult to a physical body because burial rights were important to the safe passage of the soul. This is where the play opens.

Antigone, sister to Polynices and Eteocles, is determined to bury her dishonoured brother in defiance of the king's command. The play begins as Antigone tries, without success, to persuade her sister Ismene to join her in this act of disobedience. She then goes off alone to do what she knows she has to do. Creon is enraged to hear that his orders have been disobeyed. He orders Polynices' body to be dug up and a guard posted to watch over it. As Antigone returns a second time to perform the rites, she is seized and brought before Creon.

CREON: Well, what do you say—you, hiding your head there: Do you admit, or do you deny the deed?
ANTIGONE: I do admit it. I do not deny it.
CREON: Now tell me, in as few words as you can, Did you know the order forbidding such an act?

ANTIGONE: I knew it, naturally. It was plain enough.

CREON: And yet you dared to contravene it?

ANTIGONE: Yes — that order did not come from God. Justice, that dwells with the gods below, knows no such law. I did not think your edicts strong enough to overrule the unwritten unalterable laws of God and heaven, you being only a man. They are not of yesterday or to-day, but everlasting, though where they came from, none of us can tell. Guilty of their transgression before God I cannot be, for any man on earth. I knew that I should have to die, of course, with or without your order. If it be soon, so much the better. Living in daily torment, as I do, who would not be glad to die? This punishment will not be any pain. Only if I had let my mother's son lie there unburied, then I could not have borne it. This I can bear. Does that seem foolish to you? Or is it you that are foolish to judge me so?[1]

Creon really has no option. He is the custodian of the law, whose authority has been deliberately flouted. As he must, he finds Antigone guilty and condemns her to death — she is to die by being walled up in a cave. In a final act of defiance, Antigone takes her own life. Creon's world then collapses about him as the play descends deeper into tragedy. Creon's own son Haemon — betrothed to Antigone — first pleads with Creon for mercy for her, then defies his father, threatens him, and in utter despair, kills himself. Creon's wife, Eurydice, hearing of these tragic events, takes her own life, cursing Creon. The mood of the city is one of anger as public sympathy grows in support of Antigone. Creon is utterly, morally defeated. Overcome with remorse and humbled, he is unable to offer any recompense or remedy.

Antigone deserves our attention, not only as a great dramatic tragedy, but also because it presents the dilemma of natural law versus positive law. Creon's case was fairly straightforward. He was the king, responsible for law and order, aware that society cannot survive if the law can be defied with impunity. Creon was no tyrant. He was the legitimate ruler in Thebes, whose laws were to be obeyed. His position was the position of all governments — the law was the law, binding on all citizens. Public order and the good of the whole community had a higher priority than the wishes of any one citizen, even of his own family.

Antigone's case was different. She argued that although Creon had the authority to make and enforce laws, there was a higher law than that of kings and governments. This was the natural law, the law of God, or of reason. Man-made laws were binding only in so far as they did not violate that higher law. Her argument was that we have certain fundamental duties, imposed on us by God — duties that are universal and eternal — and there exists a natural law to enforce those duties. This natural law is superior to, and is the criterion for judging the worth of, man-made laws. *Antigone* is, in effect, the struggle between law and conscience.

In Sophocles' play, Antigone is the heroine, for although she is condemned to death, we are intended to sympathize with her as the moral victor. Sophocles' audience was familiar with the concept of such a morally superior natural law and acknowledged it. The play finds heroism and moral victory in the deliberate defiance of the law of the land in the name of some higher principle. It is the victory of an eternal natural reason over an arbitrary edict. It is not a concept that governments like, and in the 2,400 or so years since it was first performed, few regimes have been prepared to tolerate this upholding of civil disobedience as a virtue. Kings do not like the idea of kings humbled because they try to uphold the law.

NATURAL LAW AND NATURAL RIGHTS

The idea of there being such an eternal natural law is a persistent one. One of its most forceful restatements is by the Roman Stoic philosopher Cicero, writing in *The Republic* about one hundred years before the Christian era:

> There is in fact a true law — namely, right reason — which is in accordance with nature, applies to all men, and is unchangeable and eternal. By its commands this law summons men to the performance of their duties; by its prohibitions it restrains them from doing wrong. Its commands and prohibitions always influence good men, but are without effect upon the bad. To invalidate this law by human legislation is never morally right, nor is it permissible ever to restrict its operation, and to annul it wholly is impossible. Neither the Senate nor the people can absolve us from our obligation to obey this law and it requires no Sextus Aelius to expound and interpret it. It will not lay down one rule at Rome and another at Athens, nor will it be one rule today and another tomorrow. But there will be one law, eternal and unchangeable, binding at all times upon all peoples; and there will be, as it were, one common master and ruler of men, namely God, who is the author of this law, its interpreter and its sponsor. The man who will not obey it will abandon his better self, and, in denying the true nature of a man, will thereby suffer the severest of penalties, though he has escaped all the other consequences which men call punishments.[2]

It is important to note that Cicero accepted the authority of the natural law, not only because it was the command of God, but also because it was in accord with right reason, the universal principles of rationality that guided every aspect of the universe.

MARCUS TULLIUS CICERO

Born January 3, 106 B.C.; *died December 7, 43* B.C.

This Roman philosopher and statesman is remembered for his incorporation of the Stoic doctrines of natural law into the Roman legal tradition, and through that into the mainstream of Western legal philosophy until the nineteenth century. For further reading see:

Arnold, E.V. Roman Stoicism. *Cambridge: Cambridge University Press, 1911.*
Clarke, M.L. The Roman Mind. *London: Cohen and West, 1956.*
Earl, Donald. The Moral and Political Tradition of Rome. *New York: Cornell University Press, 1967.*

The natural law at this stage was still more concerned with the imposition of duties than with the protection of rights. It was a burden to those who accepted its authority, an obligation to do something, even at great cost. The shift in emphasis from public duty to individual rights did not come until the emergence of liberal ideas of individual autonomy in the seventeenth century. The English philosopher John Locke (1632–1704) appealed to the familiar concept of an eternal, universal natural law. However, in his hands the natural law became the source of the inalienable rights of the individual in the state of nature. The natural law guaranteed natural personal rights. The natural law that previously imposed obligations now also assured rights. It still imposed the obligation, but it became an obligation to respect the rights, the liberty and property, of others. Government and society were brought into existence to preserve these rights of individuals. Their indefeasibility set limits to what governments could or could not do. Rights that existed prior to the society were held as a protection against the excessive power of the society. Rights, in this sense, came to be thought of as possessions, attributes of the person. A human being has two legs, two arms, a nose, and so on, and a set of rights. In Locke, the concept that the primary function of government was to protect the inalienable rights of individuals gained new strength.[3]

The idea was even more emphatically articulated in the American Declaration of Independence of July 4, 1776, drafted at a time when Locke was one of the most influential intellectual voices in the American colonies. The Declaration embodied the purest expression of the idea of a natural law creating a set of natural rights:

> We hold these truths to be self-evident, that all men are created equal; that they are endowed by their Creator with certain inalienable rights; that among these are life, liberty, and the pursuit of happiness. That to secure these rights, governments are instituted among men, deriving their just power from the consent of the governed; that, whenever any form of government becomes destructive to these ends, it is the right of the people to alter or abolish it, and to institute a new government, laying its foundation on such principles, and organizing its powers in such forms, as to them shall seem most likely to effect their safety and happiness.

The Canadian Charter of Rights and Freedoms embodies the same principle of laws protecting certain basic rights. The Charter sets out not to create rights but to specify and protect rights assumed already to be in existence:

> The Charter enshrines certain fundamental freedoms for everyone in Canada. They are freedoms that custom and law over the years have made almost universal in our country. Now these freedoms will be protected by the Constitution.[4]

These concepts of natural law and natural rights are still part of our moral and intellectual heritage invoked whenever we assert that some particular law is unjust or unwarranted because it violates our natural rights. We call upon the natural law when we declare that we cannot obey some particular law because of a higher obligation to obey the law of God or to respect some other more binding principle. The conscientious objector who puts God's commandment "Thou shalt not kill" ahead of the state's command to take up arms to defend the country may be citing a version of the natural law. And we seem to have a sense, not easily articulated or explained, that certain actions of government may be wrong, not in a legal sense, but because they are contrary to what we believe to be our rights.

But despite the persistence of these ideas, they raise some very serious problems. In part these are linguistic difficulties, for in English the word *law* has three distinct meanings, which are often confused. First, there is the law as we commonly understand it — the set of specific injunctions, regulations, and rules normally written down or proclaimed, as the law of the land. This sense of *the law*, from the orders of Creon to the Statutes of Canada, is what we normally call the *positive* law. An element of *will* enters the positive law, for it is the law we can choose to obey or disobey, and if we choose to defy it, we may expect to suffer certain consequences. Positive laws, government laws, are laws because people made them, either by statute or by the acceptance of binding customs and conventions.

Second, there are what we call "scientific laws," or, to add further confusion, the "laws of nature" (quite distinct from the natural law). These are the laws of the natural sciences: physics, chemistry, biology, and so on. They are not strictly speaking laws at all, but observed consistent relationships, or predictions of cause and effect. Scientists, in making a number of empirical observations of the world around them, perceive that certain events always seem to be associated, with one regularly following the other. These observations are generalized into a law that A "causes" B, (meaning perhaps no more than that A is consistently followed by B), or that A and B are in some form of predictable, measurable relationship. But, for the true scientist, these laws are always provisional. As they are based on a finite number of observations and measurements, there is always the possibility that new evidence will modify the conclusions. Law here simply means regularity, or consistency, in relationships between phenomena. It is not legislated nor can it be broken by human will. We cannot decide to break the law of gravity because we don't like its consequences or because we think it immoral. Scientific laws are called laws because people believe they have discovered certain causal consistencies in nature.

Finally, there is the natural law. The natural law, variously called the law of God, or the law of reason, or the law of some other universal, eternal principle, is the law as it *ought* to be. It is the set of the *ought* statements defining those things the moral person is obliged to do, or to refrain from doing. It is the *true* law; the moral standard for judging the positive law. Throughout Western history there has been this belief in the natural law, and with it the feeling that in the good society, the positive law will reflect the principles of the natural law. But when they are in conflict, the natural law has the superior moral authority.

What, then, is this natural law? How are we to discover its content? Those who see it as of the same order as the laws of nature, or the laws of science, gloss over the problems. Cicero, for example, believed that the natural moral law was part of the broad set of laws that governed all facets of the universe, physical and moral, discoverable by the same kind of reason. But we do not arrive at our knowledge of the natural law by empirical observation. We do not observe the actual behaviour of different societies, and from this conclude that this is how all people *ought* to behave. Empirical methods are not appropriate for discovering the natural law.

Physicists, whether they be Europeans or Asians, Christians or Moslems, or communists or capitalists, can agree, more or less, at least on the basic laws of physics. There is no such agreement on the natural law; on, say, the moral obligations of the individual toward the well-being of society as a whole, on the character and permanence of marriage, on the rights of private property, or on any other moral or social principle. There is not even agreement that there are any basic moral principles.

Many are convinced that they *know* their natural rights, and the natural law that is their source, because they received them as a direct revelation from God. This is a satisfactory base for the believer, but it is not much help for the person of a different faith who believes that God has issued a different set of commandments. Nor does it solve the problems of different interpretations of the meaning or application of those commandments. And it is of no help at all to the agnostic who has difficulty in finding evidence for the existence of God at all.

This is the dilemma of Antigone. If the command to give Polynices a decent burial was in accord with the commands of God—a clear, overriding obligation to Antigone—why hadn't the gods told Creon about it? If the natural law is the universal, self-evident law of reason, why is it not self-evident to all of us? Why is it that only some seem to have access to God's will—which always seems to excuse some from having to obey the commands of others? The political problem is that those who base their defence on rights derived from the natural law are frequently in the minority: a group trying to justify its exemption from a specific obligation, perhaps in the name of some higher, more onerous obligation, or because it allegedly violates their natural rights. But when challenged, the dissenters are hard put to explain why they should be the privileged possessors of knowledge of this overriding law.

History can offer several examples where appeals to natural rights might also be interpreted by others as a self-rationalization of an individual defiance of the common will. The assertion of natural rights, or to put it in a more modern adaptation of the same idea, of universal human rights, may sometimes be nothing more than a propagandistic device to add authority to some claim, or some demand for a special favour, or some exemption from a law found inconvenient. Was Antigone in fact guided by God speaking to her conscience, or simply by her own obstinate pride? Was Antigone doing as the gods commanded, or was she doing what she wanted to do anyway, subsequently seeking legitimacy for her own self-willed behaviour? The same problem confronted Creon. His assertion that, as king, he had the supreme obligation to enforce the law is not self-evidently true. Like Antigone, he must justify his position. These questions seem to indicate a need to treat all expressions of natural law and natural right with caution.

The paradox of the natural law is that, although there is a continuing belief in its authority, we have no knowledge of its sources, no firm evidence of its existence, no proof of its validity, and no agreement on its tenets. If the concepts of natural law and natural right are to have any meaning, they ought to include two other propositions. They ought to be eternal, and they ought to be universal. But, as a matter of historical fact, we can find no principle that has been accepted unaltered through all ages. Most of the things asserted as rights today are relatively novel ideas: the right of everyone to have a vote, private property, equality before the law, freedom of speech, access to universal education, or freedom to move from place to place. Canadians rightly treasure these things. But they are scarcely eternal rights. Most would have been incomprehensible a few centuries ago. Nor can anthropologists discover a single universal moral or legal principle accepted by all peoples. Some societies condone, even approve, the murder of strangers, old people, or sickly children. Some have never heard of private property, and in some, women are held to be by nature and in law inferior to men. The dilemma is clear. No repeated assertion of the existence of a natural law, or of natural rights, can resolve the problem of interpretation and ambiguity:

> For the natural law does not provide a means for adjudicating between conflicting laws, nor can it provide such means since to do so would be tantamount to granting to a higher authority a status which it claims for itself. Disputes about conflicting natural laws are generally settled, if they are settled at all, by introducing other criteria: a theory of utility, for example, or tradition, custom, and precedence.[5]

So the natural law, and the rights which stem from it, no matter how self-evident they might appear to some, are neither universal nor eternal.

We may thus be led to conclude that the natural law is a myth and that there are no natural rights. But, and here's the rub, we would be a lot poorer in spirit if we did not believe that we did have them. An idea so persistent, clung to so tenaciously over many centuries, cannot just be casually dismissed. Perhaps the value of the natural law lies not in its objective validity but in its contribution to human civilization. We believe in natural rights, because we want to believe in them. They add purpose and meaning to life. People can become politically free when they begin to believe that a natural law has made them free. The natural law has been a powerful weapon in the humbling of tyrants. Antigone could morally defeat Creon only because she could appeal to a higher external authority than the man-made law of Creon.

But for natural law the petty laws of a small peasant community of peninsular Italy would never have become the universal law of an international civilization. But for natural law the great medieval synthesis of godly and of wordly wisdom would not have been possible. But for natural law there would probably have been no American and no French revolution, nor would the great ideals of freedom and equality have found their ways into the lawbooks after having found it into the hearts of men.[6]

We must conclude that, if not the natural law itself, at least the belief in the natural law and its dependent rights have been one of the most important contributions to the emergence of the liberal democratic idea.

It is possible that natural rights are no more than a set of very powerful, useful, and persuasive desires, or perhaps personal excuses for refusing to do as a legitimate government commands. But this does not mean abandoning the whole notion of there being any rights at all. Clearly believing in the existence of a body of rights satisfies a deep psychological desire. The belief that we are protected by a set of rights—that those who violate those rights are morally in the wrong—adds to our sense of personal worth and dignity. With rights to be upheld, we become not just subjects, but full members of a community.

RELATIVITY OF RIGHTS

The idea of rights is thus too important to be abandoned. We might, therefore, seek to approach the idea from the direction of rights acquired from society and held as a consequence of membership of that society. This approach helps resolve the problem of the universal, eternal character of rights. It lets us continue to accept the reality, the importance, of rights, but makes it easier to explain why and how our understanding of what rights we have differs from time to time. Societies will differ in their needs and in the terms of the relationship of individual to society. And, therefore, the rights claimed by the individual to fulfill the responsibilities of citizenship will vary from time to time and place to place. The rights appropriate to the citizen of ancient Athens need not be the most appropriate for the citizen of twentieth-century Canada. This is not to suggest that rights are arbitrary—mere whims of the moment, shifting from day to day. Some believers in an absolute, universal natural law find difficulty with the idea of relative changing rights. If they are not universal, it is argued, rights are nothing and stand as no protection to anyone. Relativity is dismissed as mere arbitrariness. This may be unnecessarily extreme. There is surely some balance between unyielding absoluteness, and total capriciousness; and between absolute standards, and no standards at all. Cicero and the Roman Stoics accepted the concept of a *ius gentium*, a law of the peoples meaning, in effect, the adaptation of the universal natural law to the peculiar history, traditions, and circumstances of the various peoples of the Empire. A relative set of rights can have binding authority over a long period of time—far longer than the life of any one generation—and in this period have all the moral authority of the natural law. Societies, and the rights they enshrine, which change only slowly, will preserve certain crucial elements over very long periods. The idea of relativity permits us to recognize the possibility of change over time and from society to society. Accepting such a notion of relative, society-based rights helps us avoid the arrogant chauvinism of attempting to impose our interpretation of fundamental rights on the whole world or judging the rest of the world by our moral standards.

Let us examine two versions of how relative rights might be constructed, turning first to Jeremy Bentham (1748–1832), principal exponent of the doctrines of utilitarianism. Strictly speaking, Bentham does not have a theory of rights. But he does develop some quite important ideas of relative values. In fact, he dismisses the notion of rights as binding obligations or universally valid protections for individuals, talking instead of *utilities*, things that are useful for the promotion of happiness. And he recognizes that the things that produce happiness vary over time. Bentham is particularly interesting, for although he is a key figure in the development of capitalist ideology, he discards the whole natural rights/social contract philosophy of the first generation of liberal thinkers, such as Locke, substituting as the goal and measure of the good society "the greatest happiness of the greatest number."

JEREMY BENTHAM

Born in London February 4, 1748; died in London June 6, 1832.

A child genius whose intellectual ability did not fade with age, Bentham was admitted to Oxford at the age of 12, receiving his B.A. at 15. He devoted most of his long life to philosophic writing and to the advocacy of reforms in the legal and penal systems, in government and in administration. Bentham was the principal exponent of the Utilitarian school of philosophy, which dominated English politi-

cal thought through much of the nineteenth century. His best noted works were: Fragment on Government *(1776),* Introduction to the Principles of Morals and Legislation *(1789),* Theory of Legislation *(1802), and* Rational of Judicial Evidence *(1825).*

For further reading see:

Plamenatz, J.P. The English Utilitarians. *Oxford: Blackwell, 1958.*

Parekh, Bhikhu. Bentham's Political Thought. *London: Croom Helm, 1973.*

Halévy, Elie. The Growth of Philosophic Radicalism. *London: Faber and Faber, 1949.*

Davidson, William. Political Thought in England: The Utilitarians from Bentham to Mill. *London: Home University Library, 1916.*

In one paper, A Critical Examination of the Declaration of Rights, Bentham attacked the Declaration of Rights of Man and the Citizen as decreed by the French Constituent Assembly in 1791. These so-called rights, he said, were mere fictions, high-sounding words, which confused true interests and purposes. In the course of this criticism he wrote that the Declaration of Rights contained "a perpetual vein of nonsense, flowing from a perpetual abuse of words." Further on he asserted, "Natural rights is simple nonsense: natural and imprescriptable rights, rhetorical nonsense, nonsense upon stilts." He then proceeded to examine the Declaration clause by clause:

ARTICLE 1

"Men (all men) are born free and remain free, and equal in respect of rights. Social distinctions cannot be founded, but upon common utility."

In this article are contained two distinct sentences, grammatically speaking. The first is full of error, the other of ambiguity. In the first are contained four distinguishable propositions, all of them false—all of them notoriously and undeniably false:

1. That all men are born free.
2. That all men remain free.
3. That all men are born equal in rights.
4. That all men remain (i.e. remain forever, for the proposition is indefinite and unlimited) equal in rights.

All men are born free? All men remain free? No, not a single man: not a single man that ever was, or is, or will be. All men, on the contrary, are born in subjection, and the most absolute subjection—the subjection of a helpless child to the parents on whom he depends every moment for his existence. In this subjection every man is born, in this subjection he continues for years, for a great number of years, and the existence of the individual and of the species depends upon his so doing.[7]

Bentham's assault of the other clauses continued in the same vein. Bentham, who was not easily deceived by high-sounding phrases, tore the whole language of the Declaration of Rights to shreds as pretentious nonsense. This is not to say that such declarations are not useful. But their difficulty is that their wording suggests that they are statements of fact, describing how things are, whereas in practice they much more accurately describe how one might like things to be.

Bentham found the whole language of natural rights vague, ambiguous, and misleading. In his own philosophy the only standard by which any action by individual or government could be judged was by its utility, or usefulness, in promoting the greatest happiness of the greatest number. By this reasoning there were no rights at all. There were merely a number of things, varying from society to society, that ought to be fostered or encouraged because they made societies happier and better places to live in. In short, Bentham saw the purpose of human activity in the promotion of maximum human happiness. But the things that make us happy are neither universal nor eternal. Thus, in our own society, which is hugely dependent upon the written word, literacy is a virtual necessity for anything much beyond mere subsistence living. We may therefore claim that the happiness of the greatest number demands that all have access to some minimum level of education, that education be compulsory, and that public funds be expended to ensure that everyone may receive an education without undue economic hardship. An earlier age, say, a self-supporting, pre-technological, agricultural society, having no such need for mass literacy, would be unlikely to assert a general right to an education.

For *rights* Bentham substituted the word *utility*. Things were good or valuable, not because they were eternal or God-given, but because they were useful. Of course, as Bentham acknowledged, it is highly probable that many things will be shared by many societies over long periods of time. Many of the things that some people call natural rights have had great utility in many ages and settings. Most societies will condemn murder not only as destructive of the life of the victim but also because it is socially disruptive. But murder, to Bentham, is wrong, not because it violates an inalienable right to life, but because its consequences are nearly always intolerable. Again, most societies, but far from all, will find a social utility in the protection of private property. But this common tradition, or common usefulness, does not make property a right in the sense that Locke described it — a sacred, eternal, inalienable attribute of the individual.

Instead of looking for rights, a Benthamite acknowledged only utilities bound by time and place.

The great problem with Benthamism is that it provides us with no criteria for settling disputes about utilities. If there are two or more versions of the course of action most likely to produce the maximum happiness, what standard can be introduced to determine which has the greatest utility? If utility itself is the final standard, no other values can be introduced to set priorities among utilities. Bentham himself, following the arguments developed by his friend the pioneering economic theorist Adam Smith, saw the greatest happiness of the greatest number in a free, competitive market economy. But his own theories could just as easily be used to explain or justify massive state intervention, and were so used by some of his followers. There is the problem, too, of judging what makes people happy. It would not be too difficult to portray the totally controlled, organized society of Huxley's *Brave New World* as a society of happy people. Generally today we can reject Bentham's utilitarianism as being too simplistic and ambiguous to be a practical guide to the moral basis of society, but in its own age it served an invaluable role in breaking away from an older expression of natural law and natural rights. It added a healthy touch of scepticism and relativity to our political thinking.

T.H. GREEN

An alternative version of socially derived rights can be found in the writings of T.H. Green (1836–1882). In Green's conception, rights are not something held by the individual against the state. They originate only within the state and as a result of membership of the state. The starting point of the argument is self-consciousness, or self-awareness.[8] The one certain thing I know is that I exist. I am aware of myself as a person. Further, I am aware of myself as a being with a potential, with a life to lead as an individual. I am conscious of a certain need to realize myself, to become whatever it is I am capable of becoming. I have an overwhelming desire to preserve my dignity, self-respect, and integrity; to be, in short, a complete, morally independent person. This self-consciousness is one of the most important aspects of my humanity.

But I am aware not only of my self but also of other *selves*, — other persons in the society around me. And I am aware that these other persons possess like desires and needs, also demanding self-realization and preservation of individual integrity. I know not only me and my needs but also you and your needs.

These needs come to be expressed in terms of relationships with others. When I hold that I have a need to be able to express myself freely, I am saying that others ought not to be able to obstruct my self-expression. When I claim a right of property, I am claiming more than just the capacity to possess and use something. I am claiming an exclusive possession and use, which means my possessing something denies you the right of use of it without my consent. Property means possessing something secure from the risk of losing it to someone else. And without that someone else being there, freedom of expression or the right of property is meaningless.

When, therefore, we talk about our needs, the things essential to our dignity and self-respect as individuals, we express those needs as claims upon the rest of society, claims to be allowed to pursue those things without obstruction by others. When I want property, freedom of speech, the liberty to worship, or anything else, I express this as a claim upon you that you do not hinder me in the pursuit of my ends. The individual, therefore, makes claims upon the rest of society, i.e., upon other like individuals, for the powers to achieve self-development. And these claims for powers from the rest of society are normally expressed as claims for "rights." The power to pursue a self-realizing goal is perceived as a necessary thing, the basis of a right.

I must also recognize that you are pursuing similar goals and making similar claims upon me. The recognition that others are making similar claims is thus the vital next step. As a member of an organic community, such as that envisaged by Green, I do not live in isolation, so I make my claims not only for myself but for all the members of society. I *universalize* the claims I make. This is a key notion: a universalized claim, made by one or a few members of the society on behalf of *all* its members. Before a *claim* for a right can become a *right*, said Green, it was first necessary that the claim be universalized, made on behalf of all. Wanting free speech for myself, I assert a general right of free speech. Without this universalizing aspect, the claim is merely for some special privilege. To Green, rights are, by definition, attributes of the whole society. Anything else, any particular benefit power, or advantage, is a privilege that may, or may not, be justifiable or valid on its own merits.

The second condition for the existence of a right is the recognition by the society at large of the validity or desirability of that claim. That is to say, claims become rights only when acknowledged as such by society. This is, of course, a huge departure from the natural rights tradition. Under the concept of natural rights, individuals hold rights as a protection *against* government. In Green's interpretation individuals have only those rights that society bestows upon them. The other things that may be asserted or desired are merely claims. Society is thus not the enemy of rights but their source. There is a critical distinction between the social recognition of rights and their institutionalization in law. It is the society, not the state, nor its government, that confers the right. Green allows for the very real possibility that governments may frustrate rights clearly acknowledged by the ethos of society. This, of course, raises the problem of interpretation. How are we to know when society has conferred the status of a right upon some claim? In exact terms there is no answer. But we can make use of a parallel. There is a clear, unmistakable difference between the full sunlight of noon and the darkness of midnight, but at dusk it is impossible to pin the precise moment when day becomes night. Claims and rights can be examined in a similar fashion. Some things are clearly rights, while others, equally clearly, are not. And in between there is a grey, undefined area of things that may or may not be rights. We recognize, in Canadian society, a right of all adults to vote for their choice of representatives. Voting is an established right. But, although some may claim it, polygamy is rejected. It is not a right. But what of the grey area? In recent decades we have witnessed ever stronger claims by women for a more equal social and economic status in society. These claims are not yet fully institutionalized in law. But has society in general accepted them as rights? It is difficult to say. The claims of women for equal rights are much more fully accepted than a generation ago. But there are still deep pockets of resistance, bigotry, and traditionalism. Probably because of prevailing values, women have not yet achieved equal rights, but they are closer to them than at any time in Canadian history.

This distinction between the law as enacted by government and the values of the society is vital, for it is the values of society, the social acceptance, that confers rights, not the law. In some cases, government and the law may be ahead of society. Laws in the United States, especially the federal law, recognized the equal political and educational rights of blacks long before this equality gained wide social acceptance, although the fact of equality in law went a long way to producing a change in social attitudes. For that reason, the government was far ahead of society at large in acknowledging the validity and worth of some claims. On the other hand, governments may be slow in legislating the rights acknowledged by most members of society, perhaps out of a reluctance to offend some powerful minority. In many jurisdictions the public at large is apparently a good deal more tolerant and open in such matters as liquor regulations, Sunday observances, or other moral matters than the law is prepared to recognize. The rights of private judgment in these questions, which society seems prepared to confer, may not be accepted as such by law.

Under this argument, it can be seen that many assertions of rights are merely claims for rights. And such claims may be valid to a degree. They may be valuable or useful, or would promote a greater public good, or conform to some widely accepted standard of justice or fairness. But until society at large has accepted them they are not rights. Indeed, it might be argued that the fact that we still have to claim something, to assert our need for it, might indicate that it has not yet achieved the status of a right. Unless they are threatened or violated, we don't need to assert claims to rights — we already have them. We need to claim only the things that we want to become our rights or that seem threatened by some opposing claim.

In this struggle for the acceptance of rights, many claims, many assertions and demands for some change in our conditions, are articulated as if they were already rights. The word *rights* in this sense becomes a propagandistic device for adding authority to our claims. My demand for something becomes much more impressive, much more likely to attract attention, when I can say, "Give me this, it is my right," than if I simply say, "Give me this because I want it." In short, if you want something, you may have a better chance of getting it if you can declare that you have a right to it. Many useful, valuable, and desirable things put forward as claims are asserted to be rights, but from this perspective they become rights, not by the law of God or nature, but when accepted by the society and perhaps eventually incorporated into law by the state.

This can provide us with standards for passing judgments on states and societies. In Green's scheme of things, the "good" society is one that provides appropriate machinery for the translation of at least some claims into rights recognized by law. It will provide generous opportunities for the articulation of claims; forums in which people may express their wants, and where they can try to persuade others of their validity. And it will institute procedures for listening to competing claims for rights. Here one must recognize that not all demands have an equally valid claim for popular acceptance. Some are trivial, some foolish, some socially harmful, and many are mutually incompatible. In the good society there will also be a close approximation between claims recognized by the society at large as genuine rights and those rights written into the law and protected by the full authority of the state. The necessary conditions of a good society in the modern age would include a reasonably free press, wide opportunities for public debate, adequate access to information, and so on.

The "bad" state, on the other hand, is one in which rights are frustrated, where they are systematically denied, and where, perhaps, claims cannot even be expressed. In South Africa, for example, not only are non-whites denied equality before the law, they are denied even the right to claim that equality. It is a criminal offence to seek to change the laws on race. Non-whites have few rights, and may not legally claim more. In the bad state, even widely supported claims, deeply felt needs and desires, go unrecognized. When the government of the society is in the control of an unresponsive minority, the claims of the many may be ignored.

We have seen that the concept of rights is important. Most of us want to be assured that we have rights. But when we move from the generalized assertion of unspecified rights to some more particularized principles, difficulties arise. It is not easy to explain why some things should be held as rights and others not, or why the rights claimed by some people differ from those claimed by others. We have difficulty in demonstrating where our rights arose or what is the source of their authority. These past pages have attempted to outline some versions of how these questions might be dealt with. It is up to the reader to decide which interpretation appears most satisfactory. Perhaps other interpretations might also be introduced.

Finally, let me list a number of things that some people in Canada today might like to have or to do. Which of these things would you regard as rights, and which would you not? On what basis do you make these judgments? How would you answer the person whose judgments differ from yours? Where did the rights you recognize come from?

Voting for the candidate of your choice in an election.

Being assured of enough to eat at all times.

Not being denied an education solely for economic reasons.

Worshipping, or not worshipping, in any way you wish.

Carrying a firearm.

Having a job with reasonable pay.

Watching whatever kind of movie you want to see.

Speaking your mind on any matter.

Not having to pay income tax.

Advocating violence against groups you dislike intensely.

Not being denied a job because of race, sex, or religion.

Having a decent place to live.

Not having to employ people whose race or religion offends you.

Swimming naked at a public beach.

Vacations with pay.

Smoking marijuana.

Freedom of choice on abortion.

In discussion, could you extend this list? Can you discern any pattern in the types of responses people give to these questions? Do those who agree on some questions also tend to agree on others?

CHAPTER FOUR

Freedom of Expression

From a discussion of rights in general, it is appropriate to move to a more detailed analysis of specific rights. The most fundamental right in a liberal democracy is that of freedom of expression, the right to say or print anything one wishes. Without it, no other civil liberty has much meaning. Without the liberty to speak out, no other claim can be asserted, nothing else demanded, and if any other right or claim is denied, no protest can be made. When freedom of expression is lost, there can be no protection against the loss of all other freedoms.

As is to be expected, therefore, there is a huge democratic literature on the values of free speech and a free press. It is one of the freedoms now enshrined in Canada's Charter of Rights and Freedoms. Clause IIb states: "Everyone has the following fundamental freedoms: . . . freedom of thought, belief, opinion and expression, including freedom of the press and other media of communication."

LIMITS TO FREE EXPRESSION

While in a liberal democratic society it is conventional to declare a belief in free speech and free expression, even their most ardent and sincere defenders cannot consistently uphold them as *absolute* rights. Few are able to maintain an unqualified libertarian position, for there are always some reservations or exceptions. For example, John Milton's *Areopagitica* (1644) is regularly quoted as one of the most noble defences of a free press. One can find inspiration in his declaration "Give me the liberty to know, to utter, and to argue freely according to conscience, above all liberties." Yet even Milton "put narrow limits on who should be allowed to write without hindrance." He denied the right of free expression to Catholics, royalists, atheists, and others who disagreed with him on fundamental moral and religious questions.[1]

JOHN MILTON

Born in London December 9, 1608; died in London November 8, 1674.

English poet and writer of political tracts. His appeal for freedom from censorship, Areopagitica *(1644), is one of the most famous writings on the subject in English, although in fact Milton approved of only a narrowly defined freedom of speech. He also defended the right of a people to execute a tyrant in the tract* Of the Tenure of Kings and Magistrates *(1649). He was one of the principal defenders of Cromwell's Commonwealth.*

There are powerful forces set against the idea of freedom of expression. Any organization or regime, whether it be a political party, a church, a government, or a cause, that regards itself as the custodian of absolute truth is tempted to believe that it has not only the right but the duty to suppress error. Certainty in the possession of truth or the assumption of infallibility lead inevitably to a demand for control over information. Fear of questioning and fear of controversial ideas encourages censorious minds to burn books, sack libraries, and silence critics. Free expression is always in danger whenever any group decides it is entitled to secure its environment from real or imagined attacks or to impose its version of reality upon the whole society.

The daily newspapers regularly remind us that without a free press democracy would soon perish. And while one can perhaps look a little cynically at this self-righteous special pleading by newspaper owners, the fundamental proposition is still true: without free media, liberal democracy is crippled. Dictators and the petty would-be dictators found in every society are afraid of, or suspect the motives of, a free press. There is, in even the freest society, an ongoing conflict between freedom of expression on the one hand and, on the other hand, the politicians and administrators at every level from the national government down to the smallest local councils, the civil servants, the police, and the representatives of the major corporations. The latter groups would like to conduct their affairs in private. They find the glare of public attention uncomfortable. Information in the "wrong hands" threatens their security and their monopoly of power.

The press, or at least its more irresponsible elements, may sometimes be shoddy, sensationalist, or trivial. It may be carping, bigoted, and more concerned with selling advertising space than with protecting the public interest. The priority given to private profit-making may produce some truly dreadful, shameful papers—the grosser tabloids and gossip sheets, for example—but we are still better off than with a totally subservient press existing only to advance the one official government interpretation of events, or with no press at all.

Like all rights, the right of free speech is necessarily constrained by reference to the consequences. Because rights do not exist in isolation, one must always take into account their impact on other rights. There is no right of free speech where words will have the effect of causing unwarranted harm to others. The right of free speech does not allow one to stand up in a darkened, crowded cinema and falsely yell "Fire!" You are not exercising any right if, as a member of a crowd in the street, you shout "Jump!" to a potential suicide on a window ledge. There is no right to spread false and malicious slanders about the honesty or integrity of public figures. Freedom of speech does not give anyone the right to assert, without any evidence whatever, that some candidate for public office is a thief, a traitor, or a sex maniac. There is a fine line to be drawn between the libellous and unwarranted attack on a person's reputation, and an honest and legitimate expression of opinion about that person's suitability for public office. If in print I call some political candidate an incompetent fool, am I guilty of libel or am I making a fairly outspoken editorial comment? There are limits to the right of free speech, or free expression, limits that are most critical to an understanding of what free expression is all about. The essential point to be made is that circumstances alter cases; what is permissible in one situation may be unacceptable in another. In 1919, in the United States, Mr. Justice Holmes enunciated what came to be known as the doctrine of "clear and present danger":

> The question in every case is whether the words used are used in such circumstances and are of such a nature as to create a clear and present danger that they will bring about the substantive evils that Congress has a right to prevent.[2]

This is the recognition that what would be, in some cases, a perfectly legitimate exercise of the right of free speech, might be properly curtailed in other circumstances where there was an obvious and existing danger that the same expression could have a serious or unacceptable consequence. By the Holmes doctrine there must be a realistic danger, some actual or reasonably probable intolerable consequence; and it must exist as an immediate threat, not merely some long-term, theoretical possibility. The fact that some group might dislike the ideas being advocated, or feel alarmed about the prospect of others being persuaded by them, is not sufficient ground for limiting free speech. Following this principle, the American Supreme Court has maintained that there was a difference between, say, teaching about revolution — quoting the words of revolutionaries in the classroom — and actually *preaching* revolution to a receptive audience in a revolutionary situation.

OLIVER WENDELL HOLMES

Born March 8, 1841; died March 6, 1935.

An American jurist who wrote extensively on the theory and practice of law. He was appointed to the United States Supreme Court in 1902, serving there as one of the most distinguished justices of the age until his retirement in 1932. His major opinions displayed a realistic analysis of the shift of social forces in twentieth-century America.

If in the course of these pages, prepared long before they came into your possession and read by you probably in isolation and silence, I were to urge you to overthrow the university system of Canada, set fire to your university library, and assassinate the president of your university, you might well doubt my sanity; but it is doubtful if you, or society in general, would need to feel unduly alarmed at the threat of imminent revolution. The likelihood that any large number would respond to such an exhortation is remote indeed. If, however, you were already assembled as a member of an excited and angry crowd, where tensions were high, where there had already been violent incidents, and where tempers were badly frayed, the same exhortation made in tones that could genuinely excite you to respond might justify my forceful removal from the scene.

The state has always an overriding right to survive, and to take action to protect all its other rights and liberties. This was a central point for Machiavelli in the sixteenth century:

> For where the very safety of the country depends upon the resolution to be taken, no consideration of justice or injustice, humanity or cruelty, nor of glory or of shame, should be allowed to prevail. But putting all other considerations aside, the only question should be, What course will save the life and liberty of the country?[3]

Even where freedom of speech is most highly valued, the society will put limits on a freedom of speech that would result in the loss of all other freedoms.

This is, of course, a dangerous line of argument that must be made cautiously. Societies in general, through their governments, security forces, and police, are everywhere inclined to be oversensitive to the possibilities of sabotage or treason. It is all too easy to use the excuse of national security and the need to protect other rights to suppress legitimate dissent or to silence ideas that are discomforting or embarrassing to those in authority. Closed, timid minds, as well as many self-appointed "super-patriots," do not readily accept that a liberal democratic society, enjoying substantial legitimacy, suffers less from "revolutionary" speeches and writings than from the anti-democratic implications and dangerous precedents of trying to silence them. And occasionally, over time, the disruptive ideas of a radical minority become the conventional wisdom of the many. The United States itself was brought to nationhood by the revolutionary pamphlets of Tom Paine and others. Even today's economic conservatism was once a dangerously radical doctrine. Freedom to think and to express one's thoughts are a necessary condition for human progress.

Disclosure of the activities of the RCMP in the 1970s suggest that the force was rather heavy-handed in its interpretation of threats to national security, taking a narrow approach to the tolerable bounds of democratic dissent.[4] Such attitudes were not without precedent in Canada. In 1937 Premier Maurice Duplessis of Quebec brought in the notorious "padlock law," which empowered the government to close or "padlock" any places that were, in the government's opinion, propagating communism or bolshevism. These words were deliberately left vague, giving the government great opportunity to suppress any organization that incurred its displeasure. Similarly, in South Africa, under the Suppression of Communism Act (1950), communism is so broadly defined as to include the advocacy of any industrial, social, or economic change by "unlawful acts or omissions." Opposition to the racial policies of apartheid is held to be one of the objects of communism, and is therefore illegal.[5]

DENNIS V. UNITED STATES

In the United States, too, most of the inroads on freedom of speech have been associated with periods of anti-communist hysteria. Especially virulent was the era of Senator Joseph McCarthy in the 1950s, the spirit of which has been revived with new intensity in the 1980s. The most notable case, which is worth examining in some detail because the essential arguments were so clearly articulated, was that of *Dennis v. United States* (1951). In this case, certain leading figures of the Communist party of the United States were charged

> with wilfully and knowingly conspiring (1) to organize as the Communist Party of the United States of America a society, group and assembly of persons who teach and advocate the overthrow and destruction of the Government of the United States by force and violence, and (2) knowingly and wilfully to advocate and teach the duty and necessity of overthrowing and destroying the Government of the United States by force and violence.[6]

The majority decision of the Supreme Court invoked the "clear and present danger" doctrine. What follows is part of Mr. Justice Vinson's judgment:

> Overthrow of the Government by force and violence is certainly a substantial enough interest for the Government to limit speech. Indeed, this is the ultimate value of any society, for if a society cannot protect its very structure from armed internal attack, it must follow that no subordinate value can be protected. If, then, this interest may be protected, the literal problem which is presented is what has been meant by the use of the phrase "clear and present danger" of the utterances bringing about the evil within the power of Congress to punish.
>
> Obviously, the words cannot mean that before the Government may act, it must wait until the *putsch* is about to be executed, the plans have been laid and the signal is awaited. If Government is aware that a group aiming at its overthrow is attempting to indoctrinate its members and to commit them to a course whereby they will strike when the leaders feel the circumstances permit, action by the Government is required. The argument that there is no need for Government to concern itself, for Government is strong, it possesses ample powers to put down a rebellion, it may defeat the revolution with ease, needs no answer. For that is not the question. Certainly an attempt to overthrow the Government by force, even though doomed from the outset because of inadequate numbers or power of the revolutionists, is a sufficient evil for Congress to prevent. The damage which such attempts create

both physically and politically to a nation makes it impossible to measure the validity in terms of the probability of success, or the immediacy of a successful attempt.[7]

Mr. Justice Vinson continued:

Petitioners intended to overthrow the Government of the United States as speedily as the circumstances would permit. Their conspiracy to organize the Communist Party and to teach and advocate the overthrow of the Government of the United States by force and violence created a "clear and present danger" of an attempt to overthrow the Government by force and violence. They were properly and constitutionally convicted for violation of the Smith Act.[8]

But as well as this opinion of the majority of the Court, there were two dissenting opinions. That of Mr. Justice Douglas was a most forceful argument of the dangers of a too flexible interpretation of "clear and present danger:

If this were a case where those who claimed protection under the First Amendment were teaching the techniques of sabotage, the assassination of the President, the filching of documents from public files, the planting of bombs, the art of street warfare, and the like, I would have no doubts. The freedom to speak is not absolute; the teaching of methods of terror and other seditious conduct should be beyond the pale, along with obscenity and immorality. This case was argued as if those were the facts. The argument imported much seditious conduct into the record. That is easy and it has popular appeal, for the activity of Communists in plotting and scheming against the free world are common knowledge. But the fact is that no such evidence was introduced at the trial. . . .

So far as the present record is concerned, what petitioners did was to organize people to teach and themselves teach the Marxist-Leninist doctrine contained chiefly in four books: . . .

The opinion of the Court does not outlaw these texts nor condemn them to the fire, as the Communists do literature offensive to their creed. But if the books themselves are not outlawed, if they can lawfully remain on library shelves, by what reasoning does their use in a classroom become a crime? It would not be a crime under the Act to introduce these books to a class, though that would be teaching what the creed of the violent overthrow of the Government is. The Act, as construed, requires the element of intent — that those who teach the creed believe in it. The crime then depends not on what is taught but on who the teacher is. That makes freedom of speech turn not on *what is said*, but on the *intent* with which it is said. Once we start down that road we enter territory dangerous to the liberties of every citizen. . . .

When ideas compete in the market for acceptance, full and free discussion exposes the false and they gain few adherents. Full and free discussion even of ideas we hate encourages the testing of our own prejudices and preconceptions. Full and free discussion keeps a society from becoming stagnant and unprepared for the stresses and strains that work to tear all civilizations apart. . . .

There comes a time when even speech loses its constitutional immunity. Speech innocuous one year may at another time fan such destructive flames that it must be halted in the interests of the safety of the Republic. That is the meaning of the clear and present danger test. When conditions are so critical that there will be no time to avoid the evil that the speech threatens, it is time to call a halt. Otherwise, free speech which is the strength of the Nation will be the cause of its destruction.

Yet free speech is the rule, not the exception. The restraint to be constitutional must be based on more than fear, on more than passionate opposition against the speech, on more than a revolted dislike for its content. There must be some immediate injury to society that is likely if speech is allowed.[9]

These are vastly important statements having application far beyond the activities of the Communist party or the circumstances of the United States in the 1950s. The same kind of arguments could be raised in any debate over the necessity or desirability of prohibiting racist hate literature or the advocacy of any kind of political extremism. Periodically a spate of virulent propaganda surfaces somewhere in Canada — pamphlets, speeches, recorded telephone messages, and even comic books — attacking some segment of our society. The favoured targets are Jews, Roman Catholics, and blacks. The anti-Jewish propaganda alleges that the Jews are an inferior race, there is a Jewish conspiracy to take over the world, and the Holocaust never happened. Against the Catholics it is said that the Pope is the anti-Christ and there is a Catholic conspiracy to take over the world. The blacks, it is said, are there merely to serve the superior white races and there is a black conspiracy to take over the world. How is a liberal democratic society to deal with this material? Does one argue that nothing can or should be done because in a liberal democracy all points of view, all expressions of opinion, are equally legitimate? Does one argue that some expressions should be banned because they cause unwarranted grief and suffering to the victims, violating their rights to live peacefully and free from fear? Or does one argue that extreme words that might stimulate physical violence must be banned, not so much because of what is said, but because the form of expression is likely to provoke a break down of law and order?

CENSORSHIP

The opposite of free speech is censorship and it becomes easier to approach the limits and challenges to the rights of free speech from the direction of censorship. Censorship affects not only those with something to say. It also restricts the freedom of those who want to know what is said. Indeed, in terms of the number of people involved, or the effectiveness of impediments to the spread of ideas, it can be argued that the right to speak and write is less important than the right to hear and read. We want not only to speak freely but also to hear what others have to say.

Censorship in a liberal democracy is usually discussed as a moral-political issue, and as democrats, in our public statements at least, we are expected to be unsympathetic to the idea. Censorship, we are encouraged to believe, is the instrument of dictators. Even those who most enthusiastically supported the majority opinion in *Dennis v. United States* by and large believe that free speech is a democratic virtue. But we are all a little inconsistent, for no one, in fact, is completely opposed to all censorship. There always comes that point where even the most extreme libertarian will admit some valid restriction on freedom of speech and the press. We are mostly alert to, and shocked by, the censorship by which totalitarian regimes restrict the dissemination of what we regard as the truth. We are not nearly so perceptive to, or upset by, the limits we impose on the spread of critical ideas in our own society.

Censorship can be even more damaging to the censor than to the censored. In *Dennis v. United States*, Mr. Justice Douglas was to a large extent echoing J.S. Mill's classic nineteenth-century defence of the maximum possible freedom of expression. Mill argued that freedom of opinion and freedom of expression were a necessity to the mental well-being of humanity. His four major propositions were all directed to the deleterious effect of censorship on the intellectual and mental strength of the censors and on the vitality of their own faith; the censors were the ones who suffered most from their own restrictions:

> First, if any opinion is compelled to silence, that opinion may, for aught we can certainly know, be true. To deny this is to assume our own infallibility.
> Secondly, though the silenced opinion be an error, it may, and very com-

monly does, contain a portion of truth; and since the general or prevailing opinion on any subject is rarely or never the whole truth, it is only by the collision of adverse opinions that the remainder of the truth has any chance of being supplied.

Thirdly, even if the received opinion be not only true, but the whole truth, unless it is suffered to be, and actually is, vigorously and earnestly contested, it will, by most of those who receive it, be held in the manner of a prejudice, with little comprehension or feeling of its rational grounds. And not only this, but, fourthly, the meaning of the doctrine itself will be in danger of being lost, or enfeebled, and deprived of its vital effect on the character and conduct: the dogma becoming a mere formal profession, inefficacious for good, but cumbering the ground, and preventing the growth of any real and heartfelt conviction, from reason or personal experience.[10]

JOHN STUART MILL

Born in London May 20, 1806; died at Avignon May 8, 1873.

A precocious child, subjected to an extraordinary forced program of education by his father, James, and by Jeremy Bentham, the young Mill received no normal school education. He was employed by the East India Co. from 1823 until 1858 and was a member of Parliament from 1865 to 1868. Mill's place in history is based on his passionate defence of individual liberty, and his recognition that the state may not be the only enemy of that liberty. In politics he steered an uneasy course between enthusiasm for the concept of democracy and a fear of the consequences of extending democratic political rights beyond the property-owning middle classes. His enduring fame is derived from his most carefully worked out piece of writing Essay on Liberty *(1859). Among his many other writings one should note his* Logic *(1843),* Political Economy *(1848),* Considerations on Representative Government *(1861),* Utilitarianism *(1863),* On the Subjection of Women *(1869), and his* Autobiography *(1873).*

For further reading see:

Brinton, Crane. English Political Thought in the Nineteenth Century. London: Benn, 1933.

Plamenatz, J.P. The English Utilitarians. Oxford: Blackwell, 1958.

Hamburger, Joseph. Intellectuals and Politics: John Stuart Mill and the Philosophic Radicals. New Haven: Yale University Press, 1965.

Cowling, Maurice. Mill and Liberalism. Cambridge: Cambridge University Press, 1963.

A further danger of censorship lies, not in the moral issue, although that is important enough, but in the fact that censorship limits access to the real world. The world of first hand sensory experiences, the things known by direct personal contact, is extremely limited. Our knowledge of physical reality is limited to those things we can see and hear, and perhaps smell, touch, and taste; and here it does not take much experiment to show how unreliable is the evidence of the senses. We do not always see and hear accurately or completely. Indeed, much of what we do claim to perceive is coloured by our personal backgrounds, by what was referred to in an earlier chapter as "attitude sets." A Canadian health inspector, an artist, and a Mexican farm labourer will literally see different things as they enter the same Mexican village. We do not view an objective world, but a world interpreted by our own experiences.

Apart from the limited range of personal, first-hand, sense-experienced events, we know of most of the world only through secondary sources: through the press, radio, television, film, or the reports of others. Our contact with, and therefore our range of responses to, the real world is through mediators. Other people stand between us and the events outside the range of our direct experience. We do not deal with the facts and events of the real world, but with *reports* of those events. I did not react to the war in the Falkland Islands — I was not there, I have never been there, and I have very little desire to go there. I responded to newspaper reports and to television films of the Falklands war — which are not the same thing at all. And I interpreted those reports in the light of my existing attitudes to war in general, to the Argentinian military dictators, and to the government of Mrs. Thatcher. In almost all situations the only physical reality is the reality of the newspaper column and the television film, the only things touched and seen. But a knowledge founded on print and pictures is relevant, useful knowledge only to the extent that the print and the pictures are themselves reasonably complete and reasonably accurate representations of situations and events. This is a most important fact to keep in mind. As most knowledge of the real world comes to us second hand, we can make accurate judgments about the real world only to the extent that the reports are accurate.

However, despite the good intentions and professional skills of even the best newspapers, by the very nature of the world, the reports cannot be complete. They must be selective in what they choose to say. As it is impossible to say *everything* about any organization or event, every abridgement is to some extent a distortion of the truth. On the nightly television news, for example, some complex event such as violence in the Middle East — an isolated event in a complicated history of continuing passions and hatreds

— is covered in two or three sentences, with some camera shots of guns firing and ambulances shrieking through rubble-strewn streets. But the moment of violence is not the Middle East crisis, and after seeing the moment, we are really no nearer to an understanding nor to reaching a solution. Even television's proudest boast that it can bring reality into the living room cannot be sustained. Much has been made of the assertion that television coverage of the Vietnam war showed the American people the reality of that war. But it did nothing of the kind, and could not. Truth was distorted by reduction to the size of a TV screen, by minimizing the noise, by eliminating the smell, and by the fact that the worst episodes lasted only a minute or two. The whole presentation still looked like a movie set, indistinguishable from the action-packed adventure film that preceded it. Both were expected to have a happy ending. As a medium, television is based on fantasy, with few contacts with reality. This creates in the audience a disposition to suspend belief, which affects the news programs as much as the more overt fiction.

In any report on any event some things will be seized on for attention, while others will be left out. Of necessity, the reporter must use personal judgment in the selection of specific items. One reporter might describe some things, and ignore others that you, had you been there, would have treated differently. Journalists do not report events; they report the things about events that they personally think are important. The reporters become censors between the reader and the world. If a reporter does not tell us about something, then in effect, that something does not exist. Outside the world of direct personal experience, the only truths we know are truths compiled for us by others.

THE CENSORS

A clearer understanding of censorship, or information control, as it might more accurately be described, comes through an analysis of its components: Who does what, when, and how? First, who does the censoring? Perhaps the most important censors, but the least understood, are ourselves. We impose a great deal of self-censorship on our lives. It is a censorship that may be either unconscious, meaning unrecognized, or conscious, meaning admitted and acknowledged. Unconscious censorship occurs when we close our minds to unpleasant or unfavourable ideas. In psychological terms it can be referred to as *ego protection*, the desire to maintain, intact, the whole fabric of our established ideas, the unity of the attitude set. My attitudes are part of what makes me, *me*, and I will resist intrusions that might require a restructuring or a reevaluation of some parts of that attitude system, and therefore a reordering of my own being.[11] Free speech loses much of its value if too many people refuse to expose themselves to unwelcome or unfamiliar ideas. So to be a vital democratic force, free expression requires a tolerant audience as much as it needs the uncensored communication.

Conscious self-censorship occurs when individuals deliberately refuse to read opposition newspapers, or listen to the candidates of other parties, or attend to any thoughts or ideas challenging or questioning their established convictions. Except when engaged in some academic exercise, most read and listen, not to open themselves to new ideas, but to receive confirmation and assurance in the things already believed. Most partisan newspapers, particularly the religious and political press, are read almost exclusively by the faithful, and most attend a political rally to support the speaker and to hear the "truths" they have always known. Propagandists for any cause spend an enormous amount of time presenting their case yet, more often than not, the message reaches only those who already believe it. This does not mean a complete wasted effort, because the faithful do need reassurance and they are strengthened by it. But converts are hard to reach. In Canada, for example, very few, say, Roman Catholics or Moslems, will be regular readers of the *United Church Observer*, and few convinced Liberals or Conservatives will read the *New Democrat*.

But although we are our own most severe censors, there are also external censorship agencies, those generally brought to mind when censorship is discussed. These are the official military and political censors who, in varying degrees in different countries, set themselves up as a barrier between the public and knowledge of the world. In the less democratic countries the censors are busy with their scissors and their blue pencils, invoking their regulations to cut, delete, and silence, to deny in practice any principle of a free press. Their task is to make sure that the media report only what officialdom wants reported, to make sure that dissenters and critics do not easily find an audience. But it is too simple to imagine an absolute dichotomy between the dictatorships and the democracies. There are differences of degree, often very substantial differences, but censors are at work in all regimes. Certainly there are countries where nothing may legally be published without prior official consent. We are not in that position in Canada, but even here there are severe penalties for making public any official secrets. Government and the bureaucracy have built up enormous internal defences to prevent the public having anything but the most carefully controlled access to the public's business. Always there is a quite proper, unarguable case for the withholding of some information. But the whole tendency of modern governments is to widen the area of secrecy to keep to themselves everything they are not forced to disclose.

Governments have a vested interest in secrecy. Nowhere is the contrast between the language and ideals of democracy, and its actual practice, more sharply revealed. Public officials surrounding themselves with a blanket of secrecy thereby restrict the content of public debate. This is the dilemma. Liberal democracy, as its founding idealists understood it, implied rational behaviour by informed citizens. With insufficient information, people do not have the necessary evidence to judge intelligently. But governments that claim to be democratic seldom make all that necessary information available. All liberal democratic governments, to varying degrees, persist in denying their citizens access to the information they need.[12] To a large extent, the secrecy practices of governments make it impossible to reach anything even approximately near the liberal democratic ideal.

Liberal democracy degenerates into a sham if public opinion is based only on what the government chooses to make public. Canada, at the federal level at least, is more open than many parliamentary democracies, but even here not everything can be made public. And obviously not everything should be made public. But legitimate censorship on the grounds of security, public interest, or individual privacy can all too easily be directed to more partisan goals. The undoubted right of governments to impose controls on nationally sensitive issues is easily expanded to avert criticisms that might simply be politically or administratively embarrassing or inconvenient. Political censorship in peacetime "represents a confession by the authorities of their refusal to trust the people to form sound opinions and their unwillingness to allow them to judge between conflicting views and to abide by the results as democracy requires."[13] The whole concept of censorship is thus elitist, in that it assumes that one segment of society is entitled to the possession of information that ought not to be made available to the rest. Those who would try to make it available must therefore be silenced. The few take it upon themselves to decide what the many shall see and hear. There is thus a contempt for the people implicit in the notion that they must be protected from harmful ideas, although these forbidden ideas do not endanger the protectors. The censors assume themselves to be of firmer moral fibre than the censored. Film censors who would protect us from the corrupting influence of pornographic movies seem themselves never to be corrupted by what they have witnessed.

Because information is a source of power, ruling elites resist the extension of information. The older ruling classes dreaded the social consequences when reading and writing, former mysteries understood only by priests and rulers, became accessible to the masses. It was feared that once the "lower orders" could find out things for themselves, they would become rebellious and disorderly and no longer respectful of the wisdom and guidance of their natural superiors. Once it was conceded that it was impossible to stop the lower classes from reading, their "betters" embarked on a continuing campaign to ensure that they saw and read only what was good for them, and that, as far as possible, "seditious and immoral" ideas were kept from them.[14] This is still the philosophy behind much government secrecy. The "people" cannot be trusted with too much information. Not understanding it, they would misuse it.

Beyond this overt censorship by governments and their agencies, there is another level of censorship, of restriction on the dissemination of information. This is the censorship imposed by the media themselves. It is a dangerous innocence to imagine that, because only governments impose censorship, a free market system limiting the range of government activities liberates us from the fear of censorship. This traditional liberal view that it is only governments that need to be feared is proclaimed by many of those involved in the mass media. Any information control imposed by the media owners themselves, in furtherance of their own interests, is upheld as an exercise in the freedom of the press. But private censorship can suppress ideas and dissent quite as effectively as the worst government censor. To be an instrument of liberal democracy, the marketplace of ideas would have to provide equal access to all. But nowhere is this ideal realized or even realizable.

As might be expected, in advanced capitalist societies such as our own, the mass media are largely privately owned, and by that part of the private domain associated with the largest scale capitalist enterprises. There is a consequence:

> The right of ownership confers the right of making propaganda, and where that right is exercised, it is most likely to be exercised in the service of strongly conservative prejudices, either by positive assertion or by the exclusion of such matters as owners may find it undesirable to publish. Censorship is not, in a free enterprise system, purely a state prerogative.[15]

It is unquestionably true that such corporate censorship is neither as pervasive nor as monolithic as in a totalitarian regime, but the very fact that the media are overwhelmingly in the control of one social class inclines them to influence the flow of information in the interests of that class:

> The mass media cannot ensure complete conservative atunement; nothing can. But they can and do contribute to the fostering of a climate of conformity, not by the total suppression of dissent, but by the presentation of

views which fall outside the consensus as curious heresies, or, even more effectively, by treating them as irrelevant eccentricities, which serious and reasonable people may dismiss as of no consequence.[16]

It's not only, or even mainly, the overt political commentaries and editorials that are affected. Even the quality and character of entertainment television are influenced by the fact that, in general, the multinational corporations, which are the largest source of media advertising revenue, view social change or challenge at home or abroad as a threat to their continued well-being. The main objective of the media in our society is to encourage a relaxed, confident consumerism, which it does by ignoring, playing down, or overtly rejecting any questioning of a materialistic value system. It is not a question of ramming an unremitting, strident capitalist propaganda down the throats of a helpless audience. It is much more effective not to raise political issues at all, to defuse controversy, to establish a relaxed, apolitical atmosphere in which people can go about their daily business without troubling themselves about the health or character of the system in which they live. The nightly prime-time television mix of mindless sit-coms and violent crime dramas, broken up by endless commercials, does more to divert the mind from any criticism of the prevailing political order than any sustained overt proselytizing.

One area of research today deals with *agenda setting*. This is the idea that the media define the topics, the subject matter; in short, they set the *agenda* of public debate. In a democracy the media cannot tell us what to think, and they do not have much effect when they try. But they are enormously influential in determining what we shall think about. The public can have no opinions on matters about which the media remain silent, for, in effect, they do not exist. The media not only tell us what to talk about, they even help assign priorities among the things discussed. We tend to assume that news stories feature on the front page because they are important. But it is actually the other way round. News stories come to be regarded as important because news editors have chosen to put them on the front page. A simple experiment quickly confirms this. For example, a selection of newspapers from across Canada, for one week, shows that items blazoned with major headlines in one paper, will be relegated to the back pages in another part of the country, and ignored altogether elsewhere.

Finally, censorship can arise from the society itself, by imposing the values or the mores of the majority or some particularly outspoken and articulate group upon the whole society. When majorities or crusaders of various stripes bring pressure on governments to restrict the kind of films that may be shown and the books that may be read in schools or stocked in public libraries; and bring pressure on sponsors to withhold support from television programs that displease them, they are limiting our freedom of speech and expression. One group is taking it upon itself to define the values of all members of society.

THE TIMING OF CENSORSHIP

The impact of censorship is affected not only by who the censor is but also by the timing of the act of censorship. There are two dimensions here: prior censorship and *post facto* censorship. Prior censorship means that before anything can be published, said, or shown, it must be demonstrated that it does not violate any law or regulation. In most dictatorships all, or almost all, printed material is subject to prior censorship. Nothing may be published until the censor has added a stamp of approval. Such censorship, generally strict, may embrace also books, plays, films, and public lectures. Totalitarian regimes do not welcome, or are perhaps afraid of, criticism or divergent views. They become perhaps unduly sensitive to what they interpret as slights or attacks on the solidarity of the regime. Stability and consensus are to be maintained by preserving uniformity in thinking and ideas. Dissent is interpreted as treason.

Prior censorship is, by definition, alien to the idea of democracy, yet it is not entirely unknown. Most democracies will have some version of an Official Secrets Act that makes it illegal to make mention of matters in certain reasonably well-defined categories. On occasions these categories are far more broadly drawn than would seem consistent with the ideals they are supposedly protecting. However, within the liberal democracies the newspapers are not required to submit advance copies to ensure that they have not violated the law. In other areas the media may do pretty much as they please and there are no legal constraints on political criticisms of the government of the day. In some parts of Canada, as in Ontario for example, there is prior censorship of publicly displayed films. The grounds are more likely to be obscenity or violence than political dissent. The Ontario censors do take their job quite seriously, often protecting Ontario film-goers from scenes that may be quite legally watched elsewhere in Canada.

There is also *post facto*, or after the fact, censorship. Here no official censors issue regulations on what may or may not be published. No one will demand to see any page proofs in advance or preview any film. But after the fact of publication, there may be legal action for violation of the laws of national security, libel, obscenity, or whatever. In effect, officialdom says, "You may publish, exhibit, or say what you like, but you must bear the consequences for whatever you choose to publish." In some senses, and in some situations, post facto censorship may be more repressive than prior censorship. At least if there is official government censorship, once the stamp of approval is on the copy, the editor's responsibilities are over. There is nothing more to fear. But if the regime maintains more the facade than the reality of democracy, the news editor is in a difficult position. The government will issue no regulations or directives, but it lets it be known that it will react very firmly to things it does not like. The editor will be under great pressure to act with extreme caution or circumspection. This was very much the position in the New Zealand Broadcasting Service where I worked some thirty or more years ago. The government of the day kept a very firm control over the domestic broadcasting news services. It acted, not through regulations or censors, but through a widely appreciated set of understandings of what it would do if displeased. Without putting it in so many words, the news editor was told, "You can say whatever you want — Once!" And in the United Kingdom, where libel laws are much more strictly interpreted than in Canada or the United States, newspaper editors or book publishers choose to exercise what might here be regarded as excessive caution.

THE MATERIAL CENSORED

The third area where full freedom of seeing and hearing might be restricted involves the material to be covered. Here the question is: what sort of things ought, or ought not, to be restricted? Obviously any simple-minded proposition that all censorship be abolished is neither realistic nor helpful. There are at least two broad areas, national security and public interest, where some limitation on free expression may be consistent with liberal democratic values. National security is the easiest to deal with. By no stretching of libertarian rhetoric could we justify in wartime the prior announcement of troop movements, the sailing of troop ships, the deployment of forces, the specification of new weapons, and so on. Freedom of expression does not extend to these unquestionably secret matters. The same might be said about letting the enemy have information about the effectiveness of their attacks, when we have reason to believe they do not have this information. A more difficult question arises when it comes to withholding information about losses suffered or damage done when there is no doubt that the enemy does know all about it — a sunken ship or a position lost, for example. Here the object of censorship, it is alleged, is not to keep facts from the enemy, but to protect the morale of one's own side. The military mind always seems to have a very low opinion of the civilian population's moral strength or ability to cope with bad news.[17] Yet there is a great deal of evidence indicating that people in general are more likely to be demoralized by the lack of any news at all than by the receipt of bad news. In the absence of real news they will tend to circulate their own news — rumours — which may be even more demoralizing than the facts. In practice the censorship of bad news may have the effect of protecting the reputations of military leaders who have lost battles. Losses, however, cannot be indefinitely concealed, and experience suggests that more is lost from the breakdown of credibility later than from the immediate disclosure of some disaster.

A difficult question, particularly in wartime, is the boundary between legitimate criticism of political, administrative, or military incompetence or failure designed to prevent the repetition of those errors; and disloyal opposition to the war effort threatening the security of the nation. A free press generally tries to take the view that responsible criticism is more than a right; it is a duty. Governments, on the other hand, react most strongly to suggestions that they are anything other than the noblest and wisest. In times of war, or a perceived threat of war, governments become afraid of criticism, tending to disbelieve that it can be offered honestly. Winston Churchill and his Cabinet manifested "at times a startling conviction that any opinion which they personally did not like was for that reason unpatriotic and treacherous."[18] The same might be said of President Reagan's reaction to critics of his foreign policy. This poses a very real problem. In any government, anywhere, there will be from time to time instances of gross incompetence, bad judgment, and corruption. No system can ever be totally immune from these failings. In an open society in peacetime, there is some possibility that these things will be exposed, and perhaps corrected. The threat of publicity may even reduce the incidence of corruption or malfeasance. In the defensive atmosphere of wartime, however, criticism and exposure can be silenced because they weaken confidence. But the price to be paid for protecting morale is the continuation of the incompetence or the immunity of the corrupt. It might well be argued that it is a bad bargain.

The second widely used justification of censorship is that broad umbrella called "the public interest." Here again we find defensible, ambiguous, and indefensible attitudes. As a defensible case, it could be argued that any government is entitled to prohibit the advance publication of budget details or perhaps rationing proposals. Negotiations in industrial disputes or dealings between nations might be adversely disrupted by too much publicity. Governments have the undeniable right to keep some of their activities secret. On the other hand, governments at all levels do appear to adopt the attitude that the public's business is no concern of the public. When boards, councils, and committees of enquiry conduct all their affairs in private, refusing even to announce the results of their deliberations, they may be imposing an undesirable, self-defeating level of information control. Democratic government depends on responsible voter behaviour. This is possible only with an informed public opinion, and opinions cannot be informed if government refuses to provide the information.

Finally, there is the great issue of censorship of morality. What right does society as a whole have to pass laws dealing with the portrayal of obscenity, violence, blasphemy, or any other area of concern? The problem is complicated by the fact that in a society such as Canada standards are far from uniform and are changing continually. It is difficult to say anything meaningful about what the public will or will not tolerate. There are those who feel morally outraged by the glimpse of a bare breast on television, and those who feel far more shocked by the violence of a hockey game. One person will argue that as obscenity, however defined, is an assault upon the whole moral fabric of the nation, society therefore is entitled to protect itself against such an assault. It has not only the right but the obligation to so act. Another might respond that as obscenity is in the eye of the beholder, those who are offended by particular books, films, or television shows have the unchallenged right not to read or watch them. The fact that they are offended does not give them the right to impose their views on others. Certainly the censorship of books, magazines, or films is a violation of freedom of expression. But the question is: is it a justifiable violation, an appropriate limit to a right, that is nowhere held to be absolute? The whole question of censorship on moral grounds is such an emotional one and arouses such deep reactions that no easy, generally accepted solution is possible.

Censorship, the reverse of free expression, thus involves three major variables: who does it; when it is done; and what is censored. A construction of all these variables enables us to assemble some kind of continuum between two impossible situations. No one can maintain a position of total censorship. If no one could write or say anything to anyone, anywhere, without official approval, all original thought would be stultified, and the regime would collapse under the weight of its own machinery of supervision. On the other hand, it is impossible to maintain a position of no censorship. If a society is to survive, it must put some constraints on some kinds of expression, in some kinds of circumstances. Between these impossible absolutes we can each put ourselves in a more or less libertarian position and set some limits between the permissible and nonpermissible rights of expression.

If free speech were the only right we had or wanted, there would be no problem. But the free speech of one person may endanger other rights of other persons. There is, for example, the possibility of conflict between the right of free speech and the right of privacy. This is one of many instances where two highly valued rights confront each other. In our society, privacy is held by many to be a right. So is free speech, therefore, one must decide, not in generalities, but in each specific instance, which right is to take precedence. Neither can be absolutely upheld without destroying the other. There is the very difficult question of the extent to which the media should be permitted to make public the private life of a figure in the public eye. If there is to be a guiding principle it should be, perhaps, that in so far as, say, a politician's private lifestyle does not adversely affect the capacity to carry on public duties, that lifestyle is not the public's concern. The media, and especially the sleazier tabloids, make much of what they assert to be "the public's right to know." It is, however, not at all clear where one might draw the bounds of such a right; particularly when it collides with other rights. One might ask if the real concern is in fact the public's right to know, or the newspaper's right to make money. We must balance the right of free speech against such other rights and values as property, life, the liberty to do many things, privacy, the society's own moral values, the security of the state, civil peace and order, and perhaps much more.

CHAPTER FIVE

The Meaning of Liberty

The previous chapter made the point that the most fundamental of all rights is freedom of expression, because only through it can any other liberty or freedom be demanded. But freedom as a a wider object of human desire involves an ambiguous word and an ambiguous concept. Its interpretation is, to a large degree, a product of individual understandings of the nature of the state and of the source of rights in general.

However defined, liberty is crucial to our concept of democracy, and a word of deep emotional force. The liberty of the people is set against the tyranny of kings and despots and against slavery and oppression. Liberty has been one of history's most inspiring cries. There was Patrick Henry's ringing appeal before the Virginia Convention, March 23, 1775: "But as for me, give me liberty, or give me death." The American Declaration of Independence in 1776 had as its message "Life, Liberty, and the Pursuit of Happiness," echoing Locke's natural rights of life, liberty, and property. A few years later, the French revolutionaries rallied to the call for "Liberty, Equality, and Fraternity." People have died for liberty, and many more have died or have suffered greatly because others were claiming to be setting them free. Modern armies do not admit to invading — instead they "liberate." The great fleets of merchant ships built to supply the allied armies in the Second World War were "Liberty Ships," and even one of the types of aircraft bombing enemy cities was a "Liberator."

But what is liberty? What is it that makes us free? An easy starting point would be the proposition that liberty means being able to do whatever one wants to do. Now it may be true that if I can do whatever I want, I am in some sense free. But does the converse follow? If I am stopped from doing whatever I want to do, am I therefore not free? I might want, very deeply, to be a famous opera singer — but no one will let me — principally, I imagine, because I cannot sing. Am I therefore unfree? Of course not. But would it be different if my career as an opera singer was blocked because people of my race were not permitted to perform on stage before peoples of other races? These, and other examples, seem to indicate that there may be more to liberty than just being able to do as one pleases, and more to not having liberty than just having one's inclinations frustrated. One must take into account both the nature of the desire and the nature of the impediment to its realization.

A simple exercise in imagination might make the point clearer. Suppose you live on the banks of a river too swift or rough to cross by boat or to swim across, and you very deeply desire to reach the other side. There might be many obstacles to your crossing, but for only some of these will the language of freedom, and its loss, seem appropriate. And even in those situations where freedom is at issue, it is a factor of varying importance. Feelings about it may range from mild vexation to a deep, burning personal resentment. We can contrive examples to examine this possible range:

1. Suppose, first of all, that there has never been a bridge. None of your people has ever been to the other side. While your wish to cross is a dream, it is doubtful if anyone would consider the nonrealization of that dream, the frustration of your desire, in terms of being unfree.

2. Suppose now that there had been a bridge, but it has been washed out and never replaced. Here you might feel anger at the government or whoever else was responsible for the bridge. You might rail against inefficiency, bureaucratic indifference, and so on, but again the language of freedom would seem inappropriate.

3. Your annoyance and frustration might be exacerbated if the washed-out bridge was rebuilt in another location at an inconvenient distance away. Here you might begin to feel a victim of circumstances beyond your control. Your anger might become more personalized, but it is still doubtful if there is an issue of freedom, except perhaps in the sense that others have now prevented you from doing that which you were once able to do.

4. Suppose now that the bridge is back in place but for the moment is occupied by a gang of hoodlums who will not let anyone across. Here you will want to do something about an undoubted interference with your freedom of movement. The obvious action is to call the police to clear the way. And in doing so you make a most important decision. You will be calling upon the law to secure your freedom. Traditionally we think of the state, the law, and the police as the enemies of freedom. There are, how-

ever, as is seen here, circumstances where the law can be the instrument for procuring freedom.

5.   The bridge is now clear, but it is a toll bridge, closed to you because you have no money. As you watch others pay and cross, you become conscious of the extent to which an economic disadvantage limits freedom of action. You will become aware that the poor are usually less free than the rich and that there is a close link between economic inequalities and the unequal application of social and political freedoms.

6.   A new set of considerations arises if the bridge is an international frontier. The police on the other side may have closed the frontier. Here you might, paradoxically, feel proud of your freedom, saying to yourself, "I live in a free country — thank God I don't live over there." But you still can't cross the river.

7.   You may feel very differently if it is the police on your side who have closed the border. To be shut in by forces of your own side carries a deeper psychological sense of restraint than to be shut out by the others. Here by any standard freedom is denied, and it is important to note that a major component is this psychological feeling that it is an unwarranted rebuff of your desire to go where you will.

8.   The bridge is now open, with traffic freely crossing it, but the frontier is closed to people of your race, religion, or political affiliation. Such circumstances would even further intensify the sense of freedom denied. You have been identified as one of a group that is unfree among the free. The awareness of loss of freedom is heightened by a consciousness of discrimination.

9.   Finally, the matter may be personalized. The bridge is generally open, but your passport has been withdrawn for some kind of offence against the authorities. As a political undesirable, you, individually, have been deprived of your freedom. You have been denied what others enjoy.

In one sense all these circumstances are the same: you were prevented from crossing a river. However, the significant point is that it was not the inability to go somewhere that made you unfree, but the nature of the impediment. The difference was that in some circumstances there was an expectation that you ought to have been able to cross. It was the direct action of others that stopped you. "You lack political freedom only if you are prevented from attaining your goal by human beings. Mere incapacity to attain your goal is not a lack of political freedom."[1] Freedom may thus be provisionally considered as being able to do as you want in conditions where you have an expectation that you ought to be able to do it, unfrustrated by the exercise of someone else's will. Freedom is thus not only an objective condition. It is also, at least in part, a psychological state of mind, a state of "feeling free." Freedom in this way becomes a subjective state of consciousness in which individuals feel that their actions arise from their own spontaneous motives.

This psychological dimension, this notion of expectation, is critical to a further understanding of the nature of freedom; how it has developed and how its meaning has changed. As our expectations have become enlarged, we have come to expect to be able to do more things and, therefore, to express freedom in ever wider terms. Once freedom was almost entirely a negative concept, meaning simply the absence of legal restraint. Later this view of freedom was modified by those who argued that the absence of physical or legal compulsion did not, of itself, make one free. There were situations where positive intervention was needed to secure freedom from other oppressive forces.[2] People could be enslaved as much by subjection to convention, by prejudice, by animal passions, or any obsessive desire, or by the coercive power of other individuals or associations, as by oppressive laws.

There is another circumstance to consider. Suppose you have spent your life shut off from the outside world. As your jailers have told you nothing of the river or the bridge, you are unaware of the freedoms you have been denied. It is argued later in this chapter that ignorance of the chains that bind one is of itself a form of slavery.

NEGATIVE LIBERTY

The first sense of liberty, negative liberty, meant originally freedom from the arbitrary will of kings and despots. In an age when life under the rule of absolute monarchs was generally a universal experience, it seemed enough to break the power of tyrants whose whim was law. When all law was oppressive, the removal of law was itself freedom.

Modern appeals to the desirability of freedom, in this sense of the negation of repressive laws, developed as a logical, if unintended, consequence of the Reformation in the sixteenth century. The *unintended* is stressed, for the period of the Reformation was a most complicated one in which three different forces, Protestantism, capitalism, and nationalism, began to emerge. All three were closely intertwined, strengthening and reinforcing each other, with each playing some part in the development of ideas of freedom.[3] The revolution against the centralized authority of the Roman Catholic Church expressed itself in terms of demands for freedom of conscience in religious matters. Although it was far from the original intention, these were eventually extended into demands for other kinds of political and social freedom. The first reformers had no thought of translating religious freedom into other freedoms. Inevitably, however, connections were made and the ideas of religious freedom stimulated new thinking in the realms of economics and politics.

Economic freedom, which is central to capitalism, was the most important of these new developments. The success of feudalism in restoring stability to Europe, thereby creating some surplus wealth, had stimulated the revival of cities, the resurgence of trade, the growth of a money economy, and a desire for a richer, more varied life than could be supplied by a self-supporting, agricultural economy. This was the period of the rise of the great banking houses, the expansion of money-lending, trade, exploration, and investment. This first stage in the emergence of capitalism encouraged a centralized government — which is part of the explanation for the association of developing capitalism with the growth of nationalism. A new pre-capitalist mercantilist economy called, first, for the establishment of domestic peace and regularity by subduing warring lordly factions. It required also some confidence that property would be secure and that contracts would be honoured. It was necessary that there be a stable currency, with the regulation of weights and measures. Above all, nascent capitalism wanted a government strong enough to safeguard trade routes and to enforce tariffs for the protection of home markets. The guilds played their part in ensuring quality control and standardization in what little manufacturing craftsmanship there was. Pre-capitalist mercantilism relied upon a central government regulating virtually every aspect of economic life.

Later, beginning perhaps in the seventeenth century, the new urban, wealthy, capitalist class began to chafe against the old regulations, seeing them as an inhibition on further expansion of their recently acquired power. Capitalism, which had relied on the security of the state in its formative years, later found that same security a barrier to further growth. It sought to break away from the old protective infrastructure. Capital demanded its freedom, especially a free market in labour.

From these circumstances arose the economic doctrine of laissez-faire — a term derived from the French and meaning literally "let do." Laissez-faire has become the accepted phrase for the economic philosophy that advocates the minimum possible intervention by government in the economic affairs of society. It is founded on the proposition that in buying and selling, manufacturing, and hiring labour, people should be free to make their own best bargains without let or hindrance by government regulation or control. This did not, of course, preclude combinations of manufacturers making private arrangements to keep wages low and prices high.[4]

The great exponent of laissez-faire economics was the Scotsman Adam Smith (1723–1790), whose *Inquiry into the Nature and Causes of the Wealth of Nations,* published in 1776, was the first serious work in economic theory and is still the key rationalization of capitalism. This is one of the most important works in economics ever written, for it is usually said that with it begins the modern science of economics.

Smith started with all the familiar liberal assumptions. He did not question the proposition that people are by an invariable human nature competitive, acquisitive egoists. The task was not to bemoan the fact nor seek to correct it but to create a set of institutions most appropriate for dealing with the situation. For Smith, the whole of human life was motivated by a ceaseless desire to improve one's condition. As he expressed it:

> The principle which prompts to save, is the desire of bettering our condition, a desire which, though generally calm and dispassionate, comes with us from the womb and never leaves us until we go into the grave. In the whole interval which separates those two moments, there is scarce perhaps a single instant in which any man is so perfectly and completely satisfied with his situation, as to be without any wish of alteration or improvement of any kind.[5]

To this general assessment of human nature, Smith added two further considerations:

1. The first was the phenomenon of the division of labour. People with different talents and capacities quickly learn the enormous advantage, even to the selfish individualist, of specialization combined with the exchange of goods and services. Selfish individuals help themselves most when each concentrates on doing that which he or she does best. Smith himself spoke of a natural "propensity to truck, barter and exchange one thing for another."[6] Even in the most primitive society it was acknowledged that increased productivity and ease of living came most readily from a division of labour.

2. Smith's second great consideration was what he called the "harmony of egoisms," which, together with the division of labour, is at the heart of laissez-faire economic theory. Very simply the proposition is that if selfish individuals are left free to make their own best bargains, without any interference from the state or any other agency, their voluntarily exchanged services will produce the greatest possible common good. Competitive egoism is not a failing in humans, but the source of their greatest strength, the factor that raises them above the other animals. If individuals are left free to be selfish, their rationality will lead them to the course of action that will produce the greatest good for others. Smith made the point in

one of the most frequently quoted passages in *The Wealth of Nations*:

> It is not from the benevolence of the butcher, the brewer, or the baker, that
> we expect our dinner, but from their regard to their own interest. We address
> ourselves, not to their humanity, but to their self-love, and never talk to
> them of our necessities, but of their advantages.[7]

Individuals do not consciously seek the common good, and it certainly
cannot be achieved by government direction. It arises spontaneously from
the operation of the free competitive behaviour of rational egoists. An
"unseen hand," as Smith called it, directs an "identity of interests" to a
"harmony of egoisms." And further:

> Every individual is continually exerting himself to find out the most advan-
> tageous employment for whatever capital he can command. It is his own
> advantage, indeed, and not that of society, which he has in view. But the
> study of his own advantage naturally, or rather necessarily leads him to pre-
> fer that employment which is most advantageous to the society.[8]

The freedom of the marketplace benefits not only free individuals but also
the whole society.

This was the original argument for the greatest possible economic freedom, its validity depending upon two assumptions. The first, the naturalness of the division of labour, is not a difficult proposition. The second,
the actual existence of an automatic harmony of egoisms in the market, is
much harder to establish. It might have been a realistic description of the
sort of person-to-person situation of the pre-industrial economy, where individual manufacturers — shoemakers, bakers, saddlers, etc. — made their
own goods, trading them for other goods and services or cash with the
primary consumers. It seems entirely irrelevant as an explanation of the
operations of multinational corporations or nation-wide retail chains with
centralized purchasing and pricing organizations.

LAISSEZ-FAIRE

The new liberals argued that, as individuals were the best judges of their
own interests, they should be free to pursue those interests by whatever
means they decided, within the framework of the law. This was a necessary
condition for a rising entrepreneurial class trying to liberate itself from the
restraints of an older, more restrictive economic order. The result was the
laissez-faire state, a state often called a "policeman state," a term used, not
in the modern sense of the oppressive police state of the contemporary

dictatorships, but in the sense that the *principal* task of the state was that of the policeman or, the night watchman, keeping law and order, protecting property, and maintaining security.

In practice the role of government was never as limited as this description might suggest. Adam Smith himself had acknowledged that industrial society cannot operate without a framework of public services. He was prepared to accept a proper area for government action. Among other things, the state could build roads and canals, operate a postal service, secure overseas markets, and maintain those public works and institutions from which private individuals could expect no reasonable profit. It was desirable that private individuals should, as far as possible, supply society's needed goods and services. But the state could do those things and provide those services which otherwise would not be done at all.

It was a later generation of disciples who chose to ignore Smith's original qualifications, to carry the ideas of laissez-faire to limits he had not intended. By and large most nineteenth-century economists assumed that free competition would, of itself, see to it that society was provided with most of the goods and services it needed. The competition among manufacturers and sellers would ensure quality and purity of production at a fair price and without government regulation or control. It was, therefore, not the normal business of the state to license, regulate, inspect, or supervise anybody. In more doctrinaire versions of laissez-faire, the state would have little concern for housing, education, welfare, pure foods, industrial safety, wages, working conditions, or promotion of industry. It was believed that if people were left alone, the desire for private gain would be sufficient motive to ensure that all things that needed to be done, would be done. Roads, fire services, water supply, public transport, libraries, and even education were all legitimate areas of private profit.[9]

The most overstated version of laissez-faire was put forward by Herbert Spencer (1820–1903) at a time when new laws and regulations were increasingly curbing laissez-faire practices. Spencer went further than anyone, before or since, in defining the things governments should not do:

> He opposed all organized charity, public or private, all state aid to education or industry, and all governmental operation or regulation of industry. Compulsory and public education, poor relief, and social legislation are futile attempts to change natural conditions; they attempt to perpetuate the weak and put them on the same plane as the strong, to preserve the unfit at the expense of the fit. Government should let poverty and unsanitary housing alone, so that weaker types may sooner die out; it should let industrial competition alone, however intense, for by such competition the best individu-

als come to the top. It should not operate the mint or the post office or erect lighthouses and life-saving stations because none of these activities fall within the sole justification of state activity — namely, the restraint of one man from interfering with the equal freedom of another.[10]

In the present generation, the cause of extreme laissez-faire has been taken up most prominently by F.A. Hayek, whose *Road to Serfdom* gained considerable fame when it was first published in 1944.[11] Hayek went as far in the defence of laissez-faire as it was possible for anyone still in touch with the twentieth century. In the classical tradition of political economy he condemned all central economic planning, all attempts by government to provide overall direction to the economy, as being both destructive of personal liberty and economically unproductive.

The idea of complete centralization of the direction of economic activity still appalls most people, not only because of the stupendous difficulty of the task, but even more because of the horror inspired by the idea of everything being directed from a single center. If we are, nevertheless, rapidly moving toward such a state, this is largely because most people still believe that it must be possible to find some middle way between "atomistic" competition and central direction. Nothing, indeed, seems at first more plausible, or is more likely to appeal to reasonable people, than the idea that our goal must be neither the extreme decentralization of free competition nor the complete centralization of a single plan but some judicious mixture of the two methods. Yet mere common sense proves a treacherous guide in this field. Although competition can bear some admixture of regulation, it cannot be combined with planning to any extent we like without ceasing to operate as an effective guide to production.[12]

In Hayek's mind there were only two possibilities: either a completely free society in which governments did not intervene at all, or totalitarianism, the complete subordination of economic freedom to the state. Hayek's central argument was that not only was the maximum economic freedom the most efficient form of economic organization, it was also the necessary condition for all other freedoms:

The fact that the opportunities open to the poor in a competitive society are much more restricted than those open to the rich does not make it less true that in such a society the poor are much more free than a person commanding much greater material comfort in a different type of society. Although under competition the probability that a man who starts poor will reach great wealth is much smaller than is true for a man who has inher-

ited property, it is not only possible for the former, but the competitive system is the only one where it depends solely on him and not on the favors of
the mighty, and where nobody can prevent a man from attempting to achieve
this result.[13]

INDIVIDUAL FREEDOM

Spencer represented the application of liberal individualism to the economic sphere, which he saw as the necessary condition for all other freedoms. The same set of philosophic assumptions about individual and society,
and about the nature of freedom, is also reflected directly in other aspects
of life. Economic liberty was held, as it is still held by many today, to be the
source of all other liberties. One of the clichés of the present generation is
that we live in a "permissive society," and the so-called "moral majority"
rages against the excesses of its freedoms. But although we tend today to
use *Victorian* as a synonym for a narrow-minded prudery, most of the years
of Queen Victoria's reign were characterized by a legal permissiveness far
beyond anything that could now be tolerated. Social pressures rather than
law ensured the conformity of many to middle-class social values. All
attempts at social reform legislation, no matter how dreadful the evils to
be corrected, were resisted by the doctrinaire economists on the grounds
that they were an unwarranted interference in personal liberty. In England
in 1886, when laws were finally passed prohibiting the sale of hard liquor
to children under the age of 13, a deputation of brewers and spirits merchants went to London to argue that the age should at least be lowered to
10, by which age people were perfectly capable of making their own decisions about how they wished to conduct their lives. The cry of individual
freedom, meaning simply the absence of any restrictive or controlling
legislation over manufacturers and traders, was used to rally opposition to
any efforts to involve the power of the state in correcting social abuses.

The Victorians, while on the one hand erecting a facade of rather rigid
conventions and customs, were at the same time more tolerant of non-
conforming behaviour than many in modern Canada. By way of example,
there is an account of correspondence in the London newspapers in 1894.
The issue centred round the fact that the Promenade of the Empire Music
Hall had become a parade ground and contact point for some of London's
most expensive prostitutes. A campaign to suppress the "public flaunting
of vice" ran into strong opposition from the defenders of personal freedom. Here is part of the text of a magnificently outraged letter from the
Daily Telegraph of October 14, 1894. Signed "Englishman," it went under

the title "Prudes on the Prowl" and demanded:

> How long is this great London of ours, so proud and yet so patient, to wait
> for the strong and irresistible voice of public disapprobation, that mighty
> roar of disgust which is heard today in private in every assemblage of common-
> sense men and women protesting against the execrating tyranny of the self-
> satisfied minority? How long are we patiently to endure the shrill shriek of
> the emancipated female, to say nothing of the prurient grass widow? How
> long must we listen to the impudent piety of these provincial pedlars in
> social purity who come red-hot from their Chicago platforms and tinpot
> tabernacles to tell this London of ours how she is to amuse herself and how
> she is to dispose of and harass and drive from pillar to post those unfortunate
> outcasts whom we have always had and always shall have amongst us?[14]

The general tenor of this, and the many letters that followed it, was that
the state had no business interfering with purely private conduct. The state,
as Pierre Trudeau said many years later in Canada, "has no business in the
bedrooms of the nation." The attitudes that encouraged economic laissez-
faire also produced a strong commitment to personal liberty in speech, the
press, opinions, personal habits, lifestyles and religion.

On the negative side, however, commitment to laissez-faire and the belief
in immutable economic "laws," hindered reforms for decades, with even
many of those most distressed by social injustices being persuaded that
government intervention would do more harm than good. In factory and
labour legislation reform was particularly slow, to be won only over bitter
opposition. It took twenty-five years of legislative activity and intense pressure to restrict a child of 9 to a 69-hour working week, and then only in the
cotton mills. And Lord Brougham, speaking in the House of Lords against
the first Child Labour Bill in 1833, where it was defeated, said:

> The bill is a travesty of personal liberty. Women and young persons are
> capable of making their own bargains, without interference by Government.
> The sponsors of factory legislation are victims of a misguided and perverted
> humanity.[15]

There was one notable exception to this general climate of the greatest
possible freedom of people to make their own best bargains in the marketplace without intervention by the state. There was simply no acceptance
of the freedom of workers in factories or on the farms to take common
action to improve their bargaining positions. Workers did not collectively
have the rights that they supposedly held as individuals. The general freedom of assembly did not, for a long time, include the freedom to establish
or join a union. Everywhere under liberalism, in the United Kingdom and

the United States as well as in Canada, freedom meant the freedom of the employer to set the wages, hours, and conditions of work. It did not include the freedom of employees to organize or act collectively to change those conditions. The rights to organize and to bargain collectively were won only after protracted struggles.

The possibility that the inequalities arising from the unchecked freedom of the marketplace might make a mockery of other freedoms was seldom taken into account. Nor was anyone prepared to consider the implications of the proposition that the economically dependent might not in fact be able to exercise the freedoms they theoretically held. For, although the law did not intervene to impose contractual conditions, "women and young persons" and even ordinary working men, acting independently, clearly could not bargain on equal terms with their employers. A completely unchecked marketplace did not give freedom to everyone. Liberal theorists were reluctant to admit, even to themselves, that there could be no genuine free bargaining between parties with unequal power. For the marketplace also produced the grossest inequalities, and without some external aid, the weak and poor had no protection. Those highly prized liberties could, in fact, be enjoyed only by the few.

POSITIVE LIBERTY

The social consequences of laissez-faire gradually led some to appreciate that while liberty is the absence of legal restraint, it may also be more than that. A few sceptics, realistically examining how people lived and behaved, came to suspect that untrammelled economic liberty could be the single greatest impediment to the exercise of other liberties by the many and, indeed, even to the full exercise of economic liberty by the disadvantaged. There were other dimensions to the concept of liberty. In particular, it came to be accepted that the law and the state were not the only obstacles to freedom. In some situations the law, far from being the antithesis of freedom, may be the instrument for initiating it or securing it against other forces. The law can play a positive role in protecting the liberty of individuals threatened by, say, lawless thugs, over-powerful individuals, or impersonal, unresponsive corporations, or intolerant, bigoted communities, or even the force of circumstances — the traps of poverty, ignorance, or a dehumanizing environment. The law can extend freedom to some segments of society that might otherwise be denied it. This notion of using the positive intervention of the law to secure liberty is sometimes called "positive liberty."

This wider definition of freedom began to emerge in the middle of the nineteenth century with the increasing awareness of the extent to which poverty, ignorance, economic dependence, job insecurity, or lack of access to information could all be barriers to freedom. John Stuart Mill was one of the first to expand on the notion of the law as an instrument for widening the opportunities for freedom. Mill began to explore new ideas, to see that to be free is to be rid of *all* the obstacles, not just oppressive laws, and to see that the major obstacles to the freedom of the many could be the power and the privileges of the few. If the principle of freedom for all was to have any meaning, it had to involve some notion of an approximate equality of freedom, which in turn might require some restraint on the extra freedoms of some. If all are to have some freedom, the greater freedom of some must be curbed. And only the law can ensure that the powerful, whether they be the few or the many, do not use their power to deny freedom to the weak.

All these ideas were refined, and given their most articulate formulation, as well as their strongest philosophic foundation, by T.H. Green in the last decades of the nineteenth century. It might be useful here to review some of what was said earlier, for Green's concept of liberty is derived from his philosophy of rights. Green's era, the latter part of the nineteenth century, was a period of intense reassessment of the consequences of the industrial revolution combined with laissez-faire doctrines. More and more of those who had listened to the arguments of Adam Smith, Herbert Spencer, and other liberal economists, and had then looked at the social conditions of the industrial cities — overcrowded, insanitary housing, desperate poverty, abandoned children, brutality and drunkenness, and a general air of hopelessness — were shocked by the gap between theory and reality. Unrestrained laissez-faire was not producing the greatest happiness of the greatest number of the industrial poor.[16]

THOMAS HILL GREEN

Born in Yorkshire April 7, 1836; died at Oxford March 26, 1882.

Educated at Rugby and at Balliol College, Green taught at Oxford as Professor of Moral Philosophy. He was the principal exponent of a school of philosophy known as English idealism, which drew much of its inspiration from Hegel. Green's revisions of the philosophic foundations of liberalism had a profound effect on what would later be called the welfare state. Green's philosophic approach also

led to a reappraisal of the meaning of liberty and of rights. His major political ideas are contained in his Lectures on the Principles of Political Obligation, *which were put together and edited after his death, on the basis of his lecture notes and those of some of his students.*
For further reading see:
Barker, Ernest. Political Thought in England: 1848–1914. *London: Oxford University Press, 1928.*
Richter, Melvin. The Politics of Conscience: T.H. Green and his Age. *London: Weidenfeld and Nicolson, 1964.*
Greengarten, I.M. Thomas Hill Green and the Development of Liberal Democratic Thought. *Toronto: University of Toronto Press, 1981.*
Rodman, J.R. T.H. Green: Political Theory. New York: Crofts Classics, 1964.

The mood for a reevaluation of old doctrines was strengthened by a growing evangelical humanitarianism. In some of the churches, especially in the Methodist and Wesleyan chapels, men of conscience began to campaign against the degrading circumstances of the urban poor. Some redefinition of the values of society and the meaning of liberty seemed to be called for. Green began to focus this moral outrage and intellectual reassessment. He had earlier broken away from formal ties to organized Christianity, but remained loyal to some of its ethical values, especially its humanitarian components. On this basis he made a critical redefinition of liberty. Liberty, he said, was no more the mere absence of restraint, than beauty was the mere absence of ugliness. Liberty was "a positive power or capacity of doing or enjoying something worth doing or enjoying."[17] Green here moved away from traditional concepts of liberty. From a negative lack of something, liberty became the positive *power* to do something. It is Green's argument that as well as having the abstract right to do something, one must have the actual capability of doing it before one can be said to be truly free to do it. Liberty without power was meaningless. An illustration might help the argument. Someone might say to you, "There are no laws restricting your freedom of movement and no laws requiring you take a job you don't want; therefore, you are free." But you might well respond that unless you have the economic reserves to cover the cost of moving, or to make up the wages lost while moving or training for a new job, that freedom has no substance. Without welfare, or unemployment insurance, or some other form of public assistance, an unemployed fisherman in Newfoundland, with no savings, is not free to take a job in British

Columbia, no matter what the law allows. So while it is easy to speak of an abstract freedom, freedoms carrying with them the power to act do not come into existence automatically. They must be secured and may often require the intervention of the law to so secure them.

There is second part to Green's definition of freedom: freedom is "the capacity of doing or enjoying something *worth* doing or enjoying." Here a moral component is added. Freedom becomes the instrument for the enlargement of the human potential as a moral being. Green thus distinguished freedom to do whatever one likes — to get drunk, stay ignorant, take drugs — from freedom to make the most of one's capacities. As Green saw it, it was only the freedom to make the most of one's capacities that deserved the title of freedom. Real freedom was that freedom that liberated the "spirit" or the "soul" of individuals. Green could thus talk about freeing oneself from enslavement to vice or ignorance:

> In one sense no man is so well able to do as he likes as the wandering savage. He has no master. There is no one to say him nay. Yet we do no count him really free, because the freedom of savagery is not strength, but weakness. The actual powers of the noblest savage do not admit of comparison with those of the humblest citizen of a law-abiding state. He is not the slave of man, but he is the slave of nature. Of compulsion by natural necessity he has plenty of experience, though of restraint by society none at all. Nor can he deliver himself from that compulsion except by submitting to this restraint. So to submit is the first step in true freedom, because it is the first step towards the full exercise of the faculties with which man is endowed.[18]

Green's concept of freedom developed from his understanding of an individual's self-consciousness as a moral being, that is, the ability of the individual to recognize personal responsibility for moral integrity. He asserted that the individual was entitled to demand from society the means to lead a life of dignity and self-respect. In other words, the individual's principal claim upon society was for the freedom to be a moral individual, in control of a personal destiny. Freedom was thus an essential component of self-realization. One cannot be a full person without the freedom to develop one's moral capacities. Further, as explained in chapter three, any claim for freedom must be universalized, that is, made on behalf of all members of society. My freedom to develop my potential is limited by the obligation to respect your freedom to develop yourself. Freedom is a social right, attaching not to the isolated, autonomous individual, but to the individual as member of an organic community.

For Green there were a number of obstacles to freedom, to the realization of the human personality. First there was ignorance, which limited horizons and denied one access to an awareness of the possibilities of life. Knowledge, it is said, is power; and those denied access to knowledge are denied the freedom to seek power. Ignorance of the existence of alternatives, indeed, even of the extent of one's own ignorance, can be the most confining of forces. The uneducated can be slaves for life without even being aware of their own slavery. The deliberate rejection of literacy or the refusal to be educated is a wilful abandonment of freedom. Therefore, to make education compulsory and to use the power of the state to provide the economic support for universal education were extensions of freedom, not its limitation.

Another obstacle to true liberty was poverty, which restricted the freedom of choice by reducing the destitute to total dependence on the whims of the powerful. The poverty-stricken have no choice; they must do whatever is required, simply to survive for another day. The utterly destitute have no reserves to build capital, to take time to think, to take risks, or to consider alternatives. Poverty is probably the greatest of all barriers to freedom. The indigent are dependent on the will of others, and dependence is the antithesis of freedom. Green would argue that no matter how few laws bind them, the penniless can never be free.

So freedom to Green meant the creation of a liberating environment, the removal of all obstacles to true human freedom. All of these considerations led Green to propose an enormous expansion of the involvement of the state in economic and social life. And he saw this involvement, not as adding to the power of the state as a goal in itself, nor as a restriction of liberty, but as a means of extending liberty. See, for example, part of his argument for the state's involvement in the regulation of working conditions:

> Hence restrictions may need to be placed on the sale of [labour] which would be unnecessary in other cases, in order to prevent labour from being sold under conditions which make it impossible for the person selling it ever to become a free contributor to social good in any form. This is most plainly the case when a man bargains to work under conditions fatal to health, e.g. in an unventilated factory. Every injury to the health of the individual is, so far as it goes, a public injury. It is an impediment to the general freedom; so much deduction from our power, as members of society, to make the best of ourselves. Society is, therefore, plainly within its right when it limits the freedom of contract for the sale of labour, so far as is done by our laws for the sanitary regulations of factories, workshops, and mines. It is equally within its right in prohibiting the labour of women and young persons beyond certain hours. If they work beyond those hours, the result is demonstrably physical

deterioration; which, as demonstrably, carries with it a lowering of the moral forces of society.[19]

By a similar argument, Green defended the right of the state to insist upon certain minimum standards of housing. He would also concede to the state power to control the physical environment of the city — insist upon sanitary standards, impose building codes, limit overcrowding, control traffic, separate housing from industry, create parks and green spaces, and so on. These were all part of what he considered an environment favourable to the liberation of the human spirit. Green was appalled by the setting of the industrial cities — mean minds and spirits developing in mean streets. The lack of spiritual or intellectual stimulation in the urban slums, where there was no trace of a tree, no respite from a landscape of bricks, narrow streets, noise and dirt, defeated every concept of fulfilment as the purpose of human existence. Without libraries, theatres, art galleries, open spaces, or sports facilities, and only the gin parlours for recreation, the nineteenth-century industrial city oppressed its citizens.

These conditions had grown out of rapid and haphazard industrialization, exacerbated by an exaggerated interpretation of laissez-faire economic doctrines. To remedy them it now became the task of the state to intervene and, to use Green's own words, "remove the obstacles to freedom." Once this kind of terminology is introduced, we come a long way to laying the foundations of the modern welfare state, but on an ethical base, as an interpretation of the source of freedom, rather than on an economic doctrine. This is an important point. In England, and through that route also in Canada, the origins of the welfare state owe much more to the outraged moral conscience, the religious-spiritual arguments of people such as Green, than to the doctrinaire models of the European socialists. Some pressed for the welfare state because they believed it to be morally the right thing to do. There were, of course, also other more expedient reasons. Some accepted the welfare state simply because they feared the industrial strife and increased crime that would be the consequence of failure to reform.

In the years following Green, arguments for increased government intervention in social measures were put forward, quite consistent with Green's position. Such things as government sponsored, prepaid health care schemes, for example, provided not only medical care as such but also, perhaps more importantly, freedom from the fear of the economic consequences of ill health. The point is not always appreciated today, but in an earlier generation, sickness or an accident to the family breadwinner could spell economic disaster. When the principal wage earner in the family fell ill, it might have meant that the rest of the family would be broken up to spend the rest of their days in the horrors of the poor house. Fear of the economic consequences of illness was a constant nagging pressure in a previous age, a fear surpassing even that of the pain and suffering of illness.

A PLURALITY OF FREEDOMS

This argument seems to be moving away from the concept of freedom as such and toward the idea of a freedom to do this or to do that, or the freedom from this or from that. The tendency now was to replace the singular word *freedom* by the plural word *freedoms*. In 1945 Professor Barbara Wootton wrote a little book, *Freedom Under Planning*, in direct response to Hayek's *The Road to Serfdom*. But this is how Professor Wootton introduced the idea of a plurality of freedoms:

> The freedoms that matter in ordinary life are definite and concrete; and they change with the changing ways of different ages and different civilisations. Freedom to-day might mean, for instance, freedom to ask for your cards and sweep out of an objectionable job; freedom to say what you think of the government in language of your own choosing; freedom to join, or to refuse to join, the Transport and General Workers' Union; freedom to start a rival Union of your own; freedom to be a Freemason, a Catholic or a Plymouth Brother; freedom from concentration camps, official spying and detention without trial; freedom to stand for Parliament or the Parish Council on any programme that you like; freedom to strike or not to strike; freedom to wear a nightdress or pyjamas as you prefer. No one would suggest that all these freedoms are of equal importance; nor do these examples necessarily cover all the freedoms that we actually have, can have, or ought to have. The relative value of different freedoms, and the conditions under which they can in fact be realised are difficult and debatable matters, and are, in fact, debated in the pages that follow. But a random list of typical contemporary freedoms is useful as a reminder that free*dom* has to be perpetually reinterpreted into free*doms*.[20]

Once freedom is approached as a plural concept, consideration must be given to the conflict of freedoms, or to the priority of freedoms. The old liberal individualists thought they were making the essential case for freedom. But nobody is ever opposed to freedom, one's *own* freedom, that is. Even Hitler believed in freedom — the freedom of Germany to assume its destiny as world conquerer. However, we have now come to appreciate that any one freedom may also be a restriction on another freedom. It is not freedom in general that is desired, but a number of specific, identifiable freedoms. Consider, for example, the 1974 Canadian Election Expenses Act, which limits the amount of money candidates and parties can spend on election campaigns. In one sense, especially in the traditional sense of freedom as the absence of legal restraint, the legislation is a restriction on the freedom of candidates to collect as much money as they can or wish, where they wish, and to spend as much of that money as they want to in trying to win votes. On the other hand, the law extends the freedom of many to contest elections with reasonable opportunities of winning, without being handicapped by inadequate funds.

BARBARA WOOTTON

Born at Cambridge 1897.

Professor of Social Studies at the University of London since 1948. Governor of the BBC, 1950. Research Officer for the Trade Union Congress and for the Labour Party, 1922–25. Principal of Morely College for Working Men and Women, 1926–27. Member of several British Royal Commissions and recipient of numerous honorary degrees. Created a life peer as Baroness Wootton of Abinger in 1958. Deputy Speaker of the House of Lords since 1967. Her numerous publications include Lament for Economics *(1938),* Freedom Under Planning *(1945),* Testament for Social Science *(1950),* The Social Foundations of Wage Policy *(1955), and* Crime and Penal Policy *(1978).*

"Give me liberty, or give me death" may have been an inspiring cry, a memorable phrase, but it is an inadequate guide to what precisely is protected by this freedom. How are we to determine the point at which a restraint of freedom ceases to be a matter of common sense or an accommodation to others and becomes an issue of such vital importance that death is preferable to its loss? What particular freedoms are worth dying for? After all, in the American Civil War, many from the South went to war and died in defence of their liberty to hold others in slavery. It was not just liberty they fought for, but a particular liberty, the liberty of one group to deprive others of their liberty. So, "Give me liberty, or give me death" means nothing without further information about what liberty is being demanded — liberty to do what, against whom? The slogan is too vague and ambiguous for a response other than an emotional feeling of empathy. As R.H. Tawney has noted:

> There is no such thing as freedom in the abstract, divorced from the realities of a particular time and place. Whatever else the conception may imply, it involves a power of choice between alternatives, a choice which is real, not merely nominal, between alternatives which exist in fact, not only on paper. Because a man is most a man when he thinks, wills and acts, freedom deserves the sublime things which poets have said about it; but, as part of the prose of everyday life, it is quite practical and realistic. It means the ability to do, or to refrain from doing, definite things, at a definite moment, in definite circumstances, or it means nothing at all.[21]

Once the problem is put in terms of deciding the priorities of liberties, questions can be answered. The answers may not be to everyone's satisfaction. They may not necessarily be wise or just answers, but they can at least be specific. The problems can be perceived and understood. Arguing the relative priority of liberties also makes it easier to deal with the question of the "tyranny of the majority," which will be the central theme of a later chapter. A democratic society accords enormous moral authority to majorities as the legitimizing force in our society. But majorities can be intolerant and can use their power, the sheer pressure of public opinion, to force individuals to conform to majority standards and values, often to the extent of denying simple liberties to dissenting individuals. For example, how much liberty should I have to dress as I wish, or to wear my hair as long or as short as I please, without public harassment? There was a time, not so many years ago, when fashion designers seemed to have almost autocratic power. When styles changed, men and women everywhere adjusted their wardrobes, fearing not the wrath of the designer, nor any legal penalty, but the disapprobation of their friends. It is only a few decades since a man who valued his reputation would not have dared appear in public without a hat.

At a more serious level it could be asserted that if my liberty to worship God in any way I wish, or not to worship at all, without endangering my career, is denied by the voice of public opinion, I am a victim of a tyranny quite as burdensome as that of an oppressive law. In these circumstances the force of law may be necessary to protect the freedom of the individual from the conforming pressures of the many. This then raises the broader issue of the use of law to restrain the freedom of some to behave in one way, in order to guarantee the freedom of others to behave in some other way. If, for example, a black family buys a house in a previously all-white neighbourhood, how far is it the duty of the state to intervene to restrict the liberty of the neighbourhood to preserve its all-white purity, in order to advance the liberty of the black family to live where it chooses? Or, in a related question, which freedom is to be protected: the freedom of restaurant owners to pick their own customers and serve whom they choose, or the freedom of customers not to be denied restaurant service because of race or religion?

Beyond whatever answers you give, the crucial point is that *any* liberty may involve a conflict of liberties. Almost every liberty claimed by one person to do one thing runs counter to the liberty of another person to do another thing. The liberty of the employer to refuse to have anything to do with a union is in conflict with the liberty of workers to form or join a union if they wish. Both of these are liberties, but it is not possible for them both to be granted at the same time. It is the government that must decide which will prevail.

Even the old negative freedom did not deny law altogether. It was always recognized that a condition of no law was not a condition of freedom, but of slavery. Hobbes's state of nature was a condition of dreadful subjection to a hostile environment in which individuals were unable to escape from limitations of barbarism. There is fairly general acceptance of the idea, which indeed goes back to Aristotle, that we do not lose our freedom when we obey laws that we have ourselves had some part in making or approving. Such obedience to the law extends to the community the widely shared principle that there is true individual freedom in individual self-discipline. The debate is really about how far we are to go in establishing what kind of laws to introduce, or protect, or enhance what kind of liberties, before we begin to lose on the other side more liberties than we gain. This is a debate seeking a balance between law as a liberating force, freeing us from savagery, subjection to vice, or from each other; and unwarranted extensions of law as an impediment to a fuller, freer, development of ourselves.

The old liberal individualists saw freedom primarily as economic freedom, the philosophy of laissez-faire. Any extension of the state into the supposed free market for the exchange of goods and services was a violation of the only freedom that mattered. Economic freedom was the source and the sustenance of all other freedoms. This is, in essence, still Hayek's argument in *The Road to Serfdom*. After describing freedom as it is used in this positive, pluralistic, competing sense, Hayek went on:

> The subtle change in meaning to which the word "freedom" was subjected in order that this argument would sound plausible is important. To the great apostles of political freedom the word had meant freedom from coercion, freedom from the arbitrary power of other men, release from the ties which

left the individual with no choice but obedience to the orders of a superior to whom he was attached. The new freedom promised, however, was to be freedom from necessity, release from the compulsion of the circumstances which inevitably limit the range of choice of all of us, although for some very much more than for others. Before man could be truly free, the "despotism of physical want" had to be broken, the "restraints of the economic system" relaxed. . . .

The demand for the new freedom was thus only another name for the old demand for an equal distribution of wealth. But the new name gave socialists another word in common with the liberals, and they exploited it to the full. And, although the word was used in a different sense by the two groups, few people noticed this and fewer still asked themselves whether the two kinds of freedom promised could really be combined.

There can be no doubt that the promise of greater freedom has become one of the most effective weapons of socialist propaganda and that the belief that socialism would bring freedom is genuine and sincere. But this would only heighten the tragedy if it should prove that what was promised to us as the Road to Freedom was in fact the High Road to Servitude.[22]

The counter-argument rejects the key proposition that economic laissez-faire is the condition of all other freedoms. It proposes instead that laissez-faire can, in fact, give freedom only to the few: to the possessors of capital and those with economic reserves. It denies freedom to the many who are economically dependent upon the rich. By this argument, the extension of welfare services, unemployment insurance, minimum wage laws, compulsory education, city zoning laws, and the provision of public libraries, parks, and sports facilities, all paid for out of public funds, are not, as alleged, denials of economic freedom. Nor are they purely social, economic measures. They are extensions of freedom because they remove some of the obstacles to the freedom of the many imposed by personal disadvantages, circumstances beyond individual control, other overly powerful individuals, or conforming public pressures. Their consequence is a widening of opportunities for personal development.

CHAPTER SIX

Questions of Equality

The ideas of liberty and equality are at the heart of the liberal democratic faith. The great rallying cry of the French Revolution of 1789, that massive assault on the old aristocratic order, was "Liberty! Equality! Fraternity!" Few today seem to be quite sure what fraternity means, as the concept is not much discussed except among some socialists. Liberty and equality, however, still have immense emotional appeal. One of our goals is surely a free and equal society—equally free, and freely equal. But there is an uneasy and confusing co-existence between liberty and equality. They both complement each other, and contradict each other.

They contradict each other in the sense that a totally free society, imposing no constraints on anyone, would soon become a very unequal society. The most ambitious, talented, energetic, or luckiest, or perhaps the least scrupulous, or some combination of these, would be able to gather to themselves all that was of value, leaving just the scraps for the rest. This, in fact, is what in large measure did happen in the heyday of laissez-faire. Great fortunes were made, but the mass of the urban proletariat lived in grinding hopeless poverty. Those who would have a completely free society, especially in economic activity, must abandon any possibility of equality. The converse also applies. Those who want a society of equals, must curb the liberty of those who could become too unequal. Complete equality can be maintained only if some economic liberties are curtailed. An excessive enthusiasm for equality, with its inevitable restrictions on the unequal, is thus alien to the spirit of classical liberalism.

Yet the ideas are also complementary. If liberal democracy means anything, it means a society of free people, with freedom for *all* the people.

Hence, it implies some notion of an equality of liberty, without which liberty would be the privilege of the few, impossible for the many, and therefore not true liberty at all.

INDIVIDUAL AND SOCIAL INEQUALITIES

As with liberty, equality is a complex concept that can mean several things. The first critical issue is the relationship between individual differences and the inequalities of classes and groups. A primary problem within the democratic ideal seems to be that of ensuring that natural or unavoidable individual variations do not become the basis of artificial political, social, or legal inequalities which would make a mockery of that ideal.

There seem to be three major considerations:

(1) The first is that the similarities among human beings are greater and more significant than the differences. While there may be a very large spread between the extremes in any one variable — physical strength and appearance, intellectual capacity, moral integrity, ambition, and so on — humans still have much in common. Most will cluster round some mean, common point. The bell curve below demonstrates that on any normal or standard distribution of a variable, there will tend to be a heavy concentration round some central point. In intelligence humans will range from the genius to the moron. But most fit somewhere comfortably in the middle, as in the standard distribution curve. Again, in athletic prowess, there are those unreal people who do acrobatic skiing for television beer com-

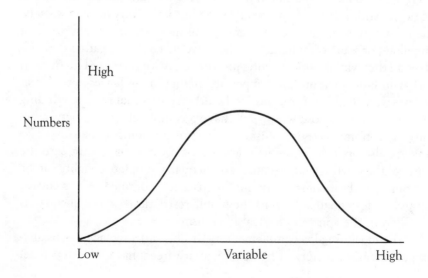

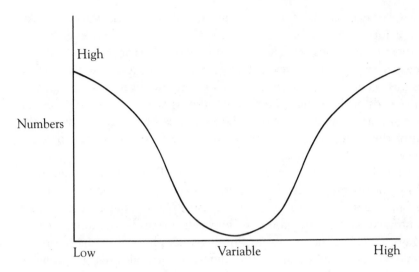

mercials, and those who become exhausted tying their own shoelaces. And once more, the majority are in the middle. Between the extremes there is a huge gulf. But few approach the extremes. Our similarities are greater than our differences. More than three centuries ago, Thomas Hobbes built his social contract around his recognition of an equality outweighing individual differences. Recognizing this equality he wrote:

> Nature hath made men so equall, in the faculties of body, and mind; as that though there bee found one man sometimes manifestly stronger in body, or of quicker mind than another; yet when all is reckoned together, the difference between man, and man, is not so considerable, as that one man can thereupon claim to himselfe any benefit, to which another may not pretend, as well as he. For as to the strength of body, the weakest has strength enough to kill the strongest, either by secret machination, or by confederacy with others, that are in the same danger with himselfe.[1]

In his further development of the topic he argued that the same principles of equality applied to other aspects of life.

If the opposite were the case, there would be such distributions concentrated at the extremes. For example, if there were a large number of highly intelligent or superstrong people and another large number of people possessing little intelligence or strength, only a very few would be left in the middle and this would produce the kind of reverse bell curve illustrated above. The case for institutionalizing inequalities would be stronger. No one denies the extremes. We all recognize those rare individuals whose brilliance amazes us, not only the superior intellect of an Albert Einstein, but also jazz pianists such as Oscar Peterson, athletes such as Wayne Gretzky, or the saintly ones like Mother Theresa. The exceptional are everywhere. But these inequalities of the very few do not destroy the essential equality of the majority. This is the key to the argument about equality and inequality. The anti-egalitarians, or elitists, compare extremes by focussing attention on the ends of the scale. Their consciousness is alert to the differences. The egalitarian, while accepting the existence of the gulf between the ends of the scale, pays more attention to the fact that most people are somewhere in the middle.

(2)   This leads to the second consideration. This is the argument that, within a democracy, individual differences ought not to be institutionalized differences. That is to say, the undeniable physical differences between certain races and ethnic groups, or between the sexes, the differences in religion, language, family origin, intelligence, physical strength, and so on, ought not to be reflected in formal differences in political, legal, social, or property rights.

At the heart of the anti-egalitarian, anti-democratic case is the belief that the differences among people are so great, so critical, that they must be reflected in institutional arrangements. The anti-democrat, in concentrating so hard on differences, becomes blind to the huge areas of commonality. The separateness is so crucial that it must be applied in all areas. Such a person will argue that people of different races or religions are so different that they must have different political rights, live in different areas, and work at different occupations. The ends of the scale are so far apart that they can never be joined. This is the intuitive attitude rationalized in racism, sexism, caste systems, class barriers, and religious bigotry.

The democratic case is that, yes, we do differ in our ethnic and racial heritage, in the colour of our skins, in the way in which we choose to worship a Creator, in the things we like to eat, and the ways in which we prefer to cook and serve them. We differ in intelligence, in moral standards, and in physical appearance and capacity. But the democrat will argue that these differences ought not to be carried over into other areas of social life. The proposition is not that we are equal, but that we ought to be treated as equal. Our differences must not be formalized into different laws or binding customs that will categorize people in terms of voting rights, treatment before the law, where they might live, and what work they might be allowed to do. The egalitarian does not deny variations, but does deny the extension of their significance.

Sex differences illustrate the point very well. It is an indisputable biological fact that on average men are physically stronger than women. But it is only *on average*. And it is also a biological fact that a great many of the strongest women are considerably stronger than a great many of the weakest men. There would, therefore, seem to be no justification for excluding *all* women from a particular type of job because "women aren't strong enough." And there certainly does not seem to be any justification for founding different political or property rights on the biological differences between male and female. Yet, in the earlier years of this century, much of the objection to women's suffrage took just this form. It was argued that because women differed physically from men, they ought not to have the same political rights. There is an almost surrealistic absurdity to the argument against women's suffrage put forward by Jean Joseph Denis in the Canadian House of Commons in 1918:

> I say that Holy Scriptures, theology, ancient philosophy, Christian philosophy, history, anatomy, physiology, political economy, and feminine psychology, all seem to indicate that the place of women in this world is not amid the strife of the political arena, but in her home.[2]

The connection between biological characteristics and the right or the capacity to cast a ballot was never really established. Those who argued in these terms never felt the necessity for offering evidence.

(3) If it is argued, as it has been here, that there are clear, natural inequalities among individual human beings, no case can be made for complete equality, meaning sameness or uniformity. On the other hand, it can also be demonstrated that the division of humanity into nations, classes, castes, or political ideologies is artificial. They are established by society and do not coincide with natural individual differences. Therefore, the extent to which any society seeks to transfer the natural inequalities of individuals into institutionalized inequalities of groups is a matter of human choice. The institutionalized inequalities that put humans into different categories with varying privileges, being human made, are therefore changeable by human will. It is the responsibility of each society to decide for itself the level of legal, economic, or political inequality it is willing to tolerate, and it must therefore accept the moral consequences of whatever choice is made. To quote from R.H. Tawney's excellent study *Equality*:

> So to criticize inequality and to desire equality is not, as is sometimes suggested, to cherish the romantic illusion that men are equal in character and intelligence. It is to hold that, while their natural endowments differ profoundly, it is the mark of a civilized society to aim at eliminating such inequalities as have their source, not in individual differences, but in its own

organization, and that individual differences, which are a source of social energy, are more likely to ripen and find expression if social inequalities are, as far as practicable, diminished.[3]

It would be a utopian fantasy to imagine that all social or political inequalities could be eliminated. The world is not made that way. But egalitarians seek to abolish the grosser inequalities and to soften the impact of those that must remain.

RICHARD H. TAWNEY

Born in Calcutta November 30, 1880; died in London January 16, 1962.

As historian, teacher, and socialist, Tawney was deeply committed to teaching in the Workers' Educational Association. His socialism, less intellectual than that of many of his colleagues, was in the Christian Socialist tradition. For a time he was a member of the Fabian Society. In the First World War he enlisted as a private and rose to the rank of sergeant but refused the offer of a commission as he later declined a peerage. Author of numerous books including Equality (1931), which was the driving force behind many of the policies of the Labour party. Note also The Acquisitive Society (1921) and Religion and the Rise of Capitalism (1926).

For further reading see:

Terrill, R. R.H. Tawney and his Times. London: Deutsch, 1973.

POLITICAL AND LEGAL EQUALITY

From these general considerations we can proceed to examine some of the specific types of equality we seek in a liberal democracy. There is, first of all, political equality. In the political sense, equality does not mean that all citizens must have the same power as, say, the prime minister. It is not a contradiction of the democratic notion of equality to suggest that some should be leaders and others followers. It is not necessary that all decisions be taken by all citizens voting equally.

But a minimum requirement of a liberal democracy is that all citizens should have more or less equal opportunity to participate in politics if they so desire, without being denied access to the system as voters or candidates by reason of race, religion, sex, or any other category. This is, alas, an ideal not readily achieved in practice even with the best will in the world. It is true that universal suffrage, from the age of about eighteen, is now the norm in all countries claiming to be liberal democracies. So today, although the right to vote was slowly won over bitter opposition, it is not now a serious issue. In this sense equality has been achieved. But not all votes count equally. In many jurisdictions, population inequalities adversely affect urban areas. Wherever there is a tendency for rural voters to support one party and urban voters another, there may be a significant partisan advantage in these inequalities. Further, a plurality election system, such as that of Canada, does not accurately translate shares of the popular vote into shares of parliamentary seats. It is a system that over-rewards winning parties, and penalizes losing parties.

Political inequalities became even more marked at the candidate level. Women, for example, have the same voting rights as men, but the representation of women in the Canadian House of Commons and in the provincial legislatures is very poor indeed. There is no evidence that women are less qualified than men to be members of parliament, but long-standing tradition and custom and, most importantly, the reluctance of nominating meetings to challenge that tradition, means it is extremely difficult for women to be selected as candidates. With a few special exceptions, all eligible voters may legally be candidates, but the costs in money, time, energy, and occupational and family ties mean that in practice only a few may seriously consider a full-time political career. In assessing the costs of politics, one must take into account more than the direct cost of an election campaign. In Canada, since the federal Election Expenses Act of 1974, which imposes limits on the amount of money spent on election campaigning and also provides for the reimbursement of a certain proportion of expenses incurred, this cost is not excessive. The actual expenses of the job, however, such as maintaining a residence in both Ottawa and the home constituency, can be a serious burden to some. But the greatest cost of all may be the loss of other earnings, and perhaps the setback of one's professional life. Not everyone can afford to interrupt a career for three or five, or more, years, and only a few can consider the break in family ties and obligations that a political career entails. So the legal position is more tolerant than the real world. In law all are equal, but in life "some are more equal than others."

Again, in theory all democratic citizens are equal before the law, but once more reality imposes limitations on this equality. Law is a costly process, especially in civil and corporate law, where the few very rich are at a great advantage. In a legal battle between an ordinary private citizen and a giant corporation, the citizen, even after winning the first round, may find funds exhausted while the corporation employs its teams of highly paid, highly qualified legal experts in endless rounds of appeals. Even where the criminal courts attempt to treat all equally, they find it difficult to do so because the impact of various penalties is not the same for all. A fine of $100 may be a financial disaster to a person with no savings, earning $120 a week. The same fine would mean little or nothing to a millionaire. On the other hand, thirty days in jail might not mean very much to an unemployed, homeless derelict, happy to get any sort of shelter from a Canadian winter. The same penalty might be a shaming, humiliating experience, perhaps even the source of great financial loss, to a senior executive, a supposed pillar of the community. Equal penalties might thus not be the same thing as equality before the law.

It is also easy to establish that despite legal assurances, we do not all have equality of speech, of movement, or of assembly. Economic differentials again affect the reality. Some will find it easier to rent meeting halls or buy space in the media. And of course it is one of the norms of the value system of capitalism that the rich and powerful are always more newsworthy than the poor and weak. Very wealthy persons, wishing to express themselves publicly on political or social issues, usually find no difficulty in commanding an audience or being reported. The common citizen, whose judgments might be as valid, will find it almost impossible to persuade anyone outside a small circle of family and friends to listen. Thus none of these other equalities, political or legal, would appear to have much effect without some large measure of economic equality. Excessive economic inequality makes any other form of equality impossible.

ECONOMIC EQUALITY

A most critical question, therefore, is that of the relationship between economic equality and other equalities. No substantial practical case can be made for *complete* economic equality, either as a thing to be desired or a thing possible to achieve. Only the most naive could propose that all could, or should, have exactly the same incomes with the same standard of living, regardless of skills, experience, ambition, energy, needs, or desires. But where economic inequalities are excessive, the very rich will come to hold almost exclusive access to political power. The rich will make the property laws, define the distribution of taxes, own all the employment opportunities, and perhaps, they will also be the major renters of housing. That same inequality will produce, on the other hand, that crushing pov-

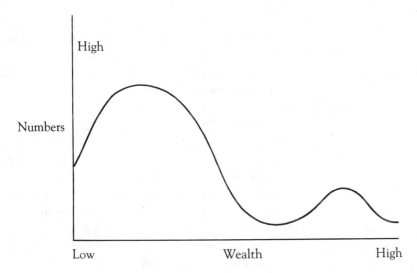

erty of the destitute who simply live from day to day close to starvation, with each day's energies entirely consumed in the struggle to survive for one more day so that the struggle might be repeated. Such an existence for the very poor is degrading and dehumanizing, and destructive of any attempt at seeking any improvement of condition. The destitute, who are denied anything approaching economic equality, will also suffer from political, legal, and social inequality.

Where the very rich are able to define the rules for society, so perpetuating their wealth and the poverty of the many, the poor may also be effectively denied the liberty even to seek these other equalities. This is a critical problem in much of Latin America. A small number of exceedingly rich rule over a very large number of extremely poor and there exists only a relatively small middle class (see diagram above), and the whole system is sustained by military dictatorships determined to crush all proposals for even the most moderate reform. In these situations the rich and poor live in two separate worlds, with few links between them and few opportunities to move from the world of the poor to the world of the rich. The many can enjoy neither political equality nor political liberty without some modification of the excesses of economic inequality.

> Freedom for the strong is oppression for the weak; and oppression . . . is not less oppressive when its strength is derived from superior wealth, than when it relies upon a preponderance of physical force. Hence, when steps to diminish inequality are denounced as infringements of freedom, the first question to be answered is one not always asked. It is: freedom for whom?[4]

There are in Canada today still some very rich people, and some very poor. But in contrast to the situation in Latin America, as indeed in much of the world in an earlier age, there are fewer of the hopelessly poor, and the income of the very rich is more strictly regulated. So, the majority of Canadians are neither very rich, nor very poor. The distribution of wealth comes closer to that of the bell curve, although a curve still skewed toward the poverty end of the scale; the majority are below the median point.

A capitalist society must admit such a level of economic inequality as will give adequate incentive and reward to talent, ambition, energy, and a willingness to take risks. There is also a need to recognize the exceptional. At the same time, a just society should also acknowledge that most are not exceptional and that this ordinary majority is entitled to an economic standard consistent with human dignity. The level of economic inequality ought not to be so great as to frustrate the development of other liberties or equalities. A democratic society, if it is to provide opportunities for liberties for all, must seek some reasonably acceptable level of economic equality.

How might this economic equality be achieved? Various possibilities, all of them having further economic or political consequences, are indicated here. There is no judgment as to their political or economic feasibility. Some, which might make sound economic sense, could be politically unacceptable, while others, although politically very popular, might be a source of economic disaster. All that is intended is to suggest some of the things a liberal democratic society could choose to do if it set a high priority on equality as a goal.

Canadians, from experience, have learned the hazards of attempting any scheme of wage and price controls. To accomplish this on any long-term, nation-wide scale would require more centralized control, with more coercive power, than the Canadian electorate seems as yet prepared to accept. But if we are unwilling to go as far as a completely controlled economy, we could, if we wished, achieve some of the same effects through other measures. It would be possible, for example, to leave income-earning potential virtually alone but at the same time introduce various other devices to redistribute income. A fairly standard practice in most Western nations, in much of this century, has been some form of graduated income tax, with higher rates for higher incomes. The current popularity of proposals for flat tax rates, which might have some merit in strictly economic terms, indicate a shift from an earlier social commitment to the easing of some inequalities.

Another route to wealth redistribution could be through government subsidies that boost prices for primary producers, or keep them low for consumers. The principle of subsidizing the cost of basic foodstuffs, public transport, or rents is adopted in many countries today, where it is often the major weapon in calming disaffection among the lowly paid working classes. It is also fairly common practice now to provide for some kind of medical and dental care programs, paid for out of public funds. Societies could redistribute wealth through unemployment insurance payments, welfare, free education, subsidized university fees, child allowances, old age pensions, and so on. From the other side, a government could impose heavy inheritance duties, capital gains taxes, excess profits taxes, absentee taxes, and so on. All these things are aimed toward the same goal. They guarantee some minimum standard to all and ease the greatest economic inequalities so that as few as possible will be blocked by economic hardship from enjoying that minimum level of political liberty necessary for participation as citizens in a democracy. Although there are undoubtedly elements of political expediency in the introduction of such measures, they nevertheless establish the intimate connection between economic equality and the other values of a liberal democratic society.

Another approach to equality might be through controlled prices and rationing so that great wealth does not lead to more than "fair shares" of necessities. The doctrine of laissez-faire assumes the free market will regulate supply and demand. Therefore, when supply falls, prices will rise, thus stimulating new production, greater supply, a falling price, and restoring equilibrium. It assumes the price mechanism will provide, of its own accord, the most efficient balance between supply and demand. But in times of inflexible supply, when rising prices are unable to stimulate further supply, as, for example, with food imports in wartime, the market may be an unsuitable instrument for social justice. There would seem to be little objection to letting the market regulate the price and the supply and demand for, say, diamonds.[5] Those who cannot afford to buy diamonds, don't have to, and are not really very much worse off if they can't. But should the same mechanism be left to control the supply of bread and milk in times of serious shortage brought about by war or some natural disaster? Certainly during the Second World War all the major nations, even those most dedicated to the spirit of laissez-faire, acknowledged that the market could not be left to regulate the allocation of food and other necessities. All introduced some system of rationing with controlled prices in an effort to ensure that all could get an equal share of what was available, and none could *legally* obtain more than a fair share.[6] It is worth noting as a sideline that in England during the war, despite acute food shortages, the poor, who were guaranteed rations at moderate prices, ate better than they had in a prewar open economy when basic commodities and the most nutritious foods were often priced out of their reach.

EQUALITY AND LIBERTY

All this has been an argument about the need or desirability of some measure of economic equality. But it should by now be obvious that there is a price in liberty to be paid for such equality, even at a moderate level. The argument becomes almost circular. It is clear that if political liberty means anything at all, it means liberty for all. That idea in turn implies equality of liberty and some equality of the rights associated with liberty: an equal liberty of speech, of assembly, and of the right to participate in politics. However, it is now clear that equal political liberty cannot become a reality without some level of economic equality. For example, there needs to be some restraint on the amounts that candidates may spend on campaigns, some effort to give the poor the same quality of legal services as the rich, and some equality of access to an adequate education. But such measures of economic equality can only be achieved by some sacrifice of economic liberty, some limitation on the power of some to accumulate and spend, and therefore:

> Political equality, save in formal terms, is impossible in the conditions of advanced capitalism. Economic life cannot be separated from political life. Unequal economic power, on the scale and of the kind encountered in advanced capitalist societies, inherently *produces* political inequality, on a more or less commensurate scale, whatever the constitution may say.[7]

Therefore political liberty for all requires some restraint on the economic liberty of some. If all are to have some liberty, none can have too much.

Neither of these democratic goals of liberty and equality exists in totality or isolation. It is always a matter of balance and of priorities. For while unlimited liberty destroys equality, and total equality makes liberty impossible, it is possible to have both *some* liberty and *some* equality. The practical problem for a liberal democratic society is not to choose between two absolutes of liberty and equality but to find an acceptable balance between them. The task is to decide how much, and what kind, of liberty is essential, and what price, in terms of sacrificing equality, is to be paid to achieve it. From the other perspective the question is what minimum level of equality in what areas is indispensable, and so, what is to be the price in the sacrifice of what liberties?

It is not being cynical to suggest that in the real world, the rich and powerful, who have already acquired a more than equal share of material goods, will put a high value on the greatest possible economic liberty even at the sacrifice of economic equality; while the underprivileged will seek to advance their political and social equality by demanding greater economic equality even at the sacrifice of the economic liberty of the economically advantaged. Liberty is a prized value of the powerful; equality is a prized value of the underprivileged. Such evaluations will also be related to interpretations of the nature of the state. Those who see the world as a collection of competing individuals will tend to give priority to individual liberty, being prepared to accept considerable inequality in order to accomplish this, while those who view the world as an organic, structural community will be more sympathetic to the idea of restraining some individual members in order to ensure that all enjoy some measure of equality.

All of this can partly explain some of the conflicts of modern politics. As long as all political power was in the hands of the propertied few, economic liberty was the dominant theme. This was the era of the unchecked adventurous entrepreneur. But as democracy extended political power to the underprivileged many through the spread of universal suffrage, thereby shifting the balance of political power to the many, there was increasing support for the idea of greater economic equality. As long as there are few rich and a large number of not so rich (even where, as today, the rich are not as rich, nor the poor as poor, as they used to be) and as long as the fate of governments is determined by numbers, the larger number of the less privileged will continue to put pressures on government to protect them from the harsher inequalities of unrestrained competition. Indeed, wherever there is a liberal democracy, there will be some sort of demand from some segment of society for more economic equality. Whatever its other justifications as a defensive measure for the survival of capitalism, the welfare state is a natural consequence of democratization.

EQUALITY OF OPPORTUNITY

So far equality has been discussed in terms of a condition of equality, a state being equal, of having equal things, and of levels of economic equality. But it is possible to pursue further developments of the concept. In one sense, equality suggests that we are equal when we all dress alike. In another sense, equality means the equal freedom of all to dress as they wish, without fear of reprisal from an employer or an intolerant public. Here one can look at equality as the equal right to become unequal, to have the right and the opportunity to be different. The point was taken up by John Stuart Mill. As a necessary corollary of his opposition to the tyranny of the majority, Mill stressed the importance of encouraging the widest possible individual diversity of mind:

> Precisely because the tyranny of opinion is such as to make eccentricity a reproach, it is desirable, in order to break through that tyranny, that people should be eccentric. . . . That so few now dare to be eccentric marks the chief danger of the time.[8]

This is, first of all, an argument for liberty. But it is also an argument for equality, for the equal right of all to express their individuality in idiosyncratic behaviour and to live according to their own standards.

Even arguments about censorship have dual implication. Primarily questions about censorship are questions about liberty. But there is also an equality element — the equal right of people to decide for themselves what they will see, read, or listen to. In obstructing my liberty, censors are asserting that as their standards of morality or their political values are superior to mine, they are entitled to impose those values on me. Thus an argument for liberty may also be an argument for equality: for an equality of liberty. In the sense of equality of condition, of being equal, all would be equal when all shared the same values and attitudes, did the same things, and lived in the same way. Within each class, all the members of Huxley's *Brave New World* were equal. But in the sense of equality of opportunity, they would also be equal if all could pursue individual lifestyles without interference; where no one person's standards could be enforced as the standards for all.

EQUAL EDUCATION FOR ALL

The problems of equality of condition versus equality of opportunity can be seen in different approaches to education. If all are to have the right to develop their talents, to make the most of their lives, all must have adequate *access* to an education. But is this necessarily the same as uniformity of education? Does equality of access mean the removal of the financial or social barriers to receiving whatever level or kind of education one is capable of receiving, or does it also imply that everyone should receive the same kind of education, in the same kind of schools?

The question has become a live political issue in England in the decades since the Second World War. In the immediate postwar years a new principle was introduced into the state-supported education system.[9] The basic concept of the new system was that all children in the publicly financed schools would attend a neighbourhood elementary school not unlike the typical Canadian grade school and serving a very similar function. In their eleventh year most children wrote a public examination administered by local authorities. This was known as the 11 + examination. The relatively small minority who were successful went on to a grammar school, which provided a higher quality academic education generally leading to university, management, or the professions. Classes in the grammar schools were generally small, teachers more qualified, and the students themselves more motivated. The general atmosphere in the grammar school was conducive to good quality academic work. Those not accepted for grammar school, or who did not write the 11 +, went on to a secondary modern, or technical school, which generally prepared students for a life in industry or in semiskilled occupations. Although the defenders of the system always denied the charge, there is no doubt that the secondary moderns were perceived as schools for losers, where there was little motivation to academic work.

The system was not totally rigid. It was possible to pass from secondary modern to grammar school, or even from secondary modern to university. But most of those who finished up in a secondary modern school accepted the fact that henceforth they were members of the working class or at best the lower middle class. While it did provide genuinely superior education for the academically qualified children, the dual system nevertheless worked principally to perpetuate a class division of society. The child's entire future was determined by the results of a public examination held at the age of eleven. This seemed unduly harsh, and one can imagine the stress, particularly in families with social/economic ambitions for their children. Eleven seemed a very early age for such critical decisions. And yet, if the successful were to take advantage of the larger opportunities of a grammar school education, the choice had to be made early.

Because of the socially divisive character of the dual secondary modern/grammar schools, the Labour party pledged itself to abolish the 11 + and replace it by a pattern of comprehensive schools. The comprehensives are not very different from the standard Canadian secondary schools, providing secondary education for all in a given catchment area, with academic and technical streams all using the same facilities. The decision on the school system was left to local government authorities, so in Labour controlled areas, comprehensive schools were gradually introduced. In Conservative areas the formality of the old 11 + examination has largely disappeared, but there are still determined efforts to preserve some equivalent of a dual system. The Labour argument was that the social divisions perpetuated by the dual system were unacceptable in a democratic society. The Conservative argument was that it was unjust and unfair to deny to the brightest students, in the name of some idealistic and unattainable equality, the superior education they were capable of receiving. The comprehensive schools provide a more uniform level of education, but the price of greater social equality and the removal of the stigma of defeatism and second class status associated with the secondary modern schools has been the loss of the high achievement and high motivation of the grammar schools.

The relevance of this description to our present topic is in the implications it has for the concepts of equality. The dual system had inequality as a goal. It was designed to produce a relatively small number of superior students destined for managerial and professional careers. But its means were equality. Every child in the country had an equal opportunity to write a common public examination, and each child's future was determined not by the parents' wealth or social status but solely by the child's own talents. Those who passed received the advantages of a better education at the state's expense.

It can be seen from this that, whatever solution was adopted, there was a price to pay. The dual system of secondary-modern and grammar schools provided an equal opportunity to become unequal. But by dividing society into winners and losers, it helped perpetuate the inequalities of a class system. The comprehensive system offered all a similar kind of education, making all more or less equal in what they did. But this was at the expense of the best, who were denied the opportunity to make the most of their superior talents. The price of raising the standards of the many was a reduction in the standards of the few.[10]

More than a century earlier, in his classic study *Democracy in America*, Alexis de Tocqueville (1805–1859) saw this as a general verdict on the egalitarian tendencies of democracy. Some of de Tocqueville's other fears about democracy will become the central theme of a later chapter, but here take note of his views on the consequences of equality:

Before I close forever the theme that has detained me so long, I would fain take a parting survey of all the various characteristics of modern society, and appreciate at last the general influence to be exercised by the principle of equality upon the fate of mankind; . . .

Nevertheless, in the midst of a prospect so wide, so novel, and so confused, some of the more prominent characteristics may already be discerned and pointed out. The good things and the evils of life are more equally distributed in the world: great wealth tends to disappear, the number of small fortunes to increase; desires and gratifications are multiplied, but extraordinary prosperity and irremediable penury are alike unknown. The sentiment of ambition is universal, but the scope of ambition is seldom vast. Each individual stands apart in solitary weakness; but society at large is active, provident, and powerful: the performances of private persons are insignificant, those of the State immense. . . . Human existence becomes longer, and property more secure: life is not adorned with brilliant trophies, but it is extremely easy and tranquil. Few pleasures are either very refined or very coarse; and highly polished manners are as uncommon as great brutality of tastes. Neither men of great learning, nor extremely ignorant communities, are to be met with; genius becomes more rare, information more diffused. The human mind is impelled by the small efforts of all mankind combined together, not by the strenuous activity of certain men. There is less perfection, but more abundance, in all the productions of the arts. The ties of race, of rank, and of country are relaxed; the great bond of humanity is strengthened. If I endeavour to find out the most general and the most prominent of all these different characteristics, I shall have occasion to perceive that what is taking place in men's fortunes manifests itself under a thousand other forms. Almost all extremes are softened or blunted: all that was most prominent is superseded by some mean term, at once less lofty and less low, less brilliant and less obscure, than what before existed in the world.[11]

Note that although de Tocqueville titled his book *Democracy in America*, it was less a description of actual conditions in the United States, and more a commentary on the characteristics and prospects of egalitarian democracy in general. It is clearly not an accurate description of the United States today.

PROBLEMS AND CONTRADICTIONS

If the contrasting concepts of equality of condition and opportunity are focussed on the economic sphere, new problems emerge. One can begin with the fairly simple proposition that in a just society all should have an equal right to pursue any kind of career, limited only by personal capacity, energy, and ambition. This would seem to many to be a most eminently reasonable principle in accordance with the concepts of competitive individualism. Note carefully that the proposition is not that all should have an equal right to be brain surgeons, managers of large corporations, professional hockey players, or even professors of political science. It is simply that all should have an equal right to try for these occupations, with their chances of success unhindered by race, sex, or social class, or, most importantly to the present discussion, by the lack of financial resources.

This concept of equality of opportunity is a fine ideal and generally widely approved. Many, indeed, appear to believe that it is part of the reality of our present society. But given the inevitable economic inequalities of capitalism, it is an extremely difficult ideal to apply in practice. If all are to have an equal opportunity of trying to be doctors or lawyers, the cost of preparation for these careers would have to be within the reach of all. That includes not only the direct cost of fees and books but also the costs of maintenance and living expenses as a student. Yet to provide this complete equality of economic opportunity would involve very heavy government expenditure, requiring extremely high taxes — higher perhaps than the community would be politically prepared to accept. Even now, in Canada, we talk of university education being accessible to all. But although the cost of a university education is heavily subsidized by the taxpayer, it is still not free, so many young people with the necessary talents and skills cannot afford a higher education.

Beyond this matter, the principle of equality of opportunity would also seem to imply that the wealthier ought not to be able to use their wealth to secure any unfair advantage. It might be suggested, for example, that the rich ought not be allowed to set their children up in business with contacts already established, or buy them superior education in private schools, or in any other way confer on them an *unfair* advantage (whatever unfair might mean in this context) at the starting gate. Obviously this would involve excessive and politically unacceptable restrictions on how people should be entitled to spend their own money. The conclusion might seem to be that that equality of opportunity is an unrealizable dream in the real world. It is a fiction, something we do not have and perhaps cannot expect to have.

Once again we appear trapped in a roundabout argument. From a variety of motives, ranging from selfishness to a love of liberty, most reject any notion of a full equality of condition. To achieve and maintain the same standard for all would involve a fairly oppressive conformity — which would be like a New Order horror out of a science-fiction story. It would deny the right of the energetic or the exceptional to raise themselves above the common standard, thereby inhibiting any raising of that common standard itself. There seems little popular support for full equality of condition. It is therefore easy to argue that democratic equality can mean only an equality of opportunity. It means no more than the right of each to use individual talents to become unequal, to rise, by personal effort, as far above the mean level as one is capable of rising. This seems to be the notion of equality most consistent with the rhetoric of liberal democracy. The conflict of the two concepts is sometimes expressed in the terminology of a race. The object, it is said, is not that all should finish together but that all should have an equal chance of reaching the starting line. But, as has been demonstrated, this is not easily achieved. If all are to reach the starting barrier together, some will need additional assistance and some will need to be curbed. An equality of opportunity, a right to become unequal, is desired because most reject the limitations, or restrictions, imposed by an equality of condition. But the equality of opportunity itself demands some equality of condition as its starting point.

One is left with this paradox. In order for people to have an equal opportunity, no one should be able to start with any inherited advantages, but many want the opportunity to accumulate wealth to pass on to the next generation. However, if there is to be equality of opportunity in the next generation, no one should be permitted to take advantage of their inheritance. It seems we can only achieve what we do want by first accepting what we do not want.

As in the case of liberty, this dilemma can be resolved only by moving away from the world of abstractions and absolutes to that of specifics and compromises. The problem of liberty became easier when, in place of high-sounding arguments about *liberty*, one began setting priorities among particular competing *liberties*. So it is with equality. It is necessary to move from the abstract to real issues in the real world. Absolute equality in any sphere—economic, social, political, legal, or whatever—is a chimera. It is hard even to conceive exactly what it would mean. If we were all suddenly to become exactly equal in our economic condition, no one could spend or buy anything without at once upsetting that equality. Yet while both liberty and equality cannot be seen as exclusive poles, each a dichotomy in itself, they can appear on a continuum. One can talk meaningfully about "more or less" equal. Imagine a line from the most absolute equality one could conceive to the most absolute inequality, say, for example, in the economic area. If real political systems were placed along such a continuum, the two ends of the scale would not be occupied. Nowhere do those absolutes exist. But there are still stages, and there are still important differences between the attitudes and policies of different states on the question of economic equality. In relative terms there is, for example, greater economic equality in Cuba than in New Zealand, more in New Zealand than in Canada, and more in Canada than in Brazil. From this kind of perspective one can begin to analyze the effects of different levels of equality. Such comparisons indicate that while excessive preoccupation with economic equality may stultify ambition, curb incentive, and imperil liberty, excessive disregard of economic equality may reduce the many to a position of helplessness and despair, which also destroys ambition, incentive, and liberty.

The issue reduces itself to the following: What level of economic inequality is a society prepared to accept or, if you like, what level of economic equality is it prepared to demand? What price is the society then prepared to pay, in terms of other equalities and other liberties, in order to achieve that level of economic equality? How equal must people be in their condition for it not to be utter nonsense to talk of their having some equality of opportunity? These are meaningful questions and you ought to try to compose your own answers to them. But they are still value judgments and personal opinions; therefore, the particular answer you give is less important than the recognition that virtually every equality and every liberty must be bought at the price of some other liberty and some other equality. We don't deal with a world of "either/or" choices; we deal with priorities, and the main political task is one of balancing and ordering priorities.

SIR WILLIAM BEVERIDGE (Lord Beveridge of Tuggal)

Born at Rangpur in Bengal March 5, 1879; died at Oxford March 16, 1963.
Graduated from Oxford in 1902. From 1919 to 1937 he was Director of the London School of Economics and Political Science and from 1937 to 1945 Master of University College, Oxford. As Chairman of the Interdepartmental Committee on Social Insurance and Allied Services in 1941–42, he was the originator of the "Beveridge Plan" (1942), which set out the framework for the whole social security, welfare, and unemployment scheme in postwar Britain. The key to the entire program was the maintenance of full employment as the major responsibility of government. The report was coolly received by the Churchill government, but was immensely popular elsewhere. His works include Insurance for All *(1924),* Changes in Family Life *(1932), and* Full Employment in a Free Society *(1944).*
For further reading see:
Harris, José. William Beveridge: A Biography. *Oxford: Clarendon Press, 1977.*
Beveridge, Janet. Beveridge and His Plan. *London: Hodder and Stoughton, 1954.*

As a final contribution to this consideration of equality let me introduce the English economist William Beveridge. In 1942 Beveridge introduced what came to be known as the Beveridge plan, which in fact became the blueprint for the whole postwar concept of social welfare as developed in the liberal democracies. In his plan Beveridge introduced the crucial phrase "A floor, not a ceiling." By this he meant that while there should not be upper limits imposed on wealth and possessions, there was a lower limit, or a floor below, to which no member of a civilized society should be allowed to sink. This would be the minimum standard of living consistent with some notion of human dignity, self-respect, and independence. It is a level considerably above that of mere survival. An earlier generation of economic theorists such as Robert Malthus (1766–1834) had assumed that economic and natural laws would keep the lowest orders of the working classes permanently at a level of bare subsistence. But by the 1940s Western societies had come to repudiate this dependence on apparently immutable economic laws and set about changing them.

THOMAS ROBERT MALTHUS

Born at Guildford, England, February 17, 1766; died December 23, 1834.

Famous as an English political economist, holding the first professorship of political economy established in the United Kingdom. In 1798 Malthus published his Essay on the Principle of Population as it Affects the Future Improvement of Society. *The principle he defined was that population increases by a geometrical progression while the means of subsistence increase only by arithmetical progression; the consequence is that population pressures will always tend to exceed the supply of food. He further concluded that crime, war, and disease were natural and necessary checks on excessive population growth.*

Beveridge also suggested that it was the moral responsibility of the whole of society to maintain that floor, even at the cost of lowering the ceiling. The Beveridge plan, in fact, moved the realities of the political world away from competitive liberal individualism in the direction of an organic society that assumed responsibility for the well-being of all its members. It proposed that any advance in a more equal social opportunity for all was conditional on some moderation of economic inequalities. And it accepted some limits on the economic liberties of some as the price for achieving this.

CHAPTER SEVEN

Democracies and Majorities

It was suggested in chapter five that liberty was threatened in many ways: repressive laws, over-powerful individuals, monopolistic corporations, certain external circumstances, and intolerant majorities. The last of these obstacles provides the theme for this chapter; the situation where the liberty of the majority frustrates the liberty of the minority; or where the majority uses its power to deny to the minority the liberty of action it claims for itself. It is a problem inherent in the nature of democratic institutions.

Before the age of democracy the masses could for the most part be ignored. Until extreme situations aroused them to occasional outbursts of violence, their opinions were of no consequence. But while the masses were never consulted on the details of policy, there has always existed a strong tradition in Western political philosophy of trusting the judgment of the common people, who have long been held to be the ultimate custodians of sovereignty. Aristotle, for one, saw greater possibilities for good in the "collective wisdom of the ages" than in Plato's philosopher king, arguing that many ordinary persons may be better than a few great ones. Of course Aristotle was not thinking of anything even remotely resembling a modern democratic franchise. And Machiavelli conceded that the people were more likely to have the general good in mind than any single tyrant.

> But as regards prudence and stability, I say that the people are more prudent and stable, and have better judgement than a prince; and it is not without good reason that it is said, "The Voice of the People is the Voice of God."[1]

In practice, of course, very few attempts were made to seek out the opinions of the many, and certainly few kings felt themselves constrained by such opinions until forced to do so.

But with the emergence of liberal democracy, public opinion, and especially majority opinion, came to new prominence in political thinking. Asked to list the components of liberal democracy, those characteristics essential to its very existence, most would begin to explore the language of liberty, equality, rights, justice, rule of law, and so on. Somewhere in this catalogue of democratic attributes would be the idea of majority rule. Majority rule is essential to the machinery of democracy, the necessary procedure for translating its ideals into practice or for institutionalizing its goals. Against the concentration of power by kings, dictators, cliques, and juntas is set the idea of government by the people, which, by a little sleight of hand, easily becomes the government elected by the majority of the people or, by a further sleight of hand, by the largest number of those actually voting, which may not be the same thing at all. Whenever complete consensus is lacking, government by the people must necessarily mean government by the majority — a point that had been made as early as the seventeenth century by John Locke:

> Men being, as has been said, by nature all free, equal, and independent, no one can be put out of this estate and subjected to the political power of another without his own consent, which is done by agreeing with other men, to join and unite into a community for their comfortable, safe, and peaceable living, one amongst another, in a secure enjoyment of their properties, and a greater security against any that are not of it. This any number of men may do, because it injures not the freedom of the rest; they are left, as they were, in the liberty of the state of Nature. When any number of men have so consented to make one community or government, they are thereby presently incorporated, and make one body politic, wherein the majority have a right to act and conclude for the rest.
>
> For, when any number of men have, by the consent of every individual, made a community, they have thereby made that community one body, with a power to act as one body, which is only by the will and determination of the majority. For that which acts any community, being only the consent of the individuals of it, and it being one body, must move one way, it is necessary the body should move that way whither the greatest force carries it, which is the consent of the majority, or else it is impossible it should act or continue one body, one community, which the consent of every individual that united into it agreed that it should; so every one is bound by that consent to be concluded by the majority. And therefore we see that in assemblies empowered to act by positive laws where no number is set by that positive law

which empowers them, the act of the majority passes for the act of the whole, and of course determines as having, by the law of Nature and reason, the power of the whole.[2]

The alternative to majority rule is minority rule. When the majority cannot act in the name of all, effective power passes to a minority who, by withholding agreement, would be able to block any proposals that they disliked. Very few things can be decided at all when unanimity is required. Overall, therefore, we accept the principle of majority decision-making. In common language, to decide things democratically means to decide by taking a vote in which the will of the majority prevails. We take it for granted that the selection of a governing body for any association, whether it be the government of the country or the executive of the local tennis club, will be by majority vote. We then expect that within these governing bodies, individual decisions will be taken by counting heads.

TYRANNY OF THE MAJORITY

Before delving into the many difficulties in applying the principle to the real world, we must confront the more fundamental question of the validity of the assumption itself. Is it in fact the case that majority rule is always the same as democratic rule?[3] The mere fact of posing the question suggests at least the possibility of a "no" answer. We can gain some initial insight from a French writer who, more than a hundred years ago, began to analyze the impact of democracy on the world. Alexis de Tocqueville (1805–1859) was an aristocrat who, having resigned himself to the defeat of the French aristocracy, sought to discover what the New World might have to offer. The old order of kings and aristocracies was over: what might the alternative be like? With this question in mind he made an extended visit to the United States in the 1830s, America then being the only country where liberal democratic, egalitarian ideas were beginning to take hold. The results of his studies appeared in his book *Democracy in America*, published in two volumes in 1835 and 1840. This is a classic study and one of the most significant works on the nature and consequences of democracy. It is still highly regarded and may be read today with ease and pleasure. It was called *Democracy in America*, but its value lies less in the comments on America than in its perception of liberal democracy.

By democracy de Tocqueville meant generally a society in which distinctions of rank had been abolished. It was an egalitarian society in which all were equal not in economic terms but in terms of social class and political authority. In such a condition, he argued, where only numbers could distinguish people, majorities would prevail. Even in de Tocqueville's day, America was less egalitarian than he imagined. (From the perspective of a French aristocrat, any slackening of social barriers would seem to indicate total equality.) And of course today there are huge inequalities in American life. But, as has been stated, de Tocqueville was not really writing about America; he was writing about egalitarian democracy. The object of the American visit was to study this new democracy in action in order to see what might be in store for Europe. He wanted to discover how to preserve and enhance the virtues of democracy while controlling its supposed defects and guarding against its abuses.

His general attitude to democracy was ambivalent. By and large, while he welcomed it, he was also afraid of it. As a passionate believer in the liberty of the individual, de Tocqueville was aware that the old order of absolute monarchs had denied liberty to the many. If all people were to be free, the old regime with its privileges had to go. Its demise and the growth of democracy were both necessary and inevitable. Democracy was the instrument for freeing humanity from age-old oppression and for giving new meaning and dignity to the lives of the many. But de Tocqueville, with an aristocrat's natural distrust of equality and of the many, feared that democracy would introduce a new tyranny, the tyranny of the majority, which he considered almost synonymous with the mob. Implicit in de Tocqueville's writings is the unverified assumption that the majority will be less rational, less informed, and less wise than the minority.

He believed it would be a misfortune if society, in liberating itself from the old despotism, should subject itself to a newer and more pervasive tyranny. In de Tocqueville's mind, the great danger of democracy lay in the tyranny of the majority. He believed there could be no greater oppressor than an intolerant public opinion given unqualified, unrestrained political and social power. The dissident has much to fear from a tyrant, a king, or a dictator. However, a tyrant king has many enemies, willing to risk offering shelter or protection to the critic. But a dissident who offends a majority, having nowhere to hide, may be stifled without hope because there are few with the courage, or the facility, to challenge an all-pervasive majority.

It was de Tocqueville's argument that if the laws are made by a legislature elected by majorities who insist that members be constantly answerable to public opinion, that they in fact be committed delegates, rather than independent representatives, such laws will offer little comfort or protection to unpopular minorities. The legislature would have to bend constantly to the whims of the majority. If, further, the same laws are admin-

istered by public servants holding their positions as patronage appointments, at the pleasure of the party in office, to be replaced by new favourites if
suspected of "disloyalty" by that governing party, no independent action
can be expected from that quarter. In a democracy overly enthusiastic about
the power of the people, even the courts could provide little protection,
for the juries, being representatives of the majority, would be held responsible for their verdicts by the majority. And if judges and police chiefs are
elected by the majority, as they still are in parts of the United States, they
can scarcely be expected to exercise independent judgments against the
wishes of an intolerant majority. We can add to de Tocqueville's fears another
variable peculiar to our own age. If we have mass media dependent upon
advertising revenue and if that revenue is based on the size of the media
audience, no newspaper or TV program will permit policies or support causes
that will consistently drive away too many of the majority audience. The
non-conformist has few friends, few supporters, few places to hide, or few
opportunities to make a voice heard in a democracy convinced of its own
righteousness and infallibility. This is the crux of the real problem that
disturbed de Tocqueville.

Once we make that step, a step which is a matter of practical necessity,
of moving from the will of all the people to the will of the majority of the
people, there is always the danger that that majority will use its power to
ride roughshod over the interests or rights of the minority. Let us follow de
Tocqueville's fears in his own words, remembering that this was written in
1835:

> I know no country in which there is so little true independence of mind and
> freedom of discussion as in America. . . .
>
> In America the majority raises very formidable barriers to the liberty of
> opinion: within these barriers an author may write whatever he pleases, but
> he will repent it if he ever steps beyond them. Not that he is exposed to the
> terrors of an *auto-da-fé*, but he is tormented by the slights and persecutions
> of daily obloquy.[4]

In short, de Tocqueville argued that there was considerable latitude within a
country like America, but it was a latitude with bounds clearly defined by
public opinion. There was no room for expression beyond those limits and
little support for those who transgressed them. To continue:

> Fetters and headsmen were the coarse instruments which tyranny formerly
> employed; but the civilization of our age has refined the arts of despotism,
> which seemed, however, to have been sufficiently perfected before. The
> excesses of monarchical power had devised a variety of physical means of

oppression: the democratic republics of the present day have rendered it as entirely an affair of the mind as that will which it is intended to coerce. Under the absolute sway of an individual despot the body was attacked in order to subdue the soul, and the soul escaped the blows which were directed against it and rose superior to the attempt; but such is not the course adopted by tyranny in democratic republics; there the body is left free, and the soul is enslaved. The sovereign can no longer say, "You shall think as I do on pain of death"; but he says: "You are free to think differently from me, and to retain your life, your property, and all that you possess; but if such be your determination, you are henceforth an alien among your people. You may retain your civil rights, but they will be useless to you, for you will never be chosen by your fellow-citizens if you solicit their suffrages, and they will affect to scorn you if you solicit their esteem. You will remain among men, but you will be deprived of the rights of mankind. Your fellow-creatures will shun you like an impure being, and those who are most persuaded of your innocence will abandon you too, lest they should be shunned in their turn. Go in peace! I have given you your life, but it is an existence incomparably worse than death."

Monarchical institutions have thrown an odium upon despotism; let us beware lest democratic republics should restore oppression, and should render it less odious and less degrading in the eyes of the many, by making it still more onerous to the few.[5]

Reading this passage, one recalls the enthusiasm with which the majority of American people supported the efforts of Senator Joe McCarthy to silence all critical opinion during the 1950s; and the absence of any popular outcry against the blacklisting of scores of people in the television and film industries for alleged communist sympathies during the same era. For a Canadian illustration we can note the lack of any widespread public protest against the uprooting of Japanese Canadians from the Pacific coast during the Second World War. The government of that time, with the full support of public opinion, inflicted a grave injustice on a minority of Canadian citizens and was able to do so with the confidence of that support. Governments generally do not run into too much criticism when they seek to curb those with unpopular views.

A public opinion intolerant of dissent can be the most vicious of tyrants. It does not need even to enshrine its intolerance in law; sheer public pressure is often enough to crush a minority into silence. Nor does it really matter much who is right or wrong, for majorities do not need to listen to reasoned argument. The simple force of numbers is an adequate substitute for evidence.

ALEXIS CHARLES HENRI CLEREL DE TOCQUEVILLE

Born in Paris July 29, 1805; died at Cannes April 16, 1859.

De Tocqueville was born of a minor noble family. His first career was in the study of law. His thoughts reflect a curious combination of enthusiasm for liberal ideas and respect for the ancient aristocratic traditions. In 1830 de Tocqueville, accompanied by Gustave de Beaumont, set out to study the emergence and future prospects of democracy in America. The necessary official approval for the travels was based on their proposal to report on the American prison system; but their study extended far beyond that into the whole character of American political society. The result of de Tocqueville's study, Democracy in America, *was published in two volumes in 1835 and 1840. In them he sought, as he wrote, "the image of democracy itself, with all its inclinations, its character, its prejudices, and its passions, in order to learn what we have to fear or hope from its progress." For the modern reader the most useful edition of* Democracy in America *is the Worlds Classics edition, translated by Henry Reeve.*

For further reading see:

Mayer, J.P. Alexis de Tocqueville: A Biographical Essay in Political Science. New York: Viking Press, 1940.

Lively, Jack. The Social and Political Thought of Alexis de Tocqueville. Oxford: Clarendon Press, 1962.

Stone, John, ed. Alexis de Tocqueville on Democracy, Revolution and Society. Chicago: University Press, 1980.

PROBLEMS OF MAJORITY RULE

Before one starts equating majority rule with democracy one needs to know something about the kind of majority it is. How was the majority arrived at? How was it created and who composes it? How does it use its power and against whom? A majority can easily be created or manipulated by the propagandist, by mass psychology, or by intimidation, or arise simply from ignorance of alternatives. Those who know only one point of view, who never receive any counter-information, are easily persuaded of the rightness of their established ideas. They are also easily persuaded that they have the right, indeed the obligation, to suppress opposing views that, almost by definition, must be treason or heresy, or both. In most of the modern dictatorships, where the government has exclusive control over what is taught in the schools or revealed by the media, the mass of population do not have to be coerced. They believe quite genuinely in the prevailing orthodoxy, having never been exposed to alternatives.

On a smaller scale we can look at the lynch mob as the aroused voice of the majority. Many western movies have depicted the fierce power of the lynch mob with its utter contempt for those who would restrain it. In a stock film situation, we find the victim in jail. Generally in the plot he will turn out eventually to be innocent. In front of the jail the lone sheriff, the enforcer of the rule of law, perhaps aided by the hero, confronts the angry mob who will brush the sheriff aside and perhaps injure or kill him as he tries to save one person from the many. Now, there have always been mobs that have done dreadful things. They are not unique to the American South or West. Marc Antony was inciting the mob. But a peculiar fact of a democracy that enshrines public opinion and majority rule is that the mob is easily convinced of its own righteousness because it is the will of the majority. Believing it expresses the will of the people, it convinces itself that it is behaving democratically and that the sheriff, in upholding the law, is somehow the enemy of the people.

We do not need to refer to the extreme methods of the lynch mob to understand the dangers of pressures to conform to majority rule. The majority wants game shows and soap operas on television, so this is what is largely available for all to watch, on all channels. Christians are a majority in our society, so Jews and Hindus might be ridiculed or reduced to second-class status. Friday is the Islamic Holy Day of rest, but in Christian Canada the Moslem must work on Friday and rest on Sunday. This is what de Tocqueville feared: that the majority in attempting to impose its standards on all, would become not the vehicle of liberty, as promised, but the instrument of a new and sometimes terrifying oppression. It was central to de Tocqueville's argument that the evil of oppression lies in the fact of the oppression, unaffected by the number of the oppressed or the number of the oppressors. If I am imprisoned for my political views, it is no comfort to be told that I am imprisoned by the will of the majority of my fellow citizens rather than by a military junta.

It is the peculiar danger of democracy that it tends to bestow upon majorities and mobs a kind of moral infallibility and to assume that what the majority wants must, for that reason alone, be right, and therefore, the majority is entitled to insist that its view shall become the universal view. The dilemma arises from two contradictory propositions: Democracy implies the freedom of all to hold and assert whatever opinions they wish. Democracy also requires that the majority will prevail. But majorities are not inclined to extend to outsiders the freedom of expression they claim for themselves. Nor do they easily accept that sometimes they may be wrong. To quote again from *Democracy in America*:

> If it be admitted that a man possessing absolute power, may misuse that power by wronging his adversaries, why should a majority not be liable to the same reproach? Men are not apt to change their characters by agglomeration; nor does their patience in the presence of obstacles increase with the consciousness of their strength. And for these reasons I can never willingly invest any number of my fellow-creatures with that unlimited authority which I should refuse to any one of them.[6]

Majorities, in other words, being no more noble-minded than the single individual, are no more likely to be right. Indeed, because majorities are inclined to arrive at their verdicts by tradition, habit, or reinforcement, there is a real probability that the majority will be wrong. Almost all innovation, revision, or correction originates with a sceptical individual. Thus, where majorities can silence critical voices, old errors will remain uncorrected, and obsolete orthodoxies will continue unreformed.

John Stuart Mill, who learned so much from de Tocqueville,[7] made much the same point: opinions are not necessarily correct simply because they are held by a large number of people. And he too, as is evident from the following quote, was unwilling to grant to a majority the power he would not give a minority or a single despot:

> If all mankind minus one were of one opinion, and only one person were of the contrary opinion, mankind would be no more justified in silencing that one person, than he, if he had the power, would be justified in silencing mankind.[8]

Mill had the strongest reservations about the power that society ought to wield over the behaviour of its members. He would not grant the majority the right to impose its standards on the non-conforming individual, whether it exercised that power through law, or merely through the pressure of public opinion. Mill's conclusion determines that

> the sole end for which mankind are warranted, individually or collectively, in interfering with the liberty of action of any of their number, is self-protection. That the only purpose for which power can be rightfully exercised over any member of a civilised community, against his will, is to prevent harm to others. His own good, either physical or moral, is not a sufficient warrant. He cannot rightfully be compelled to do or forbear because it will be better for him to do so, because it will make him happier, because, in the opinion of others, to do so would be wise, or even right. These are good

reasons for remonstrating with him, or reasoning with him, or persuading him, or entreating him, but not for compelling him, or visiting him with any evil in case he do otherwise.[9]

Mill, in the liberal tradition, would protect the individual as much from majority opinion as from the lone despot.

In another major work, *On Representative Government* (1861), reflecting his "love-fear" relationship to democracy, Mill proposed elaborate voting procedures to ensure that while the right to vote should be extended to all, effective political power would remain in the hands of the "responsible," propertied middle classes. Some of the most notable figures in eighteenth and nineteenth-century American political thinking also directed themselves to the problem of granting equal rights to all and at the same time preventing the majority (by implication, also the lower classes) from becoming too powerful. The original intention of the United States Constitution, with its indirect election of the president and the selection of senators by the state legislatures,[10] was to put an effective curb on excessive democracy. In Canada, the wording and the intent of the British North America Act of 1867 was far from democratic, granting enormous discretionary powers to the governor-general as the representative of the British Crown.

Even when the principle is accepted, and apart from the threat of majority tyranny, there are problems in translating the idea of majority rule into the realities of everyday political life. One difficulty that disturbs the tidiness of the model is the discrepancy between majority vote, meaning something more than half, and the largest vote, which may be something quite considerably less. If there are three or more serious candidates in a constituency, as is commonly the case in Canadian federal and provincial elections, a full majority is not easily achieved. More often than not, the winning candidate, who will have more votes than any other single candidate, will have less than 50% of the total. In total there will be more votes cast for the losing candidates than for the winner. For example, in the 1957 federal elections in the B.C. riding of Burnaby-Richmond, the winning candidate received only 26% of the vote, while the other three candidates received 25.8%, 24.9%, and 23.2%. Results of this kind have a cumulative effect; at only two elections since universal suffrage was introduced in Canada in 1921 has the government party won a clear majority of the popular vote. In 1972, for example, the Liberals formed the government, having won more seats than any other party. But only 38% of the electorate voted Liberal, meaning 62% of the votes were for the other parties. Majority rule does not necessarily mean what it says.

Yet, despite all the caveats and doubts, majority rule cannot be completely dismissed. It still remains a central component of liberal democracy. Whatever may be the dangers of a majority becoming a tyrant, the notion that the will of the people, and especially the will of the ordinary people, is somehow at the heart of our understanding of good government. In a liberal democracy we believe in the idea of majority rule and do our best to make it work. Majority rule becomes in turn an institutionalized expression of the further democratic principle of government by public opinion, which is based on the instinctive feeling that in a democracy the government is there to give the people what they want. If, for example, the majority favour a return to capital punishment, and it is probably true that in Canada today the majority do favour this, it is argued that the government has no right to refuse what the majority want.

This, of course, raises the question of whether it is the government's responsibility to govern—to lead and direct—or whether it is there simply to reflect the whims and shifts of popular opinion. Does "government by the people" mean that governments must do exactly as the people tell them, or does it mean merely that the people have the right to elect or remove their governors.

Although there is much popular sentiment in favour of the concept of an immediately responsive legislature, the tradition of our parliament is that our government be a government, and not just a mere recorder of public opinions. There would be no point in this activity if all that members were required to do was to vote as their constituents directed. Of course today, under the influence of more or less tightly disciplined parties, parliamentary debates are less exercises in which individuals try to persuade each other than they are exercises in which parties try to influence the electorate. In its extreme form, the notion of complete subservience of government to public will would lead to a kind of push-button democracy, with instant referenda on every issue. Frequently touted today are fantasies about the wonderful opportunities of the electronic age. Dreamers imagine that we would all sit by our television sets, listen to a brief debate, press the appropriate button, and record a vote binding on Parliament. This is a naive notion, taking no account of the realities of opinion formation and making impossible any continuity in government policy making. A television debate might produce a lot of hot air, or it might have some entertainment or educational value or provide great opportunities for high-pressure media manipulation. But it would not be an appropriate instrument for creating an informed electorate.

Government is more than a head count. It requires *informed* decision-making, set in the context of overall policy, and taking into account the impact of each decision on other decisions and the anticipated reaction of affected groups. It also requires a great deal of patient, tedious examination of legal and technical fine points. But most of us, for whom politics is at best a diversion after a full day's work, have neither the time nor the capacity, nor the interest to inform ourselves fully on any major issue. It is not difficult to predict what most viewers would choose if offered a choice between a popular television show and a debate on amending clauses to the Income Tax Act. And our further experience is that on many issues of greatest importance, those with the firmest convictions will be the least ready to expose themselves to further or conflicting information on the issue. Those who know the least about anything are readily persuaded that they know everything. Most would approach a debate not to learn but to receive reassurance about what they already believe. Push-button democracy would greatly increase the opportunities for extremist groups convinced of their own righteousness to impose their version of reality on the whole society.

Our constitution provides that Parliament may continue for up to five years between elections, in part to save it from just this constant subservience to instant opinions.[11] Instead, we give governments a chance to govern, to implement and justify their policies. After a reasonable interval we have the opportunity to return the same party to power or to replace it with another one. We are not governed by Gallup polls, so there is absolutely no moral or legal obligation for a government apparently unpopular in the polls to resign or change its policies. To use the terminology of an earlier chapter, elections are institutionalized ways of changing governments; public opinion polls are not.

In determining the appropriate relationship between members of parliament and their constituents, an important distinction has to be made between a delegate and a representative. A delegate is chosen to present the views of the constituents, acting as they command. The task of delegates is to promote in some higher assembly the views of those who chose them. In the American system, there are very strong traditions and pressures that legislators should be delegates, directly answerable to the electors. Although the reality is far removed from the ideal, there are at various levels elaborate procedures of initiative, referendum, and recall elections to keep reminding members that they are there to voice and defend the opinions of their electors.

Although many Canadians look to American models, and many candidates make promises which would indicate that they think of themselves as delegates, the Canadian parliamentary system is not a delegate system. It is a representative system, drawn from British traditions. The point at the moment is not to argue that one system is "better" than the other, but simply to draw attention to the fact that they are different, and ought not to be confused. Representatives are expected to express their own views and make their own independent decisions.[12] They do not take instructions from their constituents. The classic statement of the doctrine of representation, contained in a letter written by the great English conservative statesman Edmund Burke (1729–1797) and addressed to the electors of Bristol in 1774, reads:

> Certainly, gentlemen, it ought to be the happiness and glory of a representative to live in the strictest union, the closest correspondence, and the most unreserved communication with his constituents. Their wishes ought to have great weight with him; their opinions high respect; their business unremitted attention. It is his duty to sacrifice his repose, his pleasure, his satisfactions, to theirs — and above all, ever, and in all cases, to prefer their interest to his own.
>
> But his unbiased opinion, his mature judgment, his enlightened conscience, he ought not to sacrifice to you, to any man, or to any set of men living. These he does not derive from your pleasure — no, nor from the law and the Constitution. They are a trust from Providence, for the abuse of which he is deeply answerable. Your representative owes you, not his industry only, but his judgment; and he betrays, instead of serving you, if he sacrifices it to your opinion.
>
> My worthy colleague says, his will ought to be subservient to yours. If that be all, the thing is innocent. If government were a matter of will upon any side, yours, without question, ought to be superior. But government and legislation are matters of reason and judgment, and not of inclination; and what sort of reason is that in which the determination precedes the discussion, in which one set of men deliberate and another decide, and where those who form the conclusion are perhaps three hundred miles distant from those who hear the arguments?
>
> To deliver an opinion is the right of all men. That of constituents is a weighty and respectable opinion, which a representative . . . ought always most seriously to consider. But *authoritative* instructions, *mandates* issued, which the member is bound blindly and implicitly to obey, to vote, and to argue for, though contrary to the clearest convictions of his judgment and conscience — these are things utterly unknown to the laws of this land, and which arise from a fundamental mistake of the whole order and tenor of our constitution.
>
> Parliament is not a congress of ambassadors from different and hostile interests, which interests each must maintain, as an agent and an advocate, against other agents and advocates; but Parliament is a deliberative assem-

bly of one nation, with one interest, that of the whole — where not local purposes, not local prejudices, ought to guide, but the general good, resulting from the general reason of the whole. You choose a member, indeed; but when you have chosen him, he is not a member of Bristol, but he is a member of *Parliament*.[13]

Even in Burke's day, members were not always the free agents his words might suggest. By the twentieth century, at least in parliamentary-cabinet systems where party solidarity is necessary to keep a government in office, Burke's model of the independent representative had become an anachronism. Most members of parliament, most of the time, vote and speak according to the demands of their parties. Members are largely elected on the basis of their party label and are expected to support loyally the policies of that party. But while party discipline means that members of parliament cannot act completely as representatives, part of the old understanding remains. Members are not now, as they have never been, delegates answerable to the majority opinion of their constituents.

It remains virtually impossible to explain Western democracy in terms that do not include some notion of majority decision-making. Perhaps here is the clue. It might be a wonderful world, although possibly a very dull one, in which all would agree about everything and where all government decisions reflected the unanimous opinion of all the people. In practice there will be few proposals of any consequence in which such a complete consensus is likely. And while it is desirable that we should freely discuss and debate matters in an effort to persuade each other, there eventually comes the time when the debate must cease and a decision be taken. At this point, the only acceptable mechanism within the democratic model is that of counting votes — by ballot or show of hands, or whatever. The majority will is the only will that can be allowed to prevail. But let us keep in mind what is happening. A decision is taken because a decision has to be taken. That is all. The decision does not establish ultimate truth, moral righteousness, or the absolute good. The decision taken may be misguided, foolish, or wrong, although we may never know this.

The fact that democracy implies the priority of the majority still leaves unresolved the plight of the dissenter. If, as so many have stated, the individual's rights are genuinely indefeasible, it is no great comfort to be deprived of them by a majority rather than a tyrant. "Nor is there any good reason why an individualist should resign his private judgment merely because those who disagree with him are numerous."[14]

As Mill and de Tocqueville tried to make clear, the majority is simply the largest number and is not, by that fact alone, either right or wrong. As long as that is kept in mind, the majority may be persuaded to restrain its intolerant inclinations. Majorities must be allowed to rule because there is no acceptable alternative, but when majorities assume infallibility or fail to recognize the tentative nature of their decisions, they cease to be democratic. To be democratic, a majority must admit to itself the limits to its own wisdom and virtue. The whole argument about minority rights also raises the more basic questions of the nature of these rights. What rights does a minority have, and why should these be protected against the determination of the majority? At one level the argument can be conducted in purely pragmatic terms such as social stability, reduction of tension, compromise, moderation, "give-and-take", and so on. Respect for the rights of minorities can mean a happier, more peaceful, more comfortable society living by some implicit principle of fair play. Deeper than this, however, is the very basic assumption that all members of a society do indeed have a body of inalienable natural rights. If these are held equally by all members of the society, those of the minority cannot be taken away by any action of the majority. Consider some of the minority groups in your own community — an ethnic or religious group, for example. In what way might majority opinion make an unwarrantable attack on the rights of that group? In light of the discussion in chapter three on the sources of rights, what sort of rights might a minority have that could be endangered by the majority? If rights have their origin in the consent of the society, as T.H. Green proposed, how could it be argued that the majority voice of the community could deprive some segment of the community of its rights? Does the notion of minority rights, therefore, demand some acceptance of the principles of natural law and natural rights? Perhaps this question could be debated in terms of French language rights in English Canada or English language rights in Quebec.

PERMANENT MINORITIES

There is, finally, the special problem of permanent minorities, those racial, ethnic, or religious communities that cannot suddenly decide to join the majority and are equally incapable of recruiting new members to become the majority. A permanent majority, whether it be founded on religion, race, or language, that uses its power to maintain the subordinate status of a permanent minority, is a threat to the other values supposedly protected in a liberal democracy. A majority of, say, Presbyterians, who used their majority power to deny jobs, housing, or anything else to a permanent Catholic or Jewish minority in their community, solely because the minor-

ity was Catholic or Jewish, could not validly claim to be acting democratically because it had the largest support. Permanent minorities pose a heavy
strain on democratic idealism. They make demands on us that are not
easily met. Many research studies by sociologists and psychologists indicate that we have no natural inclination to be tolerant of those markedly
different from ourselves. Discrimination comes easier than acceptance. The
plight of permanent minorities has, in recent years, come to greater public
attention as *affirmative action* programs have attempted to improve their
position. The results have not always been what was intended.

The distinction between a permanent and a temporary majority is an
important one. Much of the literature on the tyranny of the majority seems to
envisage two more or less permanent blocs: a majority (always the oppressor) and a minority (its victim). This is far from our political reality. The
supposedly evil effects of majority tyranny may be mitigated by the fact
that on many issues the majorities and minorities will be shifting alliances,
not permanent categories. On some questions I am with the majority, and
on others I am very much with the minority. And the people I am allied
with are not the same on all issues. Any inclination, when in the majority,
to run roughshod over my opponents is likely to be moderated by the recognition that some of those opponents will be in the majority against me
on other questions.

We are brought to two views about democracies and majorities:

1.   As a machinery of decision-making, majority rule is essential to
democracy. When decisions have to be made, when the debate is over,
and when no more effort can be made to reach consensus, the will of the
majority becomes binding on all.

2.   But majority rule is only a decision-making procedure. The majority is not necessarily factually or morally right. Majorities must be prepared to allow that they may be wrong and that the minority may be right.
They must, therefore, resist the temptation to translate their voting power
into assumptions of infallibility.

So we see that in the association of democracy and majorities, there are
two necessary components. If either is missing, the democracy is faulty.
Clearly the principle of rule by the majority, or by a government approved
by the majority, is essential as the decision-making machinery. The alternative, decision-making by a self-appointed individual or an elite chosen
by only a few, is inconsistent with any other liberal democratic value. The
second component is some spirit, some attitude, a philosophy of life that
imposes a sense of self-restraint on the majority. The majority must recognize that it is only the temporary victor as a matter of political convenience. The minority are not necessarily in error, or wicked, or foolish.

They continue to exist in the community as equal citizens and have the same rights as the majority.

Democracy thus goes beyond simply the mechanics of government to include, as an even more important component, the spirit with which those mechanics are used. As Robert Dahl noted, "Every advocate of democracy of whom I am aware, and every friendly definition of it, includes the idea of restraints on majorities."[15]

CHAPTER EIGHT

The Right to Dissent

At the heart of the debate about the rights of majorities lay the fundamental liberal democratic assumption that government must be by the consent of the governed. But it is not always clear just what is meant by consent. More than fifty years ago, A.D. Lindsay drew attention to this problem. After proposing that democracy would seem to require that we insist "governors should come for our consent for everything they do," he continued:

> But when we set our minds to bring this about, certain puzzling questions and disquieting facts arise. Is democracy a means of bringing about that the people shall consent to what the government proposes to do, or that the government shall do what the people want? The two things are very different, and yet if all we want is to produce consent, it can be got in either way.[1]

This is basically the question of initial responsibility. Is it the task of government to introduce proposals for which it then seeks popular support, or is it up to the people themselves to initiate proposals that the government must then implement? This raises the question of the extent to which consent also involves participation, a theme more fully developed in the last chapter.

However it is conceived or interpreted, the notion of consent is so vital to our understanding of democracy that we must examine its origins and limits a little more closely. While the principle of tacit consent has always been implicit in Western political thought, the larger issue of consent first became a salient question in the period of the English civil war in the seventeenth century. This was a time of great political ferment as people began a reexamination of the principles by which they were governed. The old concepts of kings ruling by divine right had been discredited. Ideas of individual rights and individual conscience were beginning to supplant ideas of community obligation.

OLIVER CROMWELL

Born April 25, 1599; died September 3, 1658.

English revolutionary leader and Lord Protector of the Realm. As the English civil war between the forces of Charles I and the supporters of Parliament developed, Cromwell organized a regiment on the parliamentary side, emerging as the most powerful figure in the anti-royalist cause. After Charles was defeated, Cromwell was one of the foremost in demanding his death (1649). As leader of the army he led a brutal incursion into Ireland. The defeat of the royalists did not bring peace. Increasing conflict arose between the Presbyterian controlled parliament and Cromwell's army; Cromwell was victorious. In effect he was able to establish himself first under the title of Captain-General and then as Lord Protector of the Realm. After his death the power of his army collapsed and the Stuarts were restored to the throne (1660), whereupon Cromwell's remains were dug up, beheaded and quartered, and publicly displayed.

By great good fortune there happens to survive from this period a document most relevant to the present discussion. This is a verbatim account of a debate within the Councils of Cromwell's army.[2] The discussion took place on October 25, 1647. It has on one side Cromwell and some of his senior offices and, on the other side, a group of officers who were mostly members of an early radical group known as the Levellers. One of the Levellers, a Colonel Rainboro, expressed what Lindsay described as "the authentic note of democracy," before going on to draw some rather large conclusions. Rainboro said, "Really, I think the poorest he that is in England hath a life to live as the richest he."[3] This is the basic argument that every person, irrespective of rank, wealth, or learning, has a certain human dignity, and a certain set of basic rights, which no person or government can rightfully take away. It is an assertion of the essential equality of all members of society. But then Colonel Rainboro expanded upon the implications of his original act of faith:

And therefore I truly think, Sir, it is clear that every man that is to live under a government ought first by his own consent to put himself under that government and I do think that the poorest man in England is not at all bound in a strict sense to that government he hath not had a voice to put himself under. . . . Every man born in England, cannot, ought not, neither by the law of God nor the law of nature, be exempted from the choice of those who are to make laws for him to live under and for aught I know, to lose his life under.[4]

Here, in the seventeenth century, far ahead of their time, the Levellers were arguing for something close to universal male suffrage. In place of a parliament representing primarily the interests in property ownership, the Levellers advocated representation of the personal interests of all individuals.

While this is at first sight an attractive argument, it does create a number of problems. It seems to suggest that people ought not to be bound by any government they have not consented to and, therefore, by implication they ought not be obliged to obey the laws passed by such a government. Taken literally this would seem to mean that those Canadians who didn't vote for the government party (usually more than half the voting population) would not be obliged to obey the laws of that government. This is obviously not a tenable proposition. The solution of the difficulty is found in that sleight of hand referred to earlier by which we move from the consent of the people, to the consent of the majority of the people, and then to the consent of the largest number of people who are interested enough to vote. It had been Locke's argument that those who voluntarily remained members of a community tacitly consented to the arrangements by which the community was governed and were, therefore, bound by the decisions of the majority:

And thus every man, by consenting with others to make one body politic under one government, puts himself under an obligation to every one in that society to submit to the determination of the majority and to be concluded by it.[5]

In this way all who participate in an election, no matter how they cast their ballot, are assumed to have consented to the propriety of the election process and therefore to have given their consent to abide by the outcome. Despite its importance in the justification of democratic representation, the validity of this assumption is questionable. There is no evidence that any large number of people, when voting, have in mind any conscious endorsement of the political system of which they are part.[6]

However, while we properly accept consent by the majority of the governed as an essential criterion of democracy, we must bear in mind that some level of consent or legitimization by the people, however achieved or expressed, is a necessary condition for the maintenance of any regime. Not even the most despotic of rulers can survive long without some high level of public acceptance, even if it is only a resigned agreement to what cannot be changed. The appearances of consent can be imposed by terror or by the threat of terror. We can be easily persuaded to display unanimity. Consent, therefore, while it is a necessary condition, is not, of itself, a sufficient condition for democracy. Consent can also be induced by a combination of indoctrination, socialization, or propaganda, on the one hand, and the limiting of non-conforming information on the other. Here, as in the case of freedom of speech, this is not a world of absolutes, of either/or choices, but of "more or less." All societies make some effort to socialize the new generation to system-supporting beliefs and behaviour. All make some effort to exclude or denigrate dysfunctional ideas and actions. But there may be very substantial differences of degree between societies that demand an undeviating, unquestioning loyalty to every action of its leaders, and those which have a more relaxed expectation of popular support and accept that opposition to particular policies or governments can be properly combined with consent to the system as a whole. While all governments would like all their citizens to agree with them, this agreement is not everywhere pursued with the same single-minded intensity. In contrast to the attitudes of authoritarian regimes, it is intrinsic to the idea of liberal democracy that consent should not be limited to a passive acquiescence in whatever the government decides to do. There is the further notion that consent ought to be freely offered as a voluntary choice among viable options. It is implicit in the liberal democratic ideal that governments will at least sometimes do as the people want, and will sometimes bow to dissenting voices.

When it comes to evaluating a regime claiming popular consent we need, therefore, to ask more about the nature of that consent. It is not enough to know that the people consent to their government. We need to know something specific about how that consent is created, how freely it is offered, on what information of, or access to, alternatives is it based, and how detailed or direct are the relationships between the consent of the governed and the policies of the governors? These are questions of empirical fact to be answered by direct observation of specific situations at specific times. Nevertheless, the more general proposition remains that in a liberal democracy governments find their legitimacy in the freely offered consent of the governed.

WITHHOLDING CONSENT

The notion that consent is voluntary, however, implies that it might some-times be withheld or withdrawn. So there is also, as part of the liberal democratic tradition, a persistent principle that there are circumstances in which people are entitled to withhold consent, even to the extent in extreme cases of disobeying the law. The main object of this chapter is to explore further the ideas of withdrawing consent not just as a matter of occasion-ally breaking some particular law but also of opposing the government as such, or some of its laws, as a matter of conscience. In what circumstances would citizens feel entitled to say that as their government is behaving improperly, they will not obey it and that they will, if need be, resist by force?

We are not concerned here with the criminal who breaks the law in full knowledge of what the law is, but violates it because there is a profit in so doing. Thieves and burglars are not opposed to the laws of property. They want them in place to protect their own possessions while they break those laws for their own convenience. Nor do I have in mind the occa-sional violators of traffic laws or people who cheat a little on their income tax returns. All of us, being human, are slightly less than perfect in our obedience to the laws we generally respect. The crucial point centres on those persons of good conscience, those honest and honourable individu-als who as a matter of principle defy the law because they believe the law itself is wrong. There are, for example, those who hid Jews or helped allied airmen escape, against the laws of the Nazi occupiers of Europe, often fac-ing torture or death for their disobedience. There are those who, as a mat-ter of conscience, refuse military service or, contrary to law, support demonstrations, strikes, and sit-ins, or perhaps those who secretly give their children religious instruction in defiance of the law of an atheistic state. As well there are the newspaper reporters who may face criminal charges for refusing to reveal their sources of information about matters the gov-ernment of the day would rather have kept secret. Some will break what they regard as *minor* laws of property or trespass in order to draw public attention to what they believe are greater moral or social evils: on such matters, for example, as nuclear weapons or industrial pollution. In all these instances, the law is broken not for personal advantage or convenience but as a matter of principle and often at great cost.

An appropriate starting point to the rights and wrongs of the issue is the original Christian doctrine, which set the values of Western society for 1,500 years or more. It was a doctrine of absolute individual obedience to the civil power. The crucial New Testament text, which was the political guide until the Reformation, was Saint Paul's letter to the Romans:

> Let every soul be subject unto the higher powers. For there is no power but of God: The powers that be are ordained of God. Whosoever therefore resisteth the power, resisteth the ordinance of God; and they that resist shall receive to themselves damnation. For rulers are not a terror to good works but to the evil. . . . Wherefore ye must needs be subject, not only for wrath, but for conscience sake. For this cause pay ye tribute also; for they are God's ministers, attending continually upon this very thing. Render therefore to all their dues: tribute to whom tribute is due; custom to whom custom; fear to whom fear; honour to whom honour.[7]

This for many centuries remained the orthodox doctrine of the relationship between the Christian citizen and the Christian state. On the eve of the Reformation, Martin Luther reasserted the traditional view:

> There are no better works than to obey and serve all those who are set over us as superiors. For this reason also disobedience is a greater sin than murder, unchastity, theft, and dishonesty, and all that these may include.[8]

MARTIN LUTHER

Born November 10, 1483; died February 18, 1546.

German religious reformer and translator of the Bible. In 1505, against the wishes of his family, Luther entered an Augustinian monastery and in 1507 was consecrated a priest. In 1508 he was appointed professor of philosophy at the University of Wittenberg. The first step to the great Reformation of the sixteenth century came with Luther's publication on October 31, 1517, of his ninety-five theses against the sale of indulgences. When this was condemned as heretical, Luther refused to recant. He went on to publish other tracts setting out the major themes of the Reformation — the formal principle that the Bible is the only rule of faith and practice, and the priesthood of all believers. In politics Luther was ultra-conservative and a determined defender of the powers of government. He condemned, without reservation, any notion that the ordinary people might have any right to govern themselves or resist the civil authorities.
For further reading see:
Green, V.H.H. Luther and the Reformation. New York: Capricon, 1964.
Troeltsch, Ernst. The Social Teaching of the Christian Churches. 2 Vols. London: Allen and Unwin, 1950.

Mueller, W.A. Church and State in Luther and Calvin. Nashville: Broadman Press, 1954.

In Geneva, John Calvin was even more emphatic in his condemnation of any resistance to the civil authority. It was implicit in this argument that the king would bear the burden of guilt before God if he commanded his people to do wrong.

After Luther and Calvin, the doctrine of unquestioned obedience was challenged by the later events of the Reformation. Cynics were not surprised to note that Catholics under Catholic kings, and Protestants under Protestant kings, both insisted on strict adherence to the doctrines of Paul; however, both Catholics and Protestants under rulers of an opposing faith argued that Saint Paul did not really mean what people thought he had meant, for members of the "true faith" had a right, even an obligation, to resist the laws of a heretical king. In Catholic Scotland, the Calvinist John Knox repudiated the doctrines of the Calvinists in Protestant Geneva:

> For now the common song of all men is, We must obey our kings, be they good or be they bad; for God hath so commanded. But horrible shall the vengeance be, that shall be poured forth upon such blasphemers of God his holy name and ordinance. For it is no less blasphemy to say that God hath commanded kings to be obeyed when they command impiety, than to say that God by his precept is author and maintainer of all iniquity.[9]

JOHN KNOX

Born c.1513; died November 24, 1572.

Scottish reformer and one of the principal figures of the Reformation of the sixteenth century. Knox began his adult life as a Roman Catholic priest but later espoused Protestantism and became one of the major forces in the establishment of a Calvinistic form of Protestantism as the official religion of Scotland. His principal written work, The History of the Reformation of Religioun Within the Realme of Scotland, *was not published until after his death. He also published the tract* A First Blast of the Trumpet Against the Monstrous Regiment [government] of Women *(1588).*

Despite Knox's rejection of traditional authorities, the broad scope of the original doctrine, which gave great comfort to kings and rulers, generally remained in force. Good Christians would obey the law not only through fear of human punishment but also because this was the moral command of God. Good citizens did as commanded by their lawful superiors and did not presume to question those properly set above them. Such doctrines were entirely consistent with the hierarchical structure of feudalism, where each person had a rank in society, with rights, duties, and obligations appropriate to that rank. As it was only the highest ranks that had the duty of ruling, it would be inappropriate for those of a lower rank to interfere with matters that did not concern them. It would be disruptive of the order, stability, and security so highly prized in feudal society.

Even when resistance might have corrected a great abuse of power when kings became tyrants, as they so often did, it was still held that obedience was preferable to rebellion because of the disorder that rebellion entailed. While rebellion might bring down one bad king, it was a threat to the authority of all kings, good and bad. It established a dangerous precedent to others who might have less justification for their disobedience. There was the added danger that the revolutionary overthrow of one tyrant might lead to even harsher repression as the new king sought to safeguard his throne against further revolutions.

This was the argument for authority, for preserving the status quo, and for maintaining a society of docile, obedient subjects. The argument did not die with feudalism. In the beginning of the modern era, long after the collapse of the feudal order, the bourgeois middle classes, having won *their* freedom, adopted the same attitudes in defining the role of the working classes. Throughout the social and political literature of the eighteenth and nineteenth centuries there were repeated references to the desirability of a "contented and obedient working class" and a "law-abiding, untroublesome peasantry." Disaster would follow once the "lower orders" began to question the authority and wisdom of their "natural superiors." Thus, in the British House of Commons in 1807, Mr. Davies Giddy, speaking on the foolishness of providing education for the working classes, declared:

> However specious in theory the project might be of giving education to the labouring classes of the poor, it would be prejudicial to their morals and happiness; it would teach them to despise their lot in life, instead of making them good servants in agriculture and other laborious employments. Instead of teaching them subordination, it would render them fractious and refractory, . . . it would enable them to read seditious pamphlets, vicious books, and publications against Christianity; it would render them insolent to their

superiors; and in a few years the legislature would find it necessary to direct the strong arm of the power towards them.[10]

Those agricultural or urban labourers who from time to time protested against their oppressed conditions were arrested and charged as trouble-making disturbers of peace and order, malcontents, guilty even of treason and rebellion. Many were hanged or deported.[11] All authoritarian and military regimes are, of course, founded on the virtues of an unquestioning obedience of all orders.

CORPORATE RESISTANCE

But let us return to the traditional doctrines. While civil and political leaders, with the backing of the Church, stressed the moral obligation of individual citizens to obey the law, the Church itself, as an institution, a corporate organic unity, always reserved the right to call to order those kings who defied its moral leadership. Ordinary citizens were not entitled to set their individual consciences against the law, but the Church itself, as an established authority with the direct mandate of God in spiritual matters, could command both state and individual. You will recall from history the great power and authority behind the Church's weapon of excommunication. A king cut out from the corporate body of the Church lost much of his legitimacy. It was only because other circumstances had changed and new forces come into being that Henry VIII of England was able to survive and flourish after being excommunicated.

The source of legitimate resistance to a king's power was vested only in a corporate community. The Church offered organized opposition as one organic unity challenging the authority of another. It was in no sense a democratic concept, for the unorganized citizenry, the mass of the ordinary people, were not expected to participate as individuals nor to initiate individual acts of defiance. But the people's grievances could be brought to the king's attention through properly constituted associations. It is from this notion of corporate expression that the idea of Parliament emerged. Parliament's primary purpose was to advise the king. But from the very beginnings of the first true Parliaments in the thirteenth century, Parliament was treated as more than just a gathering of individual advisers, speaking directly to the king. The king did not summon a group of men to talk things over with him. He summoned a Parliament — a body of men who met together in private to debate (parley) the issues before them, to determine their collective decision, and to tender that decision to the king through their spokesman — the Speaker. Parliament had only one voice and it was Parliament as a unity, not the members of parliament as individuals, that advised the king. These concepts, still part of Parliament, are reflected in many of the formalities of parliamentary procedure. In the first centuries of Parliament, the ordinary people, who as individuals had no right of resistance, were expected to have their grievances expressed for them through their parliamentary representatives. It was, of course, to be a very long time before the mass of the people could demand any voice in the selection of those representatives or in expressing for themselves what they believed their grievances to be.

THE DOCTRINES OF DISSENT

The traditional authoritarian argument was never totally accepted, for even in Christian strongholds there were always those prepared to challenge it. Apart from the organized corporate resistance or criticism from Church or Parliament, there continued to be from time to time individuals ready to proclaim their rights against an unjust king. This right of dissent became particularly important during the religious wars of the Reformation, when religious minorities found themselves being persecuted for their beliefs. For a long time it appeared unthinkable that those of one faith could be loyal to a king of another or that the king, for his part, could have confidence in receiving such loyalty. The case for dissent was generally based on the proposition that a king who abused the office of kingship, who exceeded his just powers or violated the rights of his subjects, ceased to be king and became, instead, an illegitimate tyrant. As the citizens' obligation to obey was to a king and not a tyrant, the tyrant could be resisted or even deposed in the name of loyalty to the office of kingship. One could honour kingship by removing a wicked king.

These issues were given dramatic formulation in a publication written under the pseudonym Stephanus Junius Brutus Celtus. This was the famous *Vindiciae Contra Tyrannos* of 1579. Beginning as a defence of the Huguenots against brutal persecution, it developed into a wider discussion of the issues of liberty and dissent. In defining the rights of private persons, the *Vindiciae* upheld the traditional view that individuals could not oppose the public authority. Faced with an ungodly state, or commands to do or believe what cannot in conscience be done or believed, the private person could choose only exile or death. But while private resistance was impossible, there was a right of public resistance: resistance by a people as a whole, in their corporate capacity, or as expressed through their Estates-General and assemblies. It is through the *Vindiciae* that many of the ideas of Contract, of corporate resistance, and of liberties of a people passed into the Western political tradition.[12] It was essential to the argument of the *Vindiciae* that the king held his power as a trusteeship for his people. When the king violated that trust, the people, through their assemblies, were entitled and even obliged to resist to the point of deposition. But it was only the people in their collective, corporate capacity, acting through their magistrates and natural leaders, who could resist, not the people as an unstructured multitude or gathering of individuals.

The concept of the social contract, further developed during the seventeenth century, strengthened ideas of resistance. The contract set limits to the powers of the government. By making the government subject to its own laws, it set definable bounds to the power or authority of government. When those bounds were exceeded, the contract was broken, so absolving the people from any obligation of obedience. Locke had been emphatic on this point:

> Whensoever, therefore, the legislative shall transgress this fundamental rule of society, and either by ambition, fear, folly, or corruption, endeavour to grasp themselves, or put into the hands of any other, an absolute power over the lives, liberties, and estates of the people, by this breach of trust they forfeit the power the people had put into their hands for quite contrary ends, and it devolves to the people, who have a right to resume their original liberty, and by the establishment of a new legislative (such as they shall think fit), provide for their own safety and security, which is the end for which they are in society.[13]

From these various sources, especially over the past two or three centuries, the idea evolved that resistance to an unjust ruler is not only the right of a free people but perhaps even a duty. There is an impressive body of literature stressing the obligation of continued resistance to a tyrant. According to the dissenting argument, it is necessary to demonstrate continually the tyrant's illegitimacy and to place oppressors on the defensive by confronting them again and again with the proposition that their rule is based on power without authority. In abandoning the old medieval arguments of civil obedience, modern radicals maintain that those who prefer obedience to resistance, leaving it to God to punish the oppressors, abrogate their responsibilities as free citizens. Because liberty is hard to win and easy to lose, those who love liberty must be prepared to fight in its defence. A few extracts from this literature are worthy of attention. The first is a well-known quotation from a letter to William S. Smith, November 13, 1787, from Thomas Jefferson:

> What country ever before existed a century and a half without a revolu-
> tion? . . . The tree of liberty must be refreshed from time to time with the
> blood of patriots and of tyrants. It is its natural manure.

This is really an argument for the virtue of periodic revolution, and while
in times of oppression it may seem an inspiring sentiment, it is a doctrine
rather hard to sustain in practice. It certainly would not be greeted with
enthusiasm by the internal security forces in any of our modern Western
democracies. The small group of Canadians who, in 1982, bombed the
Litton Systems plant and perpetrated several other acts of violence, may
have believed themselves to be fighting for freedom against an oppressive
government, but it is not likely that they would have been treated any
more sympathetically by the courts had they cited President Jefferson in
their defence. Jefferson offers no guide to the circumstances in which we
might be justified in refreshing the tree of liberty.

T.H. Green, as pointed out in previous chapters,[14] saw the state not
simply as the enemy of individual rights but as sometimes the instrument
for extending those rights. As an extension of this general argument he
gave the state a positive role in bestowing upon individuals the power to
pursue their own self-realization not in competition with others but in
pursuit of some common good. The state had an active role in promoting
the conditions in which a full human life could be lived. From this Green
concluded that, as a general principle, citizens should obey the law when
the state was acting as a "true" state, that is, when it had established procedures for the easy articulation of the claims by individuals for those things
regarded as essential to their self-realization. The true state had effective
institutionalized mechanisms for judging the validity of, and support for,
any set of claims and for translating some of them into law. In such circumstances, where the laws are to a degree a reflection of the common will,
there is an obligation on each person to obey the law. In a just society the
individual is entitled to work for the repeal of a law, or to advocate changes in
a law, or to campaign for new laws. But the law, as it actually exists at any
moment, is morally binding on all subjects. In the good society, most people, most of the time, freely elect to obey most laws. But any society is
entitled to punish disobedience and to demand that all people, all the
time, obey all the laws.

However, the obligation to obey is not universal. In any despotism, or
in any totalitarian, authoritarian regime, where demands, claims, and resent-
ments may not even be expressed or the needs of some significant section
of the people can be ignored, disobedience may be morally justified. This
is how Green expressed the principle:

The presumption must generally be that resistance to a government is not for the public good when made on grounds which the mass of the people cannot appreciate; and it must be on the presence of a strong and intelligent popular sentiment in favour of resistance that the chance of avoiding anarchy, of replacing the existing government by another effectual for its purpose, must chiefly depend. On the other hand, it is under the worst governments that the public spirit is most crushed; and thus in extreme cases there may be a duty of resistance in the public interest, though there is no hope of the resistance finding efficient popular support. . . . Its repeated renewal and repeated failure may afford the only prospect of ultimately arousing the public spirit which is necessary for the maintenance of a government in the public interest.[15]

In other words, resistance, even armed resistance, may sometimes be justified not only by what it actually achieves or might hope to achieve but also because the example of resistance may strengthen the public spirit and weaken the will of the tyrant by denying moral endorsement. Resistance is a public declaration that the ruler does not have the unanimous consent of the ruled. This is especially true where some large segment of the population perceive the law to be immoral. At this level, resistance, open defiance of the law, is more a duty than a right. Where a regime denies a people the *legal* rights necessary for self-realization, by refusing them even the possibility of claiming the right to express grievances or seek remedies within the law, they may resort to methods outside the law.

The third statement is from an essay by Pierre Elliott Trudeau. During the early 1950s Mr. Trudeau was the central figure in a small group of Quebec intellectuals who produced a French language magazine, *Cité Libre*. Its basic political purpose was to democratize the Province of Quebec in opposition to the autocratic and corrupt rule of Maurice Duplessis. A collection of essays from *Cité Libre*, translated into English, was published a few years ago under the title *Approaches to Politics*. One suspects that a prime minister who had enjoyed power might find some of his earlier radical doctrines on the limits to power rather embarrassing. But one essay, "Must the Tyrant be Assassinated?" is worth quoting at length.

Personally I dislike violence. And I shall have occasion later on to show that assassination is a very weak political instrument.

But how do we explain that eminent theologians — among them certain Jesuits, armed with their *imprimatur* and their *nihil obstat* — have brought themselves to teach that the social doctrine of the Church makes political assassination legitimate and even obligatory?

Our discussion so far has established that any political authority exists only because the citizens agree to obey it. This agreement, then, is the guarantee of all social order.

Now, this agreement — or "psychological disposition to obey," as we have called it with rather more precision — is accorded only so long as the citizens find welfare and profit in it. If the people feel themselves oppressed, appeals to vague and abstract notions of general welfare, established order, and respect for authority will not in practice compel obedience. The people obey because it is easier to do so and because they are accustomed to it; this custom will be broken if the people, feeling themselves oppressed, start thinking about the possibility of suppressing the oppressors. . . .

It is the duty of citizens, therefore, to examine their consciences on the quality of the social order they share and the political authority they acknowledge. If the order is rotten and the authority vicious, the duty of the citizen is to obey his conscience in preference to that of authority. And if the only sure way of reconstituting a just social order is to stage a revolution *against tyrannical and illegal authority* — well, then, it must be done.

So when you teach the people to obey authority, you ought to add that it is possible to disobey it with an equally good conscience. If you did so you would find, on the one hand, that the rulers would grow rather more respectful towards the governed; on the other, that the latter would become more sensitive to the notions of liberty and justice.

It follows from all this that no government, no particular regime, has an absolute right to exist. This is not a matter of divine right, natural law, or social contract: a government is an organization whose job is to fulfil the needs of the men and women, grouped in society, who consent to obey it. Consequently the value of a government derives not from the promises it makes, from what it claims to be, or from what it alleges it is defending, but from what it achieves in practice. And it is for each citizen to judge of that.

But by what standards will he form his judgement? In a society of egoists, clearly, every citizen will want a government that will cater to him personally even at the expense of others: he will therefore pledge his loyalty to a government that will give him, as circumstances require, a bottle of beer, a refrigerator, a church pavement, or a university subsidy.

But a society of egoists quickly becomes a society of slaves for no man by himself is capable of overturning an established government. Such a government is not weakened at all when one discontented citizen refuses to obey the authorities, for they simply put him in prison.

To remain free, then, citizens must seek their welfare in a social order that is just to the largest number; in practice only the majority has the power to make and unmake governments. It follows that men can live free and at peace only if their society is just.[16]

Mr. Trudeau would be the first to admit that there are serious difficulties with this line of thought. He makes it clear that it is not up to disgruntled citizens to decide individually that, as the government is personally oppressive to them, they will exercise their rights to disobey it. The argument is not intended as a vindication of the paranoid nor to justify the assassination of presidents by those with their own private delusions. The lone discontented individual is not entitled to attempt the overthrow of an established government. Those who do make such attempts are quite properly punished. So what do Green and Trudeau mean? In what circumstances would they acknowledge a right to resist by force? Perhaps all the circumstances can be combined under the one heading—when no other channel of dissent is open.

A group which, after being given fair access to public opinion, fails to gain popular support cannot acquire a right to resort to force. Force is not a legitimate weapon for the frustrated, the unpopular, or the unsuccessful. It is not simply a second option for losers. I have, perhaps, a right to speak my mind. But I have no right to demand that others shall listen to me, nor do I have any right to resort to violence because the majority chooses to ignore what I have to say. A society does not become oppressive simply because it refuses to agree with *me*, because it refuses to follow my preferred policies, or because it compels me to do some things I would rather not do. It becomes oppressive when it denies me the right to propose alternatives, but not when it chooses not to accept those alternatives. Force is a legitimate remedy only to those denied the right even to seek popular support, or to make public their grievances.

PIERRE ELLIOTT TRUDEAU

Born in Montreal October 18, 1919.

Pierre Trudeau began practising law in Quebec in 1943, specializing in labour law and civil liberties cases. He was a founding member of the Montreal Civil Liberties Association and was one of the principal writers for the journal Cité Libre. *He held an appointment as Associate Professor of Law at the University of Montreal. He was first elected to the House of Commons in 1965 and became*

Leader of the Liberal Party in 1968. He was Prime Minister of Canada 1968–79 and 1980–84. Mr. Trudeau has published numerous articles and papers on social, economic, and political themes, and is the author of Federalism and French Canadians *(1968) and* Responses *(1967).*

RESISTANCE BY FORCE

This would seem to suggest that within a liberal democracy there can be no right to resist by force. Indeed, this is almost a tautology. A society in which the circumstances are such that some group would be morally justified in resorting to force as the only means of making its case known is, by that fact alone, not a liberal democracy. We could reasonably describe a liberal democracy as a system that so opens itself to the articulation of claims, to the expression of demands, and to the legal voicing of discontents or counter-proposals that no resort to force or violence is necessary or legitimate.

Whenever some group, some segment of society — a racial, ethnic, or religious group or an economic class — is denied equality before the law and is further denied any avenue of protest against that inequality, there may be justification for rebellion. An oppressed group, especially a permanent minority such as described in the previous chapter, which is denied access to the normal political processes and precluded by law from using the political system to articulate claims, may well be justified in resorting to force to remedy its situation. The same can be said of political opponents in a dictatorship. Where there is no legal dissent and where critics of the regime are hounded by a secret police or are silenced or imprisoned, or quietly and mysteriously disappear forever, armed resistance may be the only honourable recourse. Those who live in a free society ought to give such resistance their full moral support. But an important note of caution is warranted here. In most circumstances it would be improper in peacetime for any government or private group to attempt to foment rebellion in another country. To encourage revolution in another country by deceiving people of that country with false promises of assistance, when failed revolt may invoke the severest penalties, would be cruelly wicked and irresponsible.[17] Apart from the potentially disastrous consequences, there are the larger legal and moral issues raised by any attempt by one state to initiate or encourage the destabilizing of the political system of another with which it is not at war.

The situation of a foreign occupation, where the legitimate government of a people is overthrown by an alien military command, is particularly important. Even Thomas Hobbes in the seventeenth century, after proposing a form of government with absolute power to preserve law and order, conceded that where a country was occupied by foreign armies, or where the sovereign had surrendered himself to foreign forces, the citizens were absolved of their obligations of obedience. They were free to seek their survival as best they could.[18] We have generally hailed as heroes those who join resistance movements to free their countries from the invaders (unless, of course, *we* are the invaders or the occupiers). By and large the British, for example, while enthusiastically voicing the rhetoric of independence and freedom, long opposed vigorously the armed independence movements in their own colonial territories — in Kenya, Cyprus, Zimbabwe, and elsewhere. In the double talk of international politics, resistance movements in regimes supported by "our side" are terrorists or subversives, while those active in regimes we oppose become freedom fighters. A theme of many postwar books and films has been the bravery of those inspired patriotic heroes who, in Europe during the Nazi occupation, took up arms against the occupying governments. Resistance and disobedience to the law became a positive virtue. After the war those who, in our terms, collaborated with the enemy, were condemned as traitors and punished. Similarly, the Allies rejected as invalid the line of defence that claimed Nazis charged with committing atrocities in the concentration camps were "only obeying orders." Our motives may have been politically self-serving, but at least we reaffirmed that there are occasions when obedience to the law is less than virtuous. This, of course, is what Antigone tried to tell us many centuries ago.

Behind this recognition that disobedience, even violent disobedience, is sometimes justifiable, lie our historical memories. Great social changes have rarely been brought about except as a consequence of at least some initial unlawful acts. Those in power do not normally offer to share that power with those who simply sit quietly and say "Please." The creation of the United States as an independent nation, the transfer of power from a feudal aristocracy to a middle-class Parliament, the recognition of the rights of workers to form unions, the granting of the vote to women in England, and the extension of civil rights to blacks in the United States, were all accomplished only after initial acts of violence. Democracy itself was born in the violent resistance to antidemocratic forces.

But force is always a remedy of last resort. There is always the danger that violence may become an end in itself, incompatible with the ends it is supposed to be advancing. Violence is an easy outlet to the frustrated to vent their hatreds. But violence pursued as a continuing policy may be counter-productive; it being exceedingly difficult to achieve ends nobler than the means used to achieve them. There is a cliché that the end justifies the means — that honourable ends and great goods justify shoddy and dishonourable tactics. It is easy to argue that because the intentions are good the means are thereby made right. Unfortunately the evidence of history suggests that, rather than noble ends elevating and justifying evil means, the means dishonour and debase the ends. If we apply this proposition to those contemporary terrorist groups who seek violent change in the structure of society, we see that behind the apparently senseless savagery, the taking of innocent lives, and the destruction of property, there is usually some vision of a newer, more just society. There is an anger at whatever is perceived to be the overriding evils of the existing order together with a sense of hopelessness about correcting those evils by traditional measures. But again experience indicates that terrorism often results simply in more terrorism. Revolutionary change, when forced upon a population still unprepared to accept it because it is unstable and lacks legitimacy, can usually be sustained only by force. Revolutions are seldom the liberating experience envisioned by their initiators. Too often revolutions against tyrannies achieve not much more beyond a replacement of tyrants.

THE CONSEQUENCES OF DISSENT

There is always a difficulty in assessing the consequences of violent dissent. This is the problem of drawing valid causal relationships from a historical sequence of events. It raises what the logicians call the fallacy of *post hoc, ergo propter hoc* (after this, therefore because of this). The fallacy lies in assuming that if event A is followed by event B, A must be the cause of B. But the only way to prove this connection would be by a series of experiments replicating exactly all the other conditions, while controlling A. In real life, where each event is unique, this is impossible. One can therefore do no more than speculate or theorize. From an analysis of what has in fact happened one can look to antecedent occasions for explanation or probable cause. But at best one is making intelligent guesses or setting up plausible hypotheses. As these are far short of proofs, their tentative nature needs constantly to be held in mind.

As might be expected, the evidence of the effects of political violence is ambiguous. Thus, there could be endless, but unresolvable, argument about whether, say, the terror tactics of the Irish Republican Army advance or obstruct the unification of Ireland. If, or when, the issue is finally settled, no one will ever be able to say with absolute certainty what terrorism contributed to that settlement. The same sort of questions might be asked about the demonstrations and occasional confrontations by groups opposed to nuclear energy, Cruise missiles, abortion, urban development, and so on. On the one hand, they succeed in bringing their issues to the public attention, putting them, as it were, on the public agenda. But in doing so they also provide a focus for their opposition. Publicity in favour of any one cause becomes also publicity for the counter-cause.

And when the dissenting activity is directed against the state itself, the response is often dramatic and deadly. Consider, for example, what in Canada has come to be known as the "October crisis" of 1970. In Quebec during the 1960s there developed a number of movements committed to a greater measure of Quebec national awareness, and even independence from Canada. One of these, a small group known as the *Front de libération du Québec* (FLQ), resorted to increasingly violent tactics, culminating in the kidnapping of a British diplomat and the murder of a Quebec cabinet minister. The federal government's reaction was swift and extreme (after the event most commentators seem to agree that it was excessively extreme). Under the terms of the hastily invoked War Measures Act, dozens of people, few of whom had anything to do with the FLQ, were arrested and imprisoned. The events demonstrated the capacity, and willingness, of even a normally open liberal democracy to crush a dissent it was not prepared to tolerate.

Earlier in Canadian history the government also reacted violently to what it perceived as a threat to its security, although then the dissenters won at least a partial long-term victory. The episode began as a strike among the building and metal trades workers in Winnipeg in May 1919. At issue was the refusal of employers to engage in collective bargaining. After two weeks the Winnipeg Trades and Labour Council voted overwhelmingly to strike in sympathy, bringing the economic life of the city to a virtual halt. Although the strike was firmly non-violent, the government introduced massive countermeasures in support of the employers. The regular police were replaced by "specials," while a militia and Mounted Police were organized. In the violent breaking up of a peaceful demonstration, one person was killed and thirty injured. When the leaders were imprisoned, the strike was broken. However, after the event, a royal commission reported that the strike had indeed been non-violent; that its goals were, as the strikers had stated, collective bargaining rights and an improvement in wages and working conditions; and that its leaders were British born and not, as the government had alleged, "alien scum" out to subvert British law and order. The immediate cause was lost, but within a year four of the strike leaders had been elected to the Manitoba legislature and the process of politicizing the labour movement had begun. Canadian history is full of such instances of "union bashing." Almost invariably, in major Canadian labour disputes, the police and the government come down heavily on the side of the employers.

We seem now to have reached the position that a democratic society is a law-abiding society. The members of a truly democratic society do not resort to violence to overthrow their government because, by definition, they have no need to. The emphasis is on *truly* democratic, for many societies maintain the trappings of democracy while denying its extension to the large mass of their citizens. Where the power structure is the monopoly of a closed elite — the economically most powerful, a ruling tribe or caste, a few privileged families, or whatever—those permanently excluded from the political process may feel entitled to take action outside that process. It is a spurious democracy that allows all to vote but only the few to be voted for.

In a democracy most will obey the law not because they are passive, docile, apathetic, fearful, nor because they have left the task of punishing unjust lawmakers to God, but because the democratic society makes violent dissent unnecessary. A liberal democratic society, living up to its professed ideals, will provide institutionalized procedures for the public expression of dissent, and of proposals for changing unsatisfactory laws. Indeed, liberal democracy goes so far as to legitimize the position of an official opposition, charged with the *duty* of criticizing the government, demanding that it explain and justify its actions. Liberal democracy also recognizes the right of people to organize themselves into political parties, churches, labour unions, farmers' associations, business associations, philatelists, students, home-owners, and other special interest groups, to bring together — aggregate — the demands of members and supporters, and articulate those demands in a legal public forum. As long as all the several interests can organize and act publicly, there is no reason for them to plot and scheme in secrecy, to "go underground." Once you ban the legal activity of any group, you justify its illegal activity.

Liberal democracies, when not in their periodic fits of paranoia, seem to have grasped the cathartic function of dissent. Some level of opposition, no matter how disruptive or discordant, is socially functional. A well-established regime, with dominant, if not total, control over access to the mass media and the agencies of socialization, has more to gain from permitting even intemperate assaults from angry or frustrated minorities than from attempting to crush them. They have the cathartic effect of releasing pent-up hostilities and releasing the strains of alienation. At the same time, the toleration of a dissent that does no real harm confirms a liberal democracy's self-created image of a system that tolerates dissent. Some resistance is thus functional in strengthening the system.

Hence, liberal democratic governments provide a rough and ready, and in practice, far from perfect mechanism for government by the will of the community. And they must, if they are to be democratic in fact as well as in name, provide access to the system to *all* sections of the community. No actual modern state comes anywhere near a complete realization of this democratic ideal; nor, given the complexities and contradictions of the public will and the other external pressures that limit what a government can do, could it be expected to do so. None of our liberal democracies are in practice all that in theory they ought to be. But at least we can rank states in some kind of continuum from those states which go as far as human ingenuity and good will allow in attempting to discover and act upon the will of all the people by providing a forum for the greatest possible range of political opinions; to those states which deny the relevance of anything other than the arbitrary personal command of the leader. In the latter case, violence may be the only recourse of honourable citizens.

Finally, a discussion point: We can assume that most of the time you, personally, obey the law. But why? Is it the fear of punishment or the public shame that would follow if you were caught? Is it simply a matter of habit, of doing what you have always done, because it is easier that way, because you don't want to "buck the system" or be a troublemaker? Is it a sense of social responsibility, a feeling that as this is your society, it is a part of your duty to uphold its laws, even if you personally disagree with some of them? Is it because laws and commands are an absolute obligation—because disobedience is a sin? Is it because when acting under orders you are excused moral responsibility for what you do—that responsibility devolving on the one issuing the orders? Is it a matter of mutual self-interest, a feeling that if you obey the law you have a right to expect that others will obey it too, and you have more to gain by everyone obeying the law, than by simply breaking it yourself? Is it the fear or love of an all-seeing God? Is it that your position in society is such that you can get whatever you want without breaking the law; the law itself being drafted to protect the interests of people like you?

These are not the only motives and you may think of more. Certainly you are unlikely to be guided by just one of them, but in seriously considering what motivates you to obey the law, you might come to some better understanding of why some others sometimes feel impelled to break it. Can you imagine circumstances in which *you*, in response to an overriding moral imperative, would refuse to obey the law of the land?

CHAPTER NINE

The Right of Property

Central to the capitalist ideology is a belief in a right of property as something desired by all humans as part of their nature. Property was one of the fundamental rights asserted by John Locke to belong to all individuals in a pre-society state of nature. It was a right inherent in individuals, simply by virtue of their humanity.

In exploring the idea of property, the first problem is to clarify the terminology, for the word is commonly used in several senses. First, property means the things owned. In popular usage it tends to be associated particularly with the *land* we own — "this is private property," "I have a piece of property by the lake," and so on. But this is only a conventional use, for my car, my books, my money, and even my dentures are also just as correctly described as my property. However, property, as the things owned, must be carefully distinguished from the second sense of the word: the *right of ownership*, which is the main concern here. Definitions of property include such terms as the *condition of being owned, anything owned or possessed*, and, most importantly, *the exclusive right to possess, use, or dispose of anything*. Note these terms carefully: that property is a condition of being owned that confers an "exclusive right" to possess something, giving the owner the "sole use of something", including, most importantly, "the exclusive right to *dispose* of something." So to talk of the right of property is to talk of the right to own things — any things, not just land — the right to say, "this is mine" and, as a most important corollary of this, "you can't have it unless I say so." For that is one of the essential factors of ownership — it is not only possessing or using; it is also denying others possession. However, while the *right* of property confers exclusive use and control, all governments in practice impose restrictions or limits on the *exercise* of that right. The nature and justification of such restrictions will be the central theme of the next chapter.

It is a concept intimately associated with a sense of self-identity. That is to say, the principle that some things ought to be set aside from all other things as being "mine" becomes important only if I attach significance to a "me" distinct from all of "you." My demand for property and your recognition of the validity of that demand is an acknowledgement of my existence as an individual. The right of property is thus not something external to the individual but is derived from the fact of individual autonomy. It is implicit in the liberal understanding of life that there is some psychological satisfaction to be derived from having property. It remains a core tenet of capitalist ideology that we all desire to claim things as our own. It is a desire to identify things with ourselves that goes beyond the satisfaction of using them. I don't want books just to read them, or look at them, or incorporate them in the decor of my house. I want to *own* them, to make them part of my being. The things I own become an extension of myself.

Wherever, as in certain religious communities or tribal societies, the individual is subordinated to the whole, the importance of individual ownership is diminished. Taking a vow of poverty in a religious order does more than restrict the material pleasures of life. It lessens the opportunities for individual pride of possession and individual autonomy. This was part of the reasoning for the sharing of property by the guardians in Plato's *Republic*. Private property was incompatible with the unity and exclusive devotion to the good of the state that Plato demanded of his soldiers and rulers. Having no private property the individual must share in the property, and therefore the life, of the community. The member is diminished as an individual. Wherever, too, the individual has no need, or no means, to establish individual identity as against others, there is no reason to assert a right of property. The castaway on a desert island makes no claim for property in some things abstracted from the totality of things. Things are not owned, they are simply used. It is only when another person arrives that it becomes necessary to say, "This is me, and this hut, this coconut, and this fishing line are mine."

It will then also become necessary to work out some arrangement for determining the future ownership of things not yet claimed. Green notes the implications of property thus:

> One condition of the existence of property, then, is appropriation, and that implies the conception of himself on the part of the appropriator as a permanent subject for whose use, as instruments of satisfaction and expression,

he takes and fashions certain external things, certain things external to his bodily members.[1]

An example might make clearer this distinction between the right of property and the right of use. This text is being written on some word-processing equipment supplied by my university. I have this equipment at home for as long as I need it. For the time being I am the only one with access to it, and the only one entitled to use it. But I don't have property in it, for I must eventually return it to the university, and I have no say in who gets it next. I have temporary use of it not exclusive ownership. On the other hand, it is in my study with many of my books. These I have an absolute claim to. The distinction becomes clearer as we refer to the disposal aspect of property. And again to come back to the equipment, this I must return in good order. I am not entitled to sell it, or pawn it, or paint it blue. My books, however, are mine. I may keep them, sell them, give them away, write notes all over them, or use them to light the fire. I may do whatever I want with them because they are mine; I have property in them. The most important difference between having property in something and having the mere use or control of it lies in this ultimate right of disposal.

It is also useful to distinguish various kinds of property. This is especially important when we come to consider the appropriate boundaries of public and private ownership. At the first level there is purely personal property, beginning with such things as clothing, and perhaps also embracing jewellery, sports equipment, household furnishings, books, and so on. Simplistic attacks on socialism often allege that socialists seek to abolish all private property, including personal property, but nowhere in the theoretical writings of any socialists is there any such proposal, nor do we find it the practice in any actual socialist regime. The socialist argument excludes personal property, although there may be debate about what is, or is not, personal property, and the effort to establish socialism might place limits on the amount of personal property any one individual might accumulate. The closest approximation to the full social ownership of personal possessions would be found in certain religious communities whose members take a vow of poverty. Here each individual owns only a very few personal things, everything else being the property of the community as a whole.

At a second stage there is productive property, or property used in the creation of wealth. It includes the land, natural resources such as mines and forests, factories, machines, banks, transportation facilities, water and electricity supplies, and so on. The serious debate over public or private ownership, or about the rightness or wrongness of private property, really concerns only productive property. Once again if the question is approached at various levels, it can be seen that different kinds of arguments for public or private ownership can be raised at different levels. The simplest level of productive property covers the one-person trade — the watch repairer, the hairdresser, or the artisan of some kind. Even in such highly socialized societies as the Soviet Union these are often left as private property — largely because there does not exist an administrative machinery capable of bringing them into the public domain. At the next level one finds the small business — the family concern, the retail store, or small factory employing no more than, say, half a dozen people. Again we find that even quite extreme socialists exclude such enterprises in their debates about abolishing private property. They are not the reason why socialists are opposed to the private ownership of productive property. Indeed it is central to the Marxist argument that the abolition of private ownership of the means of production is justified because capitalism had already destroyed that small-scale private ownership for the many. As Marx wrote in *The Communist Manifesto*:

> We Communists have been reproached with the desire of abolishing the right of personally acquiring property as the fruit of a man's own labour, which property is alleged to be the groundwork of all personal freedom, activity and independence. Hard-won, self-acquired, self-earned property! Do you mean the property of the petty artisan and of the small peasant, a form of property that preceded the bourgeois form? There is no need to abolish that; the development of industry has to a great extent already destroyed it, and is still destroying it daily. . . .
>
> You are horrified at our intending to do away with private property. But in your existing society, private property is already done away with for nine-tenths of the population; its existence for the few is solely due to its non-existence in the hands of those nine-tenths. You reproach us, therefore, with intending to do away with a form of property, the necessary condition of whose existence is the non-existence of any property for the immense majority of society.[2]

The right of private ownership of the means of production is a central tenet of capitalism. The abolition, or at least the modification and regulation, of such private ownership is one of the goals of socialism. But nowhere in the real world does one find a situation where productive property is either *all* public or *all* private. No viable argument can be made for leaving *everything* in private hands nor for bringing *everything* under public ownership. The next chapter will examine more closely the kinds of arguments that might be made for putting some things under public ownership, and leaving others in private hands, especially within the mainstream of political thinking of a liberal democracy such as Canada.

JOHN LOCKE ON PROPERTY

First, however, there is a need to analyze more closely the basis of the original liberal assertion that private property is a natural right. The argument was developed by John Locke in his *Second Treatise on Civil Government* (1690).[3] Locke's contribution to political thought lies primarily in his concept of eternal, inalienable, external rights, which were the possession of the individual in the state of nature and continued to be valued as the individual's protection against the abuse of power by governments. The most crucial of Locke's rights was that of property.

There is something distinctly unreal here in claiming that private property, and especially productive property, is a universal natural right — an attribute of the free individual in a pre-productive state of nature. For when we observe most primitive peoples, we find few even capable of understanding the concept of private ownership, except for a few personal possessions. Neither the Indians and the Inuit of North America nor the Polynesians of the South Pacific recognized any private ownership of land, which was the inalienable property of the tribe as a whole. And the flocks of the early nomadic peoples belonged to the tribe, not to its individual members. The anthropological evidence does not support the contention that the private ownership of productive capacity is a universal natural human desire.

JOHN LOCKE

Born August 29, 1632; died October 28, 1704

   Remembered largely as one of the greatest English political philosophers who profoundly influenced political thought in eighteenth-century America, Locke began his adult career in the study of medicine. He travelled widely as a member of the household of the First Earl of Shaftesbury. Because of his writings, and because his father had fought on the parliamentary side in the English civil war, Locke was suspected as a dangerous radical in Restoration England. He fled to Holland, where he remained until the accession of William of Orange to the throne of England in 1689. Philosophically Locke was an empiricist, believing all knowledge to originate in sense experience. Locke's lasting political fame arises from his attacks on traditional feudal bases of authority, leading to his strong defence of the rights and liberties of individual owners of property. He was the first major rationaliser of the capitalist ethic. His most famous and influential works were the Essay Concerning Human Understanding (1690) *and the* Second Treatise on Civil Government (1690).

For further reading see:

Macpherson, C.B. The Political Theory of Possessive Individualism. *Oxford: Clarendon Press, 1962.*

Laski, H.J. Political Thought in England from Locke to Bentham. *London: Home University Library, 1920.*

Cranston, Maurice W. John Locke, a Biography. *London: Longmans, Green, 1957.*

Wood, Neal. John Locke and Agrarian Capitalism. *Berkeley: University of California Press, 1984.*

But, to return to Locke. While Adam Smith is the father of the economic theory of capitalism — its laissez-faire component — Locke is its philosophic father. His influence, especially in the United States, is enormous and continuing. His argument begins with God as the source of all property, it being his contention that in the beginning the earth and its fruits were given by God to all humanity in common. For Locke this was a necessary argument to refute the claims by kings and aristocracies that they had a natural, God-given, superior title to the world's resources. So, said Locke, God gave the earth to *all* humanity:

> God, who hath given the world to men in common, hath also given them reason to make use of it to the best advantage of life and convenience. The earth and all that is therein is given to men for the support and comfort of their being.[4]

But although all the fruits of the earth belong to all humanity, in the natural state, nobody having an inherent claim to any of them, there has to be some way of appropriating some of those fruits for individual use. If we look at an apple tree standing on unclaimed land in the state of nature, there needs to be a transition from saying, "all of these apples are ours, given to all of us by God," to saying, "this particular apple is mine, therefore, I may eat it." For if all things remained in the possession of all people, nothing could belong to, or be used by, any one person.

Locke's transition from common to private ownership is made through labour. The one thing each individual has is property in his or her own person:

> Though the earth and all inferior creatures be common to all men, yet every man has a "property" in his own "person." This nobody has any right to but himself. The "labour" of his body and the "work" of his hands, we may say, are properly his.[5]

This becomes the instrument by which property can be taken out of the state of nature and into private possession. My labour mixed with what was in the state of nature becomes mine. It is thus my existence as an individual entity that is the source of my right to own property. To continue with the previous very simple example: The tree of apples in the state of nature may belong to all of us, but when I mix my labour with it, by the labour of picking one apple, that apple becomes mine. One can see here the roots of some of the ideological appeal of Locke in the United States, for this is virtually what happened on the western frontier. People moved out on to the unoccupied land and by fencing it or ploughing it — by mixing their labour with it — they made that land theirs. As Locke himself put it:

> Whatsoever, then, he removes out of the state that Nature hath provided and left it in, he hath mixed his labour with it, and joined it to something that is his own, and thereby makes it his property.[6]

Within the conditions of society it could be argued that individuals have tacitly agreed to accept this arrangement, but it is not at all clear why, in any state of nature, there should be any recognition by others of the validity of my claim to have appropriated something by adding my labour to it. It is all very well to say that labour gives me a title to something, but why should I expect others to accept that title? Then there is another difficulty. And so, Locke continued:

> And the taking of this or that part does not depend on the express consent of all the commoners. Thus, the grass my horse has bit, the *turfs my servant has cut* [italics added], and the ore I have digged in any place, where I have a right to them in common with others, become my property without the assignation or consent of anybody. The labour that was mine, removing them out of that common state they were in, hath fixed my property in them.[7]

It is easy enough to argue that *my* labour mixed with what was in the state of nature gives me a title to something. But why should the turfs *my servant* has cut belong to me, and not to the servant who cut them? If labour is the exclusive property of the labourer, how do I come to benefit from the work of my servant? This is a most critical question, and we will eventually come to Locke's answer to it.

There are, in Locke's account, limits to the amount of property I can appropriate to myself out of the state of nature. I can't, for example, pick all the apples, sit on the pile, and say, "These are mine, go away." In Locke's mind, as the things of nature are given to humanity to enjoy or use, no one is entitled to have that which will spoil before it can be used:

> The same law of Nature that does by this means give us property, does also bound that property too. . . . As much as anyone can make use of to any advantage of life before it spoils, so much he may by his labour fix a property in. Whatever is beyond this is more than his share, and belongs to others. Nothing was made by God for man to spoil or destroy.[8]

So there is a limited right to appropriate personal property from the state of nature. There is no private title to anything that would spoil before it could be used. Such things remain in the state of nature for the use of any others willing to mix their labour with it.

MONEY

So far the argument is a fairly simple one for the limited private ownership of the fruits of the earth, and it is, perhaps, of interest in a pioneer society, but of little value to a settled modern community. If this were all there was to Locke, we would scarcely bother reading him, for the amount of land or the number of apple trees still in the state of nature is extremely limited. The proposition that the only way one can acquire private property is by mixing one's labour with things in the state of nature has very little relevance to the members of a modern urban-industrial society. It certainly does not help explain why you can own a television set, an automobile, or shares in Bell Canada. The catch comes with the introduction of money— a factor that completely invalidates the original proposition about the limits on property. The introduction of money allowed people to acquire and hold more than they needed for daily consumption. It allowed for the acquisition of property other than perishables. As money does not spoil, there can be no principled objection to its accumulation. The only reason why I can't have all the apples is that some of them would go bad before I could use them. But, according to Locke, money does not suffer this disadvantage (Locke in his day was unfamiliar with the depreciation of money through inflation):

> And thus came in the use of money; some lasting thing that men might keep without spoiling, and that, by mutual consent, men would take in exchange for the truly useful but perishable supports of life.
>
> And as different degrees of industry were apt to give men possessions in different proportions, so this invention of money gave them the opportunity to continue and enlarge them.[9]

Money has no intrinsic worth of its own. Its use is entirely conventional, for notes and coins have only the value different societies have agreed to give them. By the fact of using money as a medium of exchange or as a medium of deferred consumption, society has consented to the use of money, and therefore, it must be presumed to have consented to all the further consequences of that use. And the main consequence is consent to the unequal possession of the world, or to an inequality in wealth:

> But since gold and silver, being little useful to the life of man, in proportion to food, raiment, and carriage, has its value only from the consent of men — whereof labour yet makes in great part the measure — it is plain that the consent of men have agreed to a disproportionate and unequal possession of the earth . . . they having, by consent, found out and agreed in a way how a man may, rightfully and without injury, possess more than he himself can make use of by receiving gold and silver, which may continue long in a man's possession without decaying for the overplus, and agreeing those metals should have a value.[10]

Money thus changes the whole character of society.

Locke was one of the first to appreciate the true nature of money. Money is not just a fixed asset to be stored — something to be put away in a sock under the mattress. Nor is it simply a medium of exchange — something to simplify transactions among farmers, shoemakers, and bakers. Nor is it even just an instrument of deferred consumption — something that makes it easy for me to take the money I receive now for selling you shoes and set it aside to buy something I need later. Locke recognized that in addition to all these functions, money becomes capital, a source of further money through interest on loans and through investment. Money enables those who possess it to accumulate even more of it.

As long as property was limited to perishables, all would have much the same kind of possessions and be in much the same kind of economic condition. But consent to the use of non-perishable money was consent to inequality. Money enabled some to acquire property beyond immediate consumption and to use that money to earn still more money, so some would acquire great property. Money made the unequal accumulation of property both possible and permissible. Locke expanded upon that point:

> I dare boldly affirm, that the same rule of propriety — viz., that every man should have as much as he could make use of, would hold still in the world, without straitening anybody, since there is land enough in the world to suffice double the inhabitants, had not the invention of money, and the tacit agreement of men to put a value on it, introduced (by consent) larger possessions and a right to them.[11]

The use of money also changed the significance of the original proposition that possessions were the fruit of each person's own labour. It made possible the acquiring of property beyond the labour talents of the owner acting alone — production calling for the combined labour of many individuals. The use of money altered the effect of the labour justification for the ownership of property — the principle that the way by which possessions were appropriated was by mixing labour with things in the state of nature. The argument was developed in this way: All individuals have an indisputable right to their own persons. Each individual is, in a very literal sense, his or her own person, and we have each the sole right to the property of our own labour. No one else can own me. I own myself and my labour. But here is the critical argument: the right of property, or the right of ownership, confers the right of disposal. The sole right to anything gives one the right to dispose of it as one will. Whatever I have property in is mine not only to use and enjoy but also to sell, exchange, or even, if I choose, to give away. And having once disposed of something, I have surrendered ownership; it is no longer mine, and I have no further claim on it.

If I sell you a racehorse that begins to win races, I cannot demand that you give it back nor can I demand a share in its winnings. Because you have bought it, you have all the rights to any profits it might make. And as my ownership of my own labour implies my right to sell that labour for a sum of money, having received the money, perhaps in the form of a wage, the labour is no longer mine. It belongs to the purchaser, who is entitled to any profit from that labour. This is why *the turfs my servant has cut* belong to me. The servant sold the labour for a wage. It is therefore my labour and I am entitled to its product. To quote from C.B. Macpherson in one of the most useful books about Locke: "The labour thus sold becomes the property of the buyer, who is then entitled to appropriate the produce of that labour."[12] So in Locke's hands the argument that individuals have a right to their own labour becomes an argument for the right of each person to alienate the fruits of that labour through a wage contract. The individual who sells labour sells also the product of that labour. By this reasoning, which is one of the crucial philosophic underpinnings of capitalism, labour becomes a commodity, a disposable asset, separate and distinct from the labourer. It is the labour, not the labourer, that becomes a possession, something which, like a horse or a basket of apples, can be bought, sold, or traded and thereby confer full title on the buyer. The original owner, the labourer, has title to nothing more than the wage received for it. Under slavery, the purchaser acquired the entire person of each slave and therefore had some responsibility for the slave, even if only as an investment. By Locke's reasoning, however, the purchaser gained title only to the labour, leaving the person of the labourer supposedly a free individual responsible for individual well-being.

This is a critical point in the Marxist criticism of capitalism. Marxists will argue that such alienation of the labour from the labourer is indefensible and invalid; that the full value of the produce of the labourer must be restored to the labourer. This alienation is certainly something not found in its full implications in a pre-capitalist society where the poor, although they still worked for low wages, were not alienated from the product of their labour.

Locke's analysis of the nature of property further rationalized the division of society into two mutually exclusive classes—not so much as something to be desired as the object of a conscious policy but as something inevitable. There will be, on the one hand, the class of the possessors of money and capital; those whose wisdom and providence have enabled them to accumulate much property. Having built up reserves of money, they are able to buy fine houses, rich food, or whatever else they desire including, most importantly, the labour of others. That labour becomes as much theirs as their houses or other property, and they are entitled to any profit that labour might bring. On the other hand, there is the class of wage labourers, whose idleness, folly, and short-sightedness will keep them forever at the level of mere subsistence, selling their labour and its fruits for whatever immediate cash value it will produce. It is also assumed that, as there will always be more wanting to sell labour than there are those seeking to buy it, the price of labour will always be low.

Expanding on Locke's argument that God gave the world for the "use of the industrious and rational,"[13] laissez-faire capitalists tend still to believe that the poor are poor through their own fault. As they lack either the talent or the ambition to be rich, they deserve no more than they can get by their own effort. They are also assumed to be free sellers of their own labour, bargaining on equal terms with the potential purchasers of labour, selling it because they chose to sell it, at a price they are willing to accept. There are therefore no grounds for intervention by the government to protect labour in settling the terms of the wage contract, while any combination of workers into unions is an unjust and improper interference with the freedom of each individual to make the best possible bargain. So, although Locke started from a state of nature in which free and more or less equal individuals would own all things in common, he ended with a society made up of two antagonistic classes, with virtually uncrossable barriers between them: the class of capitalists, the purchasers of labour, and the class of labour itself, the sellers of labour for wages, entitled to no more than those wages. Liberal capitalism, which began as a philosophy of competitive individualism, became the rationalization of a dichotomized, class-structured society.

In this way the possession of property became a critical identifier of class, reflected in many other aspects of life. This is illustrated, for example, in the evolution of the franchise. In the earliest medieval parliaments it was the community as such, as an organic corporate unity, that was represented. It was London or Winchester, not the people of those cities, that sent representatives to Parliament. Under this arrangement the right to vote was restricted to those very few who held title to the land of the community. Often the Lord of the Manor would be the sole landowner, all other inhabitants being his tenants. Gradually through the fourteenth to nineteenth centuries the monopoly of landownership by the feudal aristocracy (and by the Church) was eroded as more and more of the entrepreneurial capitalist class joined the ranks of the land owners. As capital displaced land as the principal measure of worth, money became an alternative to land as a qualification to vote or hold public office. From the mid-nineteenth century the franchise was gradually broadened, but at each stage the criterion was property either in land or in money. It was taken for granted that only property owners were qualified to make decisions affecting the whole of society, including those who owned no property and who were offered few opportunities for acquiring it. It was not until the present century that the right to vote became vested in the individual as a person, rather than as a property owner.

Thus, the Canadian franchise at the time of Confederation was based on the voting qualification in the provinces and, therefore, varied across the country. In each case, however, the base of the qualification was the ownership or occupancy of real estate of varying annual values. This was gradually expanded to include other property or annual income. These property qualifications were gradually broadened until finally they were abandoned altogether.

THE ASSAULT ON CAPITALIST PROPERTY

Another assumption of capitalism is that productive property ought to be, as far as possible, in private hands. It ought to be individually owned, rather than owned by the state, or by society as a whole. It is argued, most forcefully by our new conservatives, that the most productive, efficient, and equitable use of property will follow from the free exchange of such property by private individuals in a competitive marketplace. The main problem here, of course, is that in our advanced industrial societies very little productive capacity is actually owned by private individuals. The major portion of productive property is owned by giant corporations, dominating the economy on a scale undreamed of by Adam Smith. Indeed, in terms of resources, income, and number of employees the biggest multinational corporations are larger and more centralized than many of the smaller national states.

Even the most extreme advocates of laissez-faire will admit that society may, from time to time and for various reasons, control or regulate some facets of property and the market. But always it will be asserted that such intervention is the exception and perhaps a necessary amelioration of some of capitalism's harsher consequences, but it is still a departure from the norm of the maximum possible private ownership and control of property, leading to the greatest social good and human freedom. So central, indeed, is this notion of the private ownership of productive property to capitalism that attacks on capitalism must involve attacks on the institution of property.

Although the most thoroughgoing assault on the whole foundation of capitalism is contained in the writings of the Marxist socialists, they were not the first to establish the connection between the political and the economic structure of capitalism. As far back as the seventeenth century, when capitalism was just beginning to emerge as a new force in society, a radical movement known as the Diggers (an offshoot of the Levellers mentioned in chapter eight) already understood how private property, especially in land, would divide society into the two worlds of the rich and poor. The core of Digger policy was therefore the common ownership of land. But the Diggers were out of their time. Their interest to us is more as a historical curiosity than for their actual effect on the course of the world.

Of greater relevance is the more solid attack on the property basis of capitalism made in the late eighteenth and early nineteenth centuries by a collection of idealistic-minded thinkers generally known as the Utopian socialists. They were not an organized school, but simply a number of people thinking along similar lines at about the same time. The key figures among them were two Frenchmen, Henri Saint-Simon (1760–1825) and

Charles Fourier (1772–1837), a Welshman, Robert Owen (1771–1858), and the English painter and poet William Morris (1834–1896). It would go beyond the range of this present study to examine the details of the several Utopian writers, but there are some common assumptions that unite them. The Utopians were responding to the huge injustices and inequalities, and the debasing poverty, of the new urban-industrial society, a society which in practice was so at odds with the greatest happiness of the greatest number promised by liberal individualistic theory. Alongside the great wealth and privilege of the rich, who lived in conditions of opulent luxury surrounded by armies of underpaid domestic servants, there were the vast masses of the urban poor living in conditions that totally denied any concept of human dignity or human worth. Any social history of the era will tell much the same story. The novels of Charles Dickens, too, are a valuable social commentary, describing with marvelously perceptive detail a social reality that is today hard to comprehend. Although many individuals devoted themselves unstintingly to relieving the sufferings of the poor, the age itself was as selfish and as brutal as any in human history. Society at large showed little concern for the well-being of those unable to survive in an atmosphere of unconstrained competition. It was an era that accepted little collective responsibility for the good of the whole.

The starting point of all Utopian thinking was the proposition that injustice, the violation of human dignity, and crime were all the consequence of poverty amid plenty. Crime, in particular, was the inevitable outcome of the hopeless despair associated with economic destitution. Crushing poverty, the source of almost all social ills, in turn, was caused by the institution of private property, which as even Locke had acknowledged allowed for the unequal distribution of wealth. In particular capitalist property led to the accumulation of enormous wealth by the few, at the cost of the impoverishment of the many. There were many social consequences of the excessive wealth that the institution of private property encouraged — all of them bad. The Utopians believed that great wealth was of itself an unhealthy thing, even for the wealthy. It encouraged corruption, decadence, and a pre-occupation with material luxury which overrode all spiritual, intellectual, or social concerns. (The Utopians, like many socialists, tended to a rather rigid puritanism and moral disapproval of high living.) So the inequalities of wealth, which were responsible for the economic degradation of the poor, were responsible also for the moral decay of the rich.

A second consequence was that in the separation of the rich and the poor, the rich came to know nothing of the poor. The rich could not comprehend so alien a lifestyle. Their wealth made it easy for the rich to dismiss the poor from their minds, insulating their lives from contact with them. For a Dr. William Channing, travelling in England during the 1840s, it was a "crying evil" that

> two communities whose members dwell within the sound of the same bells and under the same chief magistrate should in many respects be practically as wide apart as if they resided in two quarters of the globe.[14]

And as long as the wealthy remained ignorant of the true meaning of poverty — what it did to its victims — there would be little effective pressure for reform. Because they lived separate lives, the rich tended to think of the destitute almost as a separate species who neither needed nor really desired a greater share of the benefits of an expanding economy — they were simply not equipped to appreciate such benefits.

A third consequence of the inequalities of wealth was that the ostentatious luxury of the rich was an incitement to envy and a spur to the crime of revolution. Too great an inequality would give rise to political and social disorder. Finally, with too great a concentration of wealth in too few hands, too little was left for the rest. It was part of Utopian optimism to believe that the resources of the world provided enough for all to live in reasonable comfort, but only if the few did not take too much more than a fair share.

The Utopian response to the ills of society was therefore the abolition of at least some forms of private property. They did not, like some later Marxists, contemplate a vast bloody revolution in which all power would be seized by a revolutionary proletariat. The Utopian writers, mostly intellectuals and all conscious of their own superior wisdom, did not have a great deal of faith in the working classes. Nor did they propose the take over of private property by the state. The remedy was not nationalization. This is quite understandable, for in the conditions of the early nineteenth century it was hard to imagine the state — any state — doing anything very effective about anything. There was in this era no administrative experience or expertise that would have enabled the state to take over from private enterprise. As well, governments everywhere were firmly in the control of a property-owning elite that could not be expected to take actions contrary to its own interests. The Utopian plan, to which there were many variations in detail, was to set up model communities, as good examples to the rest of society. Their vision of what might be is reflected today in certain religious communities, such as a Hutterite settlement in Canada, or perhaps a kibbutz in Israel.

Within such communities all things would be held in common. The model is generally that of an agricultural community in which the land, the livestock, the equipment, and the buildings would all be owned by the community as such, with each person sharing in the labour and enjoying the profit in common. Apart from simple personal possessions, there would be no private property and no opportunity for one person to exploit the labour of another. Individuals could neither buy nor sell labour. The community itself, however, would own property, holding that property as against other like communities. Communities would buy and sell and trade with each other as corporate individuals would. This was the general Utopian blueprint. There were of course differences in detail and structure, but these, often very meticulously planned schemes, do not concern us here.

The immediate practical impact of the Utopians in their own age was virtually nil. Few model Utopian communities were ever created, and those that were did not long survive. Few took seriously their socialism by good example. But the Utopians are important for a number of reasons, not the least of which was that they forced other people to think more seriously, more systematically, about the problems they raised. They were among the first to appreciate the very close relationship between the economic structure of society, which means the things it produces and the ways of producing them, and other social relationships such as that between those who directly produce, such as workers in farm or factory, and those who own and draw profit, or the manner in which goods are distributed between producers and consumers. The Utopians drew attention to the influence of economic variables on the political and social forms of society. This was the factor that Marx later seized on and developed into a more coherent analysis.

Marx saw how the combination of capitalist investment and ownership of the means of production with wage labour transformed the whole of society affecting every facet of its social relationships and defining the character of its class structure. It is essential to Marx's philosophy that without a change in the property relationships, there can be no change in any other aspect of society. More attention will be given to Marx's socialism in chapter thirteen. In the meantime, however, given the persistence of the belief that "communists would do away with all private property," it is well to note the very limited range of Marx's own proposals in *The Communist Manifesto*. These are the points concerning property from the immediate program of action as put forward in 1848:

1. Abolition of property in land and application of all rents of land to public purposes.
2. A heavy progressive or graduated income tax.
3. Abolition of all right of inheritance.

4. Confiscation of the property of all emigrants and rebels.
5. Centralisation of credit in the hands of the state, by means of a national bank with state capital and an exclusive monopoly.
6. Centralisation of the means of communication and transport in the hands of the state.
7. Extension of factories and instruments of production owned by the state.[15]

Note that this does not propose the total public ownership even of productive or industrial property, and it makes no reference to the abolition of private personal property. Nevertheless, it is central to the whole socialist critique of capitalism that social reform is impossible without some assault on the inviolability of the private ownership of the means of production, distribution, and exchange.

KARL MARX

Born in Germany May 5, 1818; died in London March 14, 1883.

After graduating from university in 1842 Marx became editor of the liberal newspaper Rheinische Zeitung. *When this was suppressed by the Prussian government Marx moved to Paris, where he began the serious study of socialism. It was in Paris that he met his lifelong associate Friedrich Engels and where they jointly wrote some of their important early work. After a period in Belgium, and a brief return to Germany during which time he was arrested, Marx moved to London (1849), where he remained for the rest of his life. With Engels, Marx published* The Communist Manifesto *in 1848, and in 1867 he published the first volume of his huge work* Capital. *Volumes II and III were edited and published after his death by Engels. The literature on Marx, as one of the major intellectual forces of the nineteenth century and one of the most important influences on our own century, is vast, but for an introduction see:*

Laski, H.J. The Communist Manifesto: Socialist Landmark. *London: Allen and Unwin, 1967. This contains, as well as the text of the* Manifesto, *an excellent introduction by Laski.*

Tucker, R.C. Philosophy and Myth in Karl Marx. *Cambridge: Cambridge University Press, 1961.*

Tucker, R.C., ed. The Marx-Engels Reader. *New York: Norton, 1972.*

Beer, Max. The Life and Teaching of Karl Marx. *London: National Labour Press, 1925.*
Bober, M.M. Karl Marx's Interpretation of History. *New York: Norton, 1950.*

Let me, as a conclusion to this chapter, put forward a question for debate: Is the desire for private property, the ownership of things and especially productive property, a *natural* attribute of human nature and, therefore, something to be protected against all challenge as a natural right? Or is it a socially acquired value, a product of a particular social-economic order? In short, do we seek to own property just because we are humans? If this is the case, we will seek to set up those social and political institutions that will make it easiest for us to acquire and hold property. Or do we desire property because we have already set up the kind of social and political institutions that reward the private ownership of property? If this latter is the case, a change in the institutional structure could lead to a modification in the nature of our desires. Which proposition seems most in accord with your own understanding of the world?

FRIEDRICH ENGELS

Born at Barmen, Germany, September 28, 1820; died in London August 5, 1895.

Engels, a German socialist leader, theorist, and author, was, with his close friend Karl Marx, one of the pioneers of scientific socialism. Engels was the son of a wealthy cotton-spinner, a circumstance that enabled him to provide Marx with a certain amount of financial assistance. With Marx, he was the co-author of The Communist Manifesto (1848). *His other works include* The Condition of the Working Class in England (1845), Landmarks of Scientific Socialism (1878), *and* The Origin of the Family, Private Property, and the State (1884). *He also edited volumes II and III of Marx's* Capital *after the author's death.*

See Karl Marx's biography above for further readings.

CHAPTER TEN

Limits on Property

However one approaches the question of the nature or origin of rights, the right of property is clearly fundamental to liberalism. From the traditional natural rights (natural law) argument, it can be presented as an eternal right—a response to an unchanging, universally shared human desire that compels all to seek to own property. The argument that rights are relative and socially acquired and are far from being natural attributes of the individual would still have to include property as one of those rights to which our particular society has chosen to accord high priority. Even if the very concept of rights is totally rejected, one would have to maintain at the very least that property is a greatly prized utility.

But although property, meaning the right of ownership or the right to possess and hold exclusive control over things, is a widely shared value, as a right it is nowhere held without qualification or restriction. No single right, and certainly not the right of property, has absolute priority over all other rights at all times and in all circumstances:

> Absolute private property inevitably produced intolerable evils. Absolute owners did grave damage to their neighbours and to their descendants: they ruined the fertility of the land, they exploited destructively the minerals under the surface, they burned and cut forests, they destroyed the wild life, they polluted streams, they cornered supplies and formed monopolies, they held land and resources out of use, they exploited the feeble bargaining power of wage earners.[1]

Doctrines of absolute property rights ignore the fact that the laws of property, being established by the state, can be altered by the state. Specific property laws that apply an abstract right to real situations are social creations for social purposes. Because the rights of property are secured within society, there are situations in which society claims that it may justifiably impose constraints and limitations on that right. The law will, for example, put restrictions on the kinds of property one may own—it might decide that possession of firearms, certain drugs, dangerous animals, pornographic or seditious books, or whatever, is illegal. It might impose restrictions on the uses made of some kinds of property—perhaps laying down laws about the way one must keep a house in the suburbs where one may not, for example, keep chickens in the back garden nor use a house as a restaurant. A car must be kept in safe condition and it may not be used as a taxi, without a licence. Those who own a business must preserve certain standards of safety, cleanliness, health, noise, and dirt control. The owner of a swimming pool may be required to put a fence around it. These are all restrictions on the use of property. Beyond these, the most important constraints are on the acquisition and continued possession of property, especially property in money. There will generally be laws limiting the ways in which one might acquire money — laws against fraud or misleading advertising, for example. Most societies also demand that everyone give back a part of their property as taxation to pay for those things that society decides to accomplish by collective action.

These constraints can be defended on several grounds. From the point of view of the liberal individualist there are arguments from expediency, convenience, or necessity. These are the arguments that the selfish interests of competitive individuals can best be achieved by mutual acceptance of certain rules and regulations about property. I can agree to the law prohibiting me from keeping chickens in my back garden if I can be assured that you will also agree to laws preventing you from using your property for activities creating other disturbances to my peace and comfort. From an organic perspective it is easily accepted that, as property rights are derived from the community, property is subject to shared responsibilities and duties and, therefore, must be controlled in the common interest. From other points of view it could be argued that in some circumstances state necessity, or the survival or good of the community at large, must override individual rights. Finally, property rights might be examined in the context of majoritarian democracy, where the majority might wish to define the uses of individual property. Let us examine each of these in turn.

THE ARGUMENT FROM EXPEDIENCY

In the liberal version of life, individuals who are egoistic, competitive, and acquisitive are also rational enough to see the advantages of co-operative endeavours, not out of any sense of shared interest, but because in certain circumstances social effort provides the maximum individual gratification. From such an understanding, selfish individuals have accepted many limitations on their property rights. Over time various qualifications to the rights of property, all consistent with rational selfishness, have been put forward. None have much to do with socialist assaults on the basic principles of private ownership. Some are briefly described here.

First, there is the realization of the need to ease extremes of poverty in order to prevent social discontent, or even revolution. It has been the common experience that the rich are likely to use their economic power to acquire political power and, therefore, have it in their capacity to gather some kind of legal title to virtually all wealth and property. The way in which the great English land-owning families acquired private ownership of the common lands — the enclosures — in the eighteenth century is a classic example.[2] But periodically the very rich have faced up to the dangerous social consequences of immense wealth confronting abject poverty. Out of self-interest they have made concessions, granting the poor enough to soften any revolutionary impulse. In doing so they safeguarded their own control over what was left. Many European capitalists in the nineteenth century became familiar with Marx's predictions of a revolutionary working class. This was one of the factors that led some to realize that the survival of the capitalist system as a whole demanded a significant improvement in the standard of living and the economic security of the working classes. They accepted the logical inevitability and the long-term advantages of some redistribution of property, some limits on their inclination to keep it all for themselves. Capitalism was strengthened by restraining its own worst impulses.

Another line of argument followed the recognition that, while disease and plague are the products of overcrowded, insanitary housing, disease beginning among the poor does not necessarily stop there. It easily infects the whole community. Therefore, it is good practical self-defence to insist upon certain minimum standards of housing, to ensure an efficient sewage system and a regular supply of pure water, and to provide some measure of public health education and health care. Even the most determined individualist today can appreciate the wisdom of securing such things, even if they have to be paid for from the taxes of the wealthy; that is, by the surrender of some property already acquired. Of course this understanding of the relationship between poverty and disease is relatively recent. The novels of Charles Dickens portrayed the nineteenth century's indifference to the long-term consequences of the conditions under which most of the urban poor lived. Lest it be imagined that Dickens's writings are pure fiction, there is the evidence of several official reports prepared by the Poor Law Commissioners,[3] as well as innumerable histories and social commentaries. They all describe desperate overcrowding, appalling sanitary conditions, a shortage of clean water, and a consequent high rate of sickness and death.

The nineteenth century was an age that knew much about the rights of private property but chose to ignore any related duties or any sense of property employed for social purpose. According to G.M. Trevelyan, the nineteenth century unfolded in this way:

> The modern English slum town grew up to meet the momentary needs of the new type of employer and jerry-builder, unchecked and unguided by public control of any sort. A rampant individualism, inspired by no idea beyond quick money returns, set up the cheap and nasty model of modern industrial life and its surroundings. Town-planning, sanitation and amenity were things undreamt of by the vulgarian makers of the new world, while the aristocratic ruling class enjoyed its own pleasant life apart, and thought that town building, sanitation and factory conditions were no concern of government.[4]

Reform of these conditions was slow, and achieved only over bitter opposition. That archetypal individualist Herbert Spencer objected to any attempt to use public funds to upgrade the housing of the poor. Crowded, unsanitary housing should be left alone, he said, because disease is nature's way of wiping out the unfit members of society to the general improvement of the species. Reform came from two sources. First, the new mood of humanitarianism and social responsibility began to develop from the midcentury, largely from the awakened Christian conscience coming out of the Wesleyan and Methodist chapels. Second, there came a new awareness that the foulness born in the slums weakened the whole society. There was not only the direct spread of sickness, but also a continuing physical and mental deterioration of the working classes needed to operate the factories. Without some improvement of the conditions of the working poor, capitalism faced the prospect of wiping out the supply of cheap labour on which its existence depended. The continued prosperity of employers required that more attention be paid to the health and well-being of employees. The crisis that accelerated reform was the discovery at the beginning of the

First World War that tens of thousands of men called up from the city slums were physically unfit to serve even as cannon fodder in the trenches.

A third area of change in attitudes to the inviolability of property stemmed from the increasing technological sophistication of our productive capacity. It gradually dawned on factory owners that an impoverished, uneducated, unmotivated proletariat is not an efficient productive instrument. Brute labour, not much more than animal power, was adequate in the early days of the industrial revolution. It became increasingly inefficient as factories adopted evermore complicated machinery, while introducing a greater variety of skilled trades. Again, in purely practical, self-centred expedient terms, there was an economic payoff in providing for the education, especially the technical education, of the working classes. In order to produce this more qualified work force it became necessary to build and support schools out of public funds, and to pay higher wages so that parents could afford to keep their children at school.

Finally, there was a more sophisticated argument: the realization that the poor are not consumers. The industrial revolution had solved virtually all the problems of mass production. A bewildering array of increasingly advanced and varied manufactured products began to appear on the market. But the problem of consumption was more difficult. Goods could be produced more easily than they could be sold. It was in the interests of each manufacturer to keep *his own* labour costs as low as possible. But as long as wages everywhere were low, the working classes could not buy the goods that could so easily be produced. A higher standard of living everywhere improved the purchasing power of the huge mass of the urban proletariat. The whole economic development of the twentieth century has been founded on the assumption that rising wages have put automobiles, television sets, refrigerators, and so on, in the reach of the working classes. The old belief that wages must necessarily be kept at mere subsistence level, a cost of production to be kept as low as possible, was found to hurt the manufacturer as much as the workers. The recession of the 1980s, with the growth of unemployment, reminded us that lowering the consumer power of wage earners also dramatically affects the profits of manufacturers and retailers.

All the previous factors justify some restraint on the power of property owners. All imply some redistribution of income, which entails some mandatory taking of some wealth from those who have, to provide some benefits to the have-nots. All approach the problem not from some ideological principle of equality but from a pragmatic assessment of the consequences of excessive inequality. They are, admittedly, a violation of the principles of liberal laissez-faire individualism, but liberalism itself is realistic enough to acknowledge that in order to survive exceptions must be made to principles. It is a matter of choosing the lesser of two evils.

THE ORGANIC ARGUMENT

When the question is approached from the perspective of an organic community, that of a larger whole of which each individual is a member, constraints on property become even more easily defended. The basic proposition is that the individual is not just a competitive being, alone, isolated, and surrounded by similar autonomous beings. Rather, each shares with others the membership of a larger community. The lines made familiar to the modern world by Ernest Hemingway from the English divine and poet John Donne (1571–1631) make no sense to the liberal individualist:

> No man is an *Iland*, intire of it selfe; every man is a peece of the *Continent*, a part of the *maine*; if *Clod* bee washed away by the *Sea*, *Europe* is the lesse, as well as if a *Promontorie* were, as well as if a *Mannor* of thy *friends* or of *thine owne* were; any mans *death* diminishes *me*, because I am involved in *Mankinde*; And therefore never send to know for whom the *bell* tolls; It tolls for *thee*.[5]

These words are fully consistent with an organic world view, for if all are members of a larger society, the health and well-being of every member of that society becomes the concern of each other member. To revert to the simplistic physiological analogy of chapter two, one's arm cannot be indifferent to a gangrenous toe or an inflamed appendix. As members of an organic community, each is involved in the living conditions of the poorest members, not just because those conditions impinge upon one as an individual, or because that poverty may ultimately disrupt one's security, but because all are members of the same body.

JOHN DONNE

Born c.1572; died in London March 31, 1631.

English poet and divine, the greatest of the so-called metaphysical poets. He is today best known for his love poems. Most of his prose is deeply religious and philosophical.

Concerns for housing, public health, education, economic security, or social stability are justified by liberal individualism on the grounds that the consequences of not being concerned were intolerable. These concerns are accepted by an organic community as binding moral obligations, right in themselves, apart from their practical consequences. From an organic point of view, welfare, unemployment payments, old age pensions, child allowances, universal medical coverage, and so on, are not charity hand-outs to those who do not always deserve them, but a sharing, as a right, by all members of society in the wealth of that society. It is a moral argument, not an economic one.

From this organic point of view it is of secondary importance to argue that a society cannot afford to support its aged, its unemployed, and all those who for whatever reason cannot help themselves. Instead, it is held that any society, if it is to remain a society, cannot fail to provide for all its members. As it must allocate some of its resources to achieve this, it must, necessarily, impose limits on the use some can make of some of their own property.

STATE NECESSITY OR CONVENIENCE

Another area where the right of property may be limited or where some private property may be seized by the state, comes under the heading of state necessity: the prior rights of the state over the rights of its individual members. The concept that the state does indeed have such a prior right is defended fairly easily from an organic viewpoint. Indeed, the real danger lies in granting to the state, too readily, too many powers over the individual. But even without this excess, it can properly be argued that as the good of the members of a society is dependent upon the continued survival of the society, when that survival is genuinely threatened the particular interest of any of its individual members becomes secondary. Even the committed individualist admits to state necessity because there is no alternative. Liberalism was born in the notion of the social contract by which people formed a society to provide for their mutual security. Security, being thus the justification for there being a state, takes precedence over individual demands within the state.

It is obvious that from whatever position one argues, one can quite properly grant the state extensive jurisdiction over property when security and stability are threatened. The state, any state, has a well-established right to seize property for defence purposes: to sew minefields, dig trenches or gun emplacements, build military airfields, or whatever else is considered necessary. At a lower level one can confirm the right of the community to, say, order the killing of the cattle of one farmer to prevent the spread of foot and mouth disease, or to blow up a row of buildings to block the spread of fire, or to confiscate an automobile because it is mechanically unsafe. There seems little real debate here about the principle. When the safety or stability of society, or of any of its members, is in danger, the society has a prior claim over private property. The real debate, therefore, can only be about particular measures. Serious questions, for example, can be asked about whether the real or perceived dangers confronting the society justify the specific measures taken to avert them. There are also questions of compensation or rights of appeal. But these are all matters of political application, not of fundamental principle.

Even outside the crisis situation, such as war or insurrection, it is accepted that the modern state does have the authority to appropriate land for airfields, highways, or even for building universities. Here we have gone from the area of state necessity, where the principle of the right of the state is unquestionable, to that of what can be called state convenience, or the priority of the common good of a large number of people over the private rights of a few. It is a more difficult question, but it seems that in our real world, even in our most liberal democracies, the judgment is in favour of some form of state action, although not without some qualification or reservation. The convenience and comfort of the many is preferred to that of the few.

It is not an entirely one-sided problem. Society could not permit the blocking of a needed highway because just one farmer refused to sell a small piece of land. On the other hand, the farmer does have property rights, which he cannot be called upon to surrender without good reason. It is a regrettable fact that governments, wherever they are, when they are determined on their new highways or airfields, do display a rather cavalier attitude to these property rights. Even governments that preach the virtues of private property do not always respect it as one might hope. Our acceptance of the principles of state necessity or the greatest common good does not mean that we ought blindly to accept every invasion of our property rights without question or objection. The citizens of a democracy are entitled to demand that when their government proposes to seize property for purposes of its own, it must explain fully its need and justification for appropriating this particular piece of property rather than another one. We may not have an absolute right to property, and there are circumstances where society has a prior claim. But nor is society's own claim absolute.

DEMOCRATIC PRESSURES

Finally, there is the question of the impact of democracy itself on property rights. We need to recognize that public opinion also asserts some power over the amount of property one might continue to hold and the use one might make of some of it. Perhaps the most significant question is the relationship between democracy and the welfare state. The welfare state, with its claims for the redistribution of the property of some, was a reasonably natural outcome of the growth of democracy. As soon as the vote was extended to the underprivileged many, it was to be expected that the many would use that voting power to demand concessions from the privileged few — some level of wealth redistribution — some guarantees of economic security, or some protection against the economic consequences of unemployment, sickness, old age, and disability. In the past half century, one political party might have been pledged as a matter of ideological principle to the concept of greater economic equality. Another might have intensely disliked the idea. Both, if they were to win votes, were forced to reallocate some of the private property of some members of the community in order to achieve some other goal demanded by the many. The principles of political majoritarianism and inviolable individual rights of property tend to be mutually exclusive.

Democracy may affect private property further through demands for "conforming" use of property; that is, the sheer social pressures of public approval or disapproval that are sometimes without the backing of any force of law and compel the majority, most of the time, to follow neighbourhood practices in such things as the architecture and colour of their houses, the way they keep their gardens, and even the toys they buy their children. This is a restriction not on the quantity of property but on the way in which it may be used. There may be an additional constraint in the sense that public opinion can be an enormously powerful pressure persuading some to acquire property they might not otherwise want — "keeping up with the Joneses" as it is called. We might be persuaded to buy a new car or an electric lawnmower, or to install a swimming pool, because this is what all the neighbours have done, and they will think it odd if we don't.

So one concludes that the right of ownership, of possession of property, is a value in society; but it is a value subject to many constraints imposed by the society that defined the original right. There are many circumstances that limit the amount or kind of property an individual may acquire, require the surrender of some of that property for other social purposes, and specify the use that may be made of the property. The important point is that our society acknowledges a right of private property. It accepts that individuals do have a right to acquire and own material things, whether they be land, goods, or money. It also accepts that society cannot arbitrarily violate this right without good reason. But again, from whatever source the right may have been derived, it cannot validly be maintained as an absolute. While one may own property, one also has other obligations, and society will make claims upon some private property in order to meet those other obligations. The *principle* is not really debatable — private property is not absolutely sacred. The real debate can only be about the application of the principle to particular situations. One can only ask what kind of other obligations justify the intervention of the society as a whole into the private property of some. We can sensibly ask how much of whose property ought to be used to achieve what other purpose. The right of the state to impose taxes is now too well established to be called into question. All we can argue about is how much tax, how the burden is to be allocated among the different segments of the community, what different forms the tax might take, and for what purposes the tax money is to be used.

PUBLIC VERSUS PRIVATE OWNERSHIP

So far the discussion in this chapter has focussed largely on individually owned possessions — money, land, houses, and various forms of personal property. The focus has been on how individuals acquire, keep, and use personal property. Now it is intended to turn the discussion to productive property: property in things as a source of wealth, especially industrial enterprises and services. The principal theme is the rival claims of public versus private ownership of the means of production, distribution, and exchange. As a first point it is stressed that the term *public ownership* is a more accurate, versatile word than *nationalization*. The latter carries the connotation of ownership by the centralized national state, while public ownership can also include ownership by provincial or local governments, as well as ownership by various quasi-government corporations, commissions, and boards. As far as the daily lives of most are concerned, some of the most important public enterprises are owned at the local government level.

There are occasionally confusions of terminology here, because a distinction is sometimes made between a private company, meaning one owned by one person or a small group of associates; and a public company, meaning one in which shares are offered for public sale on the stock exchange. That is not the distinction we have in mind at this time. For the purpose of this discussion, public ownership means ownership by some agency of the state at any level, which by implication is deemed to mean ownership on behalf of the public at large. As far as individuals are concerned, it is involuntary ownership, because there are no opportunities for individual discretion. All Canadians are part owners of, say, Canada Post, and all residents of a community are owners of its transit system, fire-fighting service, and public library. As there are no shareholders, there are no dividends to be paid to individual investors. Private ownership, on the other hand, is voluntary ownership. Private individuals choose to invest money either as shareholders in some corporation or as direct participants in a partnership. In either case they expect to make some profit from their investment.

The argument about public ownership is all too often carried on as if it were an argument for or against socialism. But the connection between public ownership and socialism is not nearly as direct as many imagine. It is true that many sincere socialists, as well as many bitter enemies of socialism, still view increasing state participation in the economy—the growth of public ownership—as stages in the creation of a socialist society. Others, however, again including both socialists and anti-socialists, now accept a relatively high level of public ownership as no more than a pragmatic accommodation to the realities of political life. By doing things that private enterprise does not do well, or does not do at all, some public enterprises enhance the quality of life and provide a level of social service that stabilizes capitalism. From such a perspective a mixed economy, blending public and private enterprise, may produce a stronger capitalism or a more comfortable society; but it is not socialism. While a fully socialist society must involve the social ownership of the means of production, not all socialists believe that partial public ownership is necessarily a step in the direction of socialism.[6]

Contrary to the expectations of both the friends and enemies of socialism, bringing large sectors of the economy under public ownership or control, while it has meant some quite important social and economic changes, has not done much anywhere in the Western world to bring about the model socialist world.[7] Public ownership has not produced socialism. But if public ownership is not of itself a *sufficient* cause of socialism, it is at least a *necessary* one. That is to say, there can be a large level of public ownership without there being socialism, but there cannot be socialism without some high level of public ownership. A socialist society cannot exist within a private enterprise economy.

One needs, therefore, to be constantly reminded that public ownership is *not* socialism. The principle itself is certainly not an invention of socialists. In Athens 2,400 years ago, the state made a handsome profit from the silver mines at Laurium, which might be described as the first example of a state-owned industry operated as a public corporation. In most of modern

Europe, even under the most capitalistic governments, cable and telephone systems are normally government owned. And from the very beginning, the state constructed and operated the railways in most of the British colonies. In Canada today, there are very few, if any, out-and-out socialist municipal administrations. Yet, it is commonplace to find in every city that public transport, water supply, fire and police protection, parks, sports arenas, libraries, hospitals, schools, cemeteries, animal pounds, farmers' markets, and much more, are owned, operated, or controlled by the municipality itself as public services, which are financed entirely or in part out of taxes. They are not owned by private enterprise for the purpose of making a profit. One obviously, therefore, does not have to be a socialist to accept a relatively high level of public ownership. So while there is an ideological case to be put for public ownership, it is not the only case.

THE SOCIALIST CASE

As long as public ownership of productive property is a necessary condition of socialism, it will be part of the ideological argument. The ultimate socialist goal is a socially owned economy, operated for the public good rather than for the profit of a few entrepreneurs — the general socialist conclusion being that the public good and private profit are incompatible.

The socialist argument for public ownership is what might be called a "principled" argument based on the proposition that the private ownership of the means of production, distribution, and exchange, or of the provision of services, is itself inherently *morally* wrong, irrespective of any immediate economic or political consequences. It is a repudiation of the right of one social class to buy, exploit, or draw profit from the labour of another. Socialists reject Locke's central idea that labour is a commodity properly to be bought and sold for the advantage of the purchaser. The division of society into the two antagonistic classes of the bourgeoisie, who draw profits from hired labour, and the proletariat, who are compelled to sell their labour, is attacked as intrinsically unjust. It is an injustice that is merely eased, not resolved, by raising wages or improving working conditions, for the system is wrong in principle, to be corrected only when the ownership of the means of production, distribution, and exchange is vested in society as a whole. When the society itself is the owner of all industrial activity, each person as a member of society becomes both owner and worker. It is argued that from this condition, when the alienation of the workers from their work is abolished, the once divisive forces of society will be united in one common purpose.

This is an ideological argument based on a philosophical concept of the nature and purpose of society, and of society's responsibility for the well-being of all its members. As an ideological argument, it is not directly concerned with questions of economic efficiency. To many idealistic socialists, for whom the very concept of gain from the labour of others is repugnant, data about high profits is not proof of the efficiency of private enterprise, but evidence of its moral decay. Apart from any differences about the mechanics of government, socialism is thus a rejection of the ethical basis of capitalism. From the socialist world view, capitalism ought to be replaced because it is inherently unjust. Those who look at the world through different eyes are not easily persuaded to that conclusion.

Even within the ranks of the socialists there are differences of ideological intensity. The uncompromising purists want to proceed as rapidly as possible to bring every facet of productive property under public control at whatever cost. Others want to proceed only as fast as public opinion will accept. For the latter the road to socialism is through democracy and education. Others again will see no fundamental objection to certain aspects of the economy remaining in private hands. This is the idea of the mixed economy, where some combination of publicly and privately owned activities is accepted not only as a matter of expedient necessity but also as something desirable in itself. It acknowledges that the just society must accommodate a variety of points of view.

Whatever the detailed arrangements, these are all part of the ideological case. It is the argument of those who believe that there is something intrinsically immoral or degrading about the exploitation of labour for private gain, or that it is unjust that some should make a profit from their ownership of essential services, or that such natural resources as forests, mineral deposits, or oil reserves should belong to all the people for the common good.

THE PRAGMATIC CASE FOR PUBLIC OWNERSHIP

Earlier it was demonstrated that there is a very high level of public ownership even in societies that have little direct experience of, and even less sympathy for, socialism. It must therefore be recognized that there are various purely practical, pragmatic arguments even within a capitalist framework for bringing certain kinds of activities under public control. Although there are those who, like F.A. Hayek, would argue that once a society abandons unrestrained free enterprise it has committed itself to total socialism, most would argue that some combination of public and private enterprise is necessary to deal effectively with the needs of a modern society. The principle of the mixed economy is accepted as a fact of life in all the liberal democracies. The only constructive arguments involve the details about what a capitalist society may properly operate as public enterprises without totally abandoning its capitalist character.

FRIEDRICH AUGUST HAYEK

Born in Vienna May 8, 1899.

Professor Hayek has a long and distinguished career in the fields of economic history and theory. He was Director of the Austrian Institute for Economic Research, 1927–31; Lecturer in Economics at the University of Vienna, 1929–31; Professor of Economic Sciences and Statistics at the University of London, 1931–50; Professor of Social and Moral Science at the University of Chicago, 1950–62; and Professor of Economics at the University of Frieburg, 1962–69. He received the Nobel Prize in Economic Sciences in 1974 and has received numerous other academic honours around the world. He is the author of more than twenty books on political and economic theory, many of them related to the analysis and defence of liberalism and capitalism.

The first argument deals with those services that tend inevitably and perhaps desirably to monopoly. It is possible to imagine that gas supply, water supply, public transport, and so on, could be provided by competitive private enterprise. Rival water companies could lay their mains along the same streets and rival bus companies could compete for passengers along the same routes. Indeed, for a time in the earliest days of competitive capitalism such rivalries did exist. But they were highly inefficient and cost wasteful. Compromises and amalgamations leading to monopolies inevitably developed with at best a division of the territory among a number of companies, each with a monopoly in its own area. Water, electricity, police and fire protection, street cleaning, telephones, and regular mail delivery are seldom efficient in a competitive situation. But the principal economic argument for capitalism is that competition among suppliers in the open marketplace produces the highest quality, most cost-effective service. When competition is removed that argument ceases to apply. Wherever the possibility of a new competitor is eliminated, the monopoly supplier of an essential service is in a very powerful position. The only protection consumers have is in bringing the service under some form of public ownership or supervision; thereby bringing it under political and, ultimately, electoral control. A local government that does a poor job of regulating the water supply can be voted out of office. It is much harder to reach the board of directors of a private company that has monopoly ownership of that supply. It is thus the norm in advanced industrial societies that the ownership of certain monopoly services is vested in some form of public ownership, either directly under the control of a government department or local government or some semi-autonomous public corporation such as Ontario Hydro. Even where the operations are left as private corporations, as, say, Bell Canada, they are normally subjected to tight supervision or regulation.

Because the decisions on public control of monopoly services are made on an ad hoc basis and not ideologically, one finds strange variations in practice. Basic public utilities, sewage disposal, and city passenger transport are commonly under some form of public control. On the other hand, telephones and ambulances, which are commonly under public ownership in Europe, are still widely left in private hands in North America. Outside the United States and Canada ambulances are usually regarded as similar in character to the police and fire services, all being part of the community's crisis and emergency services. As such they are commonly under the full control of the community. The concept of ambulances competing for customers at accident sites is totally implausible outside this continent. The supply of heating fuel — natural gas or oil — provides a good illustration of the importance of the monopoly factor. Natural gas requires a fairly expensive capital expenditure in the laying of pipe lines and therefore tends to be a monopoly service, perhaps conveniently brought under public direction. Fuel oil, however, is delivered in small units by trucks, and therefore, it can still be operated much more readily by competitive private suppliers.

This suggestion of high capital outlay leads to a second kind of argument for public ownership. There are certain kinds of services that provide a huge long-term economic benefit to the society as a whole but offer little, if any, immediate return on investment; in short, situations where the profit on the enterprise is likely to be small or long delayed. Classic examples are the railway networks built in most of the British colonies. In many countries, before the age of the automobile the railway was the essential communication link for overall economic development. However, a small population and high construction costs through a mountainous terrain, often made the building of railways unattractive to private investors. There would have been no railways if the state itself had not built and operated them. Similarly, in many island nations, shipping lines, ferry services, and airlines are vital economic links from which all benefit. When there is little prospect of direct profit return to investors they must be operated as state enterprises. In the same way, the huge capital costs of such activities as space exploration, even for a nation as wealthy as the United States, put them beyond the resources of private capital. Despite the fantasies of many science-fiction writers it seems unlikely that we will ever see a world of free enterprise space traders roaming the galaxies in search of profitable deals. The rapidly increasing sophistication of our technology seems to indicate that more and more of the things we can set ourselves to accomplish will require an enormous initial capital investment. Consequently, we will be forced to set our ideological preferences aside and call upon the state to act for us, at least in the foundation stages. Even where private enterprise is prepared to provide the initial capital, as in oil exploration in Canada, there are calls upon government to intervene to provide all manner of financial assistance.

A third line of argument brings in the area of essential services: things that *must* be provided, whether they result in a profit or not. National defence is a prime example. There may be a good deal of private profit to be made in supplying goods and services to the armed forces, and some nations may still resort to mercenary armies. But in most advanced societies the armed forces themselves are non-profit organizations. If the state is to be defended, all its members must contribute to that defence. There are other essential services that must also be provided. In Canada, for example, communities such as Moosonee on James Bay or Churchill in Northern Manitoba depend for survival upon a railway service that can never be expected to make a profit. The remote communities of Canada's Arctic rely upon air services whose costs will always exceed revenues. But as private enterprise cannot be expected to provide services at a loss, and as services must be provided, the state must assume responsibility. Within the cities, roads and streets need to be paved, lit, and cleaned. The health of all residents requires that there be parks and recreation facilities, clean water, and garbage disposal. In the larger cities there must be a network of public transport. These are services that must be provided, and although the consumer may through direct charges pay part, if not all the cost, we seem to have deemed it inappropriate that private individuals should try to make a profit from them. We could, each of us individually, pay a private contractor to haul away our garbage, but in most communities we have collectively decided that this is not how things should be done. In some cases a municipality may contract out some of these services to private enterprise, but the arrangements and the financing are with the municipality as such and not directly with the consumer. There may be a fear, perhaps, that while I may pay, my neighbour may be unable to pay or choose not to pay and his piles of garbage will begin to affect my comfort.

One can argue that when a service has to be supplied to all members of the society, who must receive it (one cannot really choose not to receive city water, nor to be connected to the city sewers), it is not unreasonable to expect the community at large to own and control it. One can argue that user fees ought to cover the costs of some of these services or at least a substantial part of them. But it is harder to make the case for the proposition that they are a legitimate source of private profit, paid for directly and fully by the consumers. It has thus become a widely accepted proposition, even among non-socialists, that essential public services, which are in effect mandatory on all members of the community, must be owned and financed by the community. Consider the question of elementary education. In the conditions of our society some level of education, some grasp of the rudiments of reading and writing, have become a virtual necessity. We insist that all children attend school until they have reached a certain age. And as all children are required to attend school, it is agreed that the *collectivity* must provide those schools. The community through its school boards owns and operates the schools with no direct charge to parent or pupil. We do not leave the provision of compulsory education to competitive profit-seeking entrepreneurs, although we may also permit some private schools for those who choose to support them. The principle is accepted that because the community at large owns the schools, all members of the community, even those without children or those whose children have grown beyond school age, can be called upon to share the burden of paying for them. Occasionally we may protest about the size of the tax burden for education or argue that some of the money is not wisely spent, but few object to the principle that the schools are an appropriate area of public action.

Finally, in this brief summary of non-ideological arguments for the public ownership of certain enterprises, there are those activities that are enjoyed by the whole community but offer few opportunities for giving a direct return to an investor. Even in the most triumphant moments of laissez-faire capitalism it was recognized that the state could quite properly provide such things as lighthouses, highways, or the mint. Today it is widely accepted that communities, either directly themselves, or through various boards and commissions, have the right to use public funds to provide parks, libraries, museums, arts galleries, sports arenas, exhibition halls, hospitals, public health clinics, and so on. Although the community may demand some direct contributions to the cost of some of these services, through user fees, and so on, the ownership and financial responsibility remain with the community. They are run not to make a profit but to provide some improvement in the quality of life and the general enjoyment and safety of all members of the society. They recognize that the health and well-being of each individual is to the long-term benefit of the whole society.

All this demonstrates that a great deal of public ownership and control can be introduced and defended on purely practical grounds without any reference to socialist ideology. In every modern society, even those which still publicly proclaim their adherence to uncompromising laissez-faire values, there exists alongside the private sector a level of public ownership and control unthinkable a few generations ago—although perhaps we are now witnessing the dismantling of some of this. In our complex society, which has insisted upon the provision of certain minimum services, where the private sector has been unwilling or unable to provide such services on a profit basis, the society itself has been called upon to assume responsibility.

Just how far we have come in this direction is illustrated through an extract from an essay written by Mr. Sidney Webb in 1889, roughly a hundred years ago. When Webb was writing, laissez-faire liberalism faced few challenges as the orthodox social and political faith. Most people genuinely believed in laissez-faire and thought they were practising it. Socialism at that time was an obscure economic doctrine understood only by a few intellectuals and having no impact on practical economics or politics. Yet, argued Webb, the facts of life were forcing the state in either its central or municipal forms to intervene more often in the economic life of society. It came to do for itself things that were either not done at all before, or had been regarded previously as legitimate areas of private enterprise. Webb said this in his contribution to the *Fabian Essays in Socialism*:

> In the teeth of the current Political Economy, and in spite of all the efforts of the millowning Liberals, England was compelled to put forth her hand to succour and protect her weaker members. . . . Step by step the political power and political organization of the country have been used for industrial ends, until to-day the largest employer of labor is one of the ministers of the Crown (the Postmaster-General); and almost every conceivable trade is, somewhere or other, carried on by parish, municipality, or the National Government itself without the intervention of any middleman or capitalist. The theorists who denounce the taking by the community into its own hands of the organization of its own labor as a thing economically unclean, repugnant to the sturdy individual independence of Englishmen, and as yet outside the sphere of practical politics, seldom have the least suspicion of the extent to which it has already been carried.[8]

SIDNEY WEBB (Lord Passfield)

Born London July 13, 1859; died October 13, 1947.

Social reformer and historian. In 1892 he married Beatrice Potter (1858–1943), thus establishing one of the greatest literary partnerships of the modern age — it is virtually impossible to treat their lives separately. Their output of serious, minutely researched social studies was prodigious, although they are not now as widely appreciated as when they first appeared. Their joint work began with The History of Trade Unionism, largely researched while on their honeymoon. Their work included the massive — nine volumes — English Local Government written between 1906 and 1929. Their most controversial joint work was the two volume study Soviet Communism: A New Civilisation (1935). Sidney was one of the first Fabians and contributor to the Fabian Essays in Socialism (1889). For further reading see under the heading of The Fabians in chapter thirteen.

Webb then produced a page-long catalogue of activities already undertaken in whole or in part by the community. It included such things as the regulation of currency; the provision of weights and measures; the making, sweeping, lighting, and repairing of streets; a certain amount of shipbuilding, stockbroking, and banking; and the provision for many of such services as midwifery, nursery, education, medical attendance, and interment. The community furnished and maintained its own museums, parks, libraries, concert halls, markets, slaughterhouses, lighthouses, ferries, tugboats, public baths and washhouses, pounds, harbours, hospitals, tramways, schools, churches, and reading rooms. It carried on and published its own researches in a wide variety of fields. He continued:

> Every one of these functions, with those of the army, navy, police and courts of justice, were at one time left to private enterprise, and were a source of legitimate individual investment of capital. Step by step the community has absorbed them, wholly or partially; and the area of private exploitation has been lessened.[9]

This was the crucial point of Webb's whole argument. All these activities, and the many more that have since been added to the collective responsibility of society since 1889, were once matters of private enterprise and all could still be run as private enterprises if we chose to follow that line. We could make all our schools the object of competitive private profit making. We could let all our highways and bridges be built by private investors who would recoup their investment from the tolls charged to those who used them. We could have rival fire services seeking a profit from fire fighting. But by and large we have mutually agreed that this is not the way to do some of these things. And we have decided this not because we have all been converted to socialism, but because we have found that in some areas private ownership founded on the profit motive does not provide the service we are demanding. These services have not been imposed by despotic governments but have been introduced largely in response to public initiatives.

We have also come to the practical conclusion that even when private ownership is left intact, it is often to the interest of the society to impose somewhat stringent controls on the full freedom of activity of the capitalist. Indeed, it was part of Webb's argument that society already appreciated that it was in its own interest to limit some of the freedom of free enterprise. Again the argument did not arise from ideological conviction, but as an admission within capitalism itself that such regulation was necessary in the common interest. While it was to the advantage of each individual capitalist to operate with the maximum possible freedom, it was to the advantage of the capitalist system as a whole that certain restraints be imposed upon all of them. Webb made the point that, as well as taking over certain enterprises, the state registered, licensed, controlled, and inspected virtually all industrial functions remaining in private hands. Registration or licensing were not a mere formality, for most commercial and industrial activities, especially those relating to public transport and the sale of food, were subjected to regular inspection as can be understood from the following:

> The inspection is often detailed and rigidly enforced. The State in most of the larger industrial operations prescribes the age of the worker, the hours of work, the amount of air, light, cubic space, heat, lavatory accommodation, holidays, and mealtimes; where, when, and how wages shall be paid; how machinery, staircases, lift holes, mines, and quarries are to be fenced and guarded; how and when the plant shall be cleaned, repaired, and worked. Even the kind of package in which some articles shall be sold is duly prescribed, so that the individual capitalist shall take no advantage of his position. On every side he is being registered, inspected, controlled, and eventually superseded by the community; and in the meantime he is compelled to cede for public purposes an ever-increasing share of his rent and interest.[10]

Those today who imagine that public ownership is a socialist invention or that the regulation of free enterprise, the limitation on the full operation of a free-market economy, is something only socialists propose, find it hard to appreciate the extent to which capitalism itself has extended the power of the state to replace, supplement, limit, and regulate free-enterprise activities. And few of those who are the loudest expounders of the rhetoric of free enterprise would find much support for the dismantling of most of the controls that now circumscribe the operation of a capitalist society. Nor would there be much popular support for the handing back to private ownership of many of the things that capitalist societies have themselves brought under public control. In the real world the debate about free enterprise versus a planned economy in pure terms is over. All economies are planned. And in all societies there is a greater or lesser degree of public ownership, intervention and control. The debate now is not about the principle, but about details: what activities, in what circumstances, are to be subject to what controls, for what purpose?

CHAPTER ELEVEN

The Liberal Mind

These final chapters pull together some previously discussed ideas in order to reach a clearer understanding of the ideological bases of our society. In particular they focus on the three major social philosophies that thrive and contend in the democratic nations of the Western world: liberalism, conservatism, and socialism. As a preliminary to their individual analysis, it is useful to consider their rough relationship.

It is essential to stress that the concern here is with social philosophies, world views, and ideologies, and not with political party platforms. Although some of the major political parties in the liberal democracies identify themselves by various permutations of the words *liberal, conservative,* and *socialist,* they all embrace a wide spectrum of often conflicting political beliefs. The behaviour of the parties is a most inaccurate guide to the political philosophies implied by their names.

For many centuries political power in Western Europe was concentrated in the hands of a traditional land-owning aristocracy — the old feudal lords, backed by a hierarchical church, which was also a major landowner. Compared with the hectic transformation of our own century, it was a relatively static society, changing only slowly over generations. There was little movement between the elements of a formalized class hierarchy. Apart from the few who became soldiers or priests, most would expect to live out their lives in the class and occupation to which they had been born. Although there were considerable variations in practices and organization between regions, the economy everywhere was primarily agricultural, was carried out in time-honoured ways, and was almost entirely self-supporting, with each area supplying its own needs as far as possible from its own resources. There was only limited trade and primitive household manufacturing: weaving, milling, masonry, tanning, and so on. In the absence of machinery, farming was labour intensive; hard, heavy work, for small return. Land, almost all of it owned by the nobility, was the foundation and measure of power. Below the great families was a huge army of agricultural workers, ranked according to their degree of independence and the extent to which they were tied to the land on which they were born. Between the landowners and the land workers, a small and, therefore, not particularly influential group of merchants, traders, craftsmen, and guild masters constituted the middle classes. The whole social structure — which in its detail and regional variations was far more complex than might be suggested by this simple outline — was tied together in a chain of customary obligations, duties, and rights constituting the kind of organic unity described earlier.

For the upper classes, hereditary title conferred great status and privilege, with almost exclusive access to the enjoyment of such luxuries as the community was capable of providing. Within their own lands, beyond occasional obligations to the king, powerful lords exercised an almost absolute rule. But at the same time they accepted, with very widely differing degrees of enthusiasm and effectiveness, some kind of obligation toward the "lower orders." There was a kind of paternalism that rejected consideration of any change in existing social organization but did thrust upon the upper ranks the obligation to protect the poor from the worst economic disasters. Where the very concept of social equality would have been incomprehensible, there was no sense of democracy. But there was a recognition that all the orders were members of the same corporate unity. It was a society in which the pattern of life and the established code of conduct were expected to continue as they had been from time immemorial. There were changes in all aspects of life: social organization, agricultural methods, political structures, economic development, and so on. The many changes were cumulatively quite profound, but they occurred slowly, almost imperceptibly over a very long time. This was the base of genuine conservatism, which, for convenience and to avoid confusion with the misleading use of the word *conservative* by today's right-wing politicians, will be referred to as *toryism*. The usage is not strictly correct, but it is arbitrarily introduced here to minimize verbal ambiguity.[1]

In time, more rapid, drastic change did come to European society. After the chaos of the wars and invasions following the collapse of the Roman Empire, feudalism over the centuries succeeded in restoring order and stability. Life became a little easier and more prosperous. With an increasing economic surplus there grew a demand for a variety of goods beyond the resources of a self-contained economy. There came about a pressure for more extensive trade, leading gradually to a revival of cities. The balance of economic power, and with it political power, shifted slowly from the traditional landowner to those who possessed a wealth in money (the old feudal order had made only limited use of money). Power began to shift to the bankers, money-lenders, traders, entrepreneurs, and merchant adventurers—the new middle class who would eventually also include the newer manufacturing class. (Early capitalism was almost entirely financial and investment capitalism, as there was no significant increase in industrial production or technology for another couple of centuries.) Previous chapters have already shown why the new middle classes adopted the doctrines of laissez-faire liberalism.

For a time the major political conflict was between the old order of ancestral land-owning privilege, embodied in toryism, and the newer, aggressive radicalism of the liberals. As liberalism triumphed almost universally, many of the new successful entrepreneurial capitalists tried to become the new aristocracy by buying themselves great land-holdings. Their power, however, was now in wealth and not in inherited titles. The attitudes of competitive laissez-faire came to dominate the thinking of Western economists so much so that many today seem to imagine that these once radical doctrines are the objective truth about the nature of society, describing the world as it is now, has been, and always will be.

THE TRANSFORMATION OF LIBERALISM

But liberalism itself underwent a transformation, especially as reformers drew attention to the consequences of industrialization. As the nineteenth century progressed it became increasingly apparent that, for the great mass of the urban proletariat, laissez-faire liberalism did not produce the greatest happiness of the greatest number. The middle classes, who had overpowered the old nobility to win their own freedom and prosperity, now faced the challenge of the working classes, who wanted a share of that freedom and prosperity. Those who resisted that challenge in the name of the old freedoms became the new reactionaries. As previous chapters have already described the appalling degradation of the working classes in the new manufacturing cities, there is no need to belabour the point here. But within liberalism itself men of conscience began to rethink some of the original doctrines. The basic economic tenets of laissez-faire came to be modified as a precondition for a more widespread political and social liberty. Writers such as J.S. Mill and T.H. Green argued that belief in the virtues of a basically free entrepreneurial society, with an economy rooted in the private ownership of the means of production, distribution, and exchange, did not preclude some moderating of the brutality of unrestrained competition. Nor did it need to deny any humanitarian concern for the well-being of the old, the sick, the disabled, or the unemployed. And it did not need to set society and individual in totally irreconcilable camps. It was possible, they contended, to believe in individual liberty and still display some concern for the collective good of society. From both a new mood of humanitarian concern and a greater awareness of the unacceptable social consequences of unrestrained laissez-faire, there developed an acceptance that society had to guarantee a greater level of economic equality and security. If an increasingly complex capitalist society was to surmount tendencies to chaos and discontent, it had also on its own initiative to provide those needed benefits and services which the private investors were unable or unwilling to provide. This culminated in what has come to be called moderate, or reform, or welfare liberalism. Its goal was not to introduce socialism, but to strengthen the principle of individual freedom by extending it to all.

But, of course, in any reform movement, not all are reformed. There are always those who, refusing to be convinced, remain loyal to the old faiths. So liberalism became divided between the reformers and those who continued to uphold the established doctrines of competitive individualism, the unrestrained marketplace of laissez-faire, in which all individuals were deemed responsible for their own position in life and in which society had only minimal obligations to those unable to survive by their own efforts — the losers in the competitive rat race. From this outlook, social programs were in themselves undesirable, leading to a weakening of the moral fibre of the people. They were perhaps to be tolerated only because of the unacceptable political consequences of withdrawing them. In this way the unrepentant liberals, sometimes called "classical liberals," the radicals of the early nineteenth century who finally broke the power of the old upper classes, have become today's conservatives, the upholders of an older view of the world.

The still older land-owning paternalistic tories, who are the real conservatives, cannot exist as an independent political force; so in different strengths, in different countries, they have thrown in their lot with the classical liberals. The Conservative parties of the Western world, in this latter part of the twentieth century are all uneasy alliances of toryism and traditional liberalism. In the United Kingdom, tories are still a powerful voice in the Conservative party, although under Mrs. Margaret Thatcher their influence has been considerably watered down. Mrs. Thatcher neither likes nor trusts them. In the United States toryism barely exists. Its foundations were never strong, and many of those who might have been sympathetic to its precepts fled to Canada at the time of American independence. The presence of tory values among the Empire Loyalists has had a moderating impact on the laissez-faire inclinations of the Canadian Progressive Conservative Party. In Canadian political terms they are likely to be called "red tories," who have given liberalism in Canada what is widely referred to as a "tory touch." But in the United States there is little toryism, only various shades of liberalism. And in the absence of traditional conservatism, the right wing, unrepentant, unreformed classical liberals have become the conservatives. They call themselves neo-conservatives, but they are neither new, nor conservative; for their origin is in the early nineteenth century, and they are the purest strain of radical liberalism. To these "conservative liberals," reform liberal proposals are viewed as a dangerous toying with socialism.

This leads to a consideration of the role of the working classes so far ignored in the discussion. For as long as the working class was employed almost entirely in agricultural labour or domestic service, and working in small units, almost universally illiterate and bound by traditions of obedience to service, its political influence was nil. The English Peasants' Revolt of 1381 was an aberration that was easily put down and had no lasting effect. However, one of the consequences of industrialization and urbanization was the creation of a class-conscious, increasingly educated and skilled urban proletariat that was gradually gaining confidence in its own strength and gaining genuine access to political power with the extension of the franchise. And, again like liberalism, proletarian politics moved in several directions. In some circumstances, especially in the United States, wage earners rejected the appeals of socialist working-class politics and sought instead to improve their economic position by bargaining with the older established parties. This fact can be explained by a line of argument to be more fully developed in the next chapter, which suggests that a socialist world view can flourish only where there has existed a tory tradition of an organic community.

Where socialism did emerge as the voice of the working classes, there were two basic approaches and each had several variations. There were, on the one hand, the revolutionary socialists, who were mostly followers of the theories of Karl Marx and looked to a complete transformation of the class structure of society through revolution. These revolutionary socialists did not believe that any significant improvement in their lot could be made through reforms within a capitalist economy. They dismissed parliamentary democracy as a fraud, a device for preserving the power of the capitalist middle classes. The other strand, democratic socialism, rejects as a matter of fundamental principle the doctrines of revolution. The democratic approach, indicated in a phrase coined by the Fabians, is that all effective social change must be both gradual and democratic. Indeed it was argued that if change was to be democratic, by definition it would have to be gradual. It would proceed step by step through reforms and each stage would be prepared for and accepted by public opinion before the next stage could be introduced. A fuller discussion of both strands of socialism is set aside until chapter thirteen.

So now we have reached a peculiar and complicated situation. In the major Western democracies, the tories and the classical liberals have made an uneasy peace. They are far apart in their ideologies, reflecting quite different world views, and they disagree markedly on many policy preferences and priorities. But they unite in modern conservative parties, sharing similar desires to slow down the rate of further change, anxious to protect the interests of wealth and property, and distrustful of further government regulation of the economy. On the other hand, the older liberals and the newer reform liberals, as well as all possible shades between their extremes, have the same intellectual roots derived from the same philosophic assumptions about the individualistic character of the state. Yet they may be worlds apart in the policies they pursue, in their understanding of what ought to be done to bring about the free society both genuinely believe in. In the United States, almost the entire political spectrum, and its range of political controversy, is within these bounds of liberalism. Left and right or liberal and conservative in the United States mean reform liberal and classical liberal.

On many policy issues reform liberals and democratic socialists may be in close agreement. Socialism, which like toryism is linked to an organic conception of the state, is in its intellectual assumptions and world view largely alien to the propositions of liberalism. But democratic socialist reformers and liberal reformers, both believing themselves responsive to public opinion, will often find themselves doing similar things, even if for different reasons. Both will be supportive of a wide range of welfare and social assistance measures, and both will initiate far-reaching controls and regulations to protect society collectively from predatory individualism. Liberals may believe they are simply modifying a basically sound individualistic philosophy, doing no more than to ease its harsher consequences. Socialists may feel they are moving slowly to a total transformation of capitalist society and the creation of a new world order. But at any one point in time they will have many detailed policies and programs in common.

Finally, to complete the complications, democratic and revolutionary socialists were both born in a socialist critique of capitalist society, both looking to the eventual decay of capitalism. But their concepts of how to reach that goal and the policies to be adopted in its pursuit are so utterly at odds that they have become the most bitter of political foes, each accusing the other of betraying the cause they have in common.

THE LIBERAL MIND

With this relationship between the most important liberal democratic ideologies now more or less fixed, it is appropriate to sum up the major characteristics of each, beginning with liberalism as the dominant mode of thought of the past few centuries, and indeed, so dominant that we have quite properly attached the "liberal democracy" label to such societies as Canada, the United States, the United Kingdom, Australia, and others of a similar character.

Because of its dominant role and because of the wide range of policies it encompasses, liberalism is the most complicated to summarize. While classical liberalism is the conservatism of our own age, it is essential to feel its original radicalism. One of the most important books on the development of liberalism carries the point I am trying to make simply in its title: *The Growth of Philosophic Radicalism*, by Elie Halévy.[2] Another writer, after noting that classical liberalism has, in modified form, become the conservatism of today, recalled its radical beginnings:

> The same doctrine which now feeds the defensive backfire of reaction once kindled the spreading flame of revolution. The same arguments which now bolster an established order once reduced the castles of feudalism.[3]

The arguments now put forward by the right wing in Canada and the United States as solid, safe conservatism were less than two hundred years ago feared as dangerously revolutionary and threatening to the centuries-old privileges of a powerful class. Something of the sense of the full radical character of this new political force, some feeling for how drastically it changed society, can be gathered from the writings of Harold Laski (1893–1950):

> In the period between the Reformation and the French Revolution a new social class established its title to a full share in the control of the state. In its ascent to power, it broke down the barriers which, in all spheres of life save the ecclesiastical, had made privilege a function of status, and associ-

ated the idea of rights with the tenure of land. To achieve its end, it effected a fundamental change in the legal relationships of men.

Status was replaced by contract as the juridical foundation of society. Uniformity of religious belief gave way to a variety of faiths in which even scepticism found a right to expression. The vague medieval empire of *jus divinum* and *jus naturale* gave way to the concrete and irresistible power of national sovereignty. The control of politics by an aristocracy whose authority was built upon the tenure of land came to be shared with men whose influence was derived solely from the ownership of movable capital. The banker, the trader, the manufacturer, began to replace the landowner, the ecclesiastic, and the warrior, as the types of predominant social influence. The city, with its restless passion for change, replaced the countryside, with its hatred of innovation, as the primary source of legislation. Slowly, but, nevertheless, irresistibly, science replaced religion as the controlling factor in giving shape to the thoughts of men. The idea of a golden age in the past, with its concomitant idea of original sin, gave way to the doctrine of progress, with its own concomitant idea of perfectibility through reason. The idea of social initiative and social control surrendered to the idea of individual initiative and individual control. New material conditions, in short, gave birth to new social relationships; and, in terms of these, a new philosophy was evolved to afford a rational justification for the new world which had come into being.

This new philosophy was liberalism.[4]

HAROLD J. LASKI

Born in Manchester June 30, 1893; died in London March 24, 1950.

Laski was a prominent English political scientist and professor at the London School of Economics from 1926 until his death. He took up various visiting appointments at several American universities and at McGill. He was a member of the executive committee of the Fabian Society, 1922–36, and of the Labour party from 1936. He was chairman of the Labour party 1945–46. He was the author of numerous books including Problems of Sovereignty *(1917),* Authority in the Modern State *(1919),* A Grammar of Politics *(1925),* Communism *(1927),* The Rise of European Liberalism *(1936),* Parliamentary Government in England *(1938),* The American Presidency *(1940), and* The American Democracy *(1948).*

PROGRESS

Despite the divisions within liberalism, and the wide variety of specific views it encompasses, there are certain tenets and assumptions common to the whole liberal tradition. These reflect less a coherent body of doctrine than a certain set of attitudes; what Kenneth Minogue called *The Liberal Mind*. The first is what Laski described as the doctrine of progress. In place of the relative permanence of the old feudal order, there emerged a belief that change is the norm, and not only change as such but change always for the better. The new industrialists whose factories destroyed the countryside rationalized their actions by the slogan "You can't stop progress." History was seen as a sloping continuum, with each stage being a higher development, an advance in the human condition. Marxists and Darwinists shared this prevailing confidence in a universe unfolding according to some grand design from "lower" to "higher" forms. Most in the nineteenth century believed that new technologies opened the way to the final conquest of the physical world. In the industrial nations there was a new spirit of enterprise, frenzied activity, innovation, a boundless optimism about perfectibility through unrestrained human energy. This optimism reached its peak about 1910, to suffer mortal wounds on the battlefields of the First World War.

The conviction that given sufficient time and energy all things were possible freed some elements of liberalism from the strictures of the untenable economic theories of the more doctrinaire liberals. This was one source of the parting of the ways between the old and new strains of liberalism. On the one hand were the traditionalists who felt bound by economic laws— the laws of political economy that had, they believed, the authority and scientific validity of the laws of physics and chemistry. The laws of supply and demand were thought to be genuine scientific principles that the state would tamper with at its peril. The free exchange of the marketplace was an autonomous force, producing the best possible solution to all economic problems. Any attempt to achieve short-term goals by interfering with the operation of the market would produce long-term disaster. The state had only a limited role to play in economic affairs. On the other hand there were the more flexible liberals, the reformers, who felt economic laws did no more than set outer limits within which there was considerable room to manoeuvre. To the reformers, the laws of supply and demand were neither sacred writ nor empirical scientific laws. However, they were generally convenient and workable assumptions that were in most circumstances useful guides to policy making, but in other circumstances, they could be overridden or set aside. They were only as good as the results they produced. These liberals were prepared to accept a high level of economic planning and direct state intervention in the economy to achieve goals they felt to be more in the true spirit of a liberal society offering liberty to all.

EGOISM

The second major component of liberalism was egoism — the proposition that individuals are primarily concerned with their own well-being and it is generally beneficial to the species that they should be so concerned. The critical idea is that of human nature; it being a fundamental proposition of liberalism that there is indeed a fixed human nature and that we are what we are because of inherent attributes. We do what we do because of what we are, and always will be, not because of when or where we happen to be. In the psychology of liberalism, self-interest is the principal motive of human behaviour, even that behaviour which involves co-operation with others. Because human nature is intrinsically selfish, human institutions must be devised to direct that selfishness to the maximum possible social good. The economic philosophy of liberalism postulates that the free competitive marketplace provides the most reliable mechanism for combining individual self-satisfaction with the greatest collective benefit. This is where Adam Smith's "unseen hand" produced its magic "harmony of egoisms." It was central to Smith's whole creed that the common good was served best by individuals spontaneously pursuing their own selfish ends. "By pursuing his own interest he frequently promotes that of society more effectively than when he really intends to promote it."[5] All this is a complete repudiation of the socialist belief in a human behaviour moulded and influenced by the political, social, and economic environment in which people find themselves.

ADAM SMITH

Born in Fife, Scotland, June 5, 1723; died in Edinburgh July 17, 1790.

Professor of Moral Philosophy at the University of Edinburgh. Smith's lectures on moral philosophy were divided into four parts: natural theology, ethics, jurisprudence, and political economy. His first major work, The Theory of Moral

Sentiments, was published in 1759. He spent two years in France (1764–66) as tutor to the Duke of Buccleuch. Smith's lasting fame is as the first serious economic theorist and the principal exponent of classical laissez-faire economic theory. This was contained in his An Inquiry into the Nature and Causes of the Wealth of Nations (1776), one of the most influential books of the age. He was admitted as a Fellow of the Royal Society in London in 1773 and participated in the founding of the Royal Society of Edinburgh in 1783.

For further reading see:

Gray, Alexander. Adam Smith. London: Historical Association, 1968.

O'Driscoll, G.R., ed. Adam Smith and Modern Political Economy: Bicentennial Essays on the Wealth of Nations. Ames: Iowa State University Press, 1979.

Rae, John. Life of Adam Smith. London: Macmillan, 1895; Reissued with lengthy Introduction by Jacob Viner, New York: A.M. Kelley, 1965.

RATIONALISM

This leads to the third component: rationalism. If individuals are left free to be selfish, their rationalism will guide that selfishness in the direction of the greatest common good. People co-operate not from any sense of shared responsibility, but rather because co-operative behaviour is the most rational behaviour. As demonstrated in chapter ten, this desire to gratify individual needs has been used to justify a great deal of state intervention to ameliorate intolerable social conditions. Rationalism is that attribute of human nature that enables competitive, egoistic individuals to appreciate that their selfish best interest can be fully realized in co-operative social behaviour under law. From the approach of rational egoism, one obeys the law not because it is a moral precept, nor because it is better that one should do so, but because in a community subject to law, one advances one's self-interest more effectively and more securely than in the condition of the "war of everyman against everyman." It is a secular philosophy in which morality is founded on empirical utilitarianism rather than on prescriptive authority. Lawfulness is good, because lawlessness is inimical to happiness.

Rational individualism is at the root of the liberal trust in the power of education as an instrument of social good. The liberals in the nineteenth century argued as follows: The educated will understand the shape of society and the necessity of obedience to its authority. They will appreciate the ultimate justice of its economic laws. They will, in short, think and reason like middle-class capitalists, becoming more aware of where their true best interest lies. In comprehending the working of the marketplace, they will not demand of the state that it do things it is not equipped to do. To take the liberal argument further, it would follow that an educated population understanding the structure and operation of the good society would help to sustain that society. They could safely be allowed to participate in its government. In other words, educated people could be granted the vote because they would use that vote for the common good as understood by the liberal economists. As a matter of general principle, stemming from their commitment to liberty, the liberals believed in political equality, but they were cautious enough to want to extend the vote only to those educated to use it *properly*; that is, not so as to threaten the position of the propertied middle classes.

J.S. Mill's *Considerations on Representative Government* (1861) illustrates the liberal ambivalence toward democracy. As a matter of principle and intellectual conviction, Mill was persuaded of the necessity of universal suffrage. At the same time he recoiled from the prospect of political power being vested in the propertyless, uneducated urban proletariat. While the logic of his liberal philosophy led to democracy, his matter-of-fact realism convinced him that a genuine democracy would severely weaken the entrenched interests of the liberal middle classes, who were the repository of all civic virtue. There is throughout Mill's writings, but especially in *Representative Government*, evidence of his "love-fear" relationship with democratic institutions.

ACQUISITIVENESS

One critical attribute of human nature, as understood by the liberal mind, is acquisitiveness: the desire of individuals to accumulate property. All humans are apparently motivated by an inner psychological drive to increase their possessions. Ever since Locke began to conceive society as being divided into the exclusive classes of the owners of property who could buy labour for profit and the sellers of that labour, liberalism has been a social philosophy of property owners.

The ends it serves are always the ends of men in this position. Outside that narrow circle, the individual for whose rights it has been zealous has always been an abstraction upon whom its benefits could not, in fact, be fully conferred. Because its purposes were shaped by owners of property, the margins between its claims and its performance have always been wide.[6]

Liberalism exists to explain and justify the acquisition of property and to institute mechanisms to safeguard it.

The constant political goal has been to secure private property, as much as possible, from the jurisdiction of, or regulation by, the state. It is the whole temper of liberal individualism to be distrustful of state activity, especially as it impinges on the operation of the free market. Because the pursuit of wealth is a natural human psychological drive, it need not, and ought not, be sanctioned or regulated by either state or church. Acquisitive instincts thus have their natural outlet in a laissez-faire economic order.

> The whole ethos of capitalism, in a word, is its effort to free the owner of the instruments of production from the need to obey rules which inhibit his full exploitation of them. The rise of liberalism is the rise of a doctrine which seeks to justify the operation of that ethos.[7]

QUIETISM

Another component of liberalism is what is called "quietism." In its simplest terms this complex idea proposes that things remain at rest until some force moves them, in contrast to the idea that they will move until some force stops them. Quietism, in the form of the motivation of desire, is part of the psychological creed of liberalism. It suggests that motives are the *causes* of conduct, not mere factors in conduct. We act only because certain external stimuli impinge upon us, causing us to react in a specified and predictable way. Psychologically we respond in an almost clockwork mechanical fashion to various external forces. To quote Kenneth Minogue:

> Whenever [man] wills an act, then we must assume that the act is produced by the push of a motion or motive in the mind; and these motives can only be described and classified according to the goals or ends at which they are directed.[8]

Thus, it is only when sufficiently motivated either by the desire for pleasure or the avoidance of pain that individuals will take any action. Acceptance of the reality of a fixed human nature governed by a psychology of quietism may paralyze the will to reform. There is an account of a discussion between Henry George, author of *Progress and Poverty* (1879), and E.L. Youmans, a prominent American apologist for Herbert Spencer.

Youmans had denounced the selfishness of the rich in tolerating, even promoting, the political corruption of New York. When asked what he proposed to do about it, Youmans had replied:

> "Nothing! You and I can do nothing at all. It's all a matter of evolution. We can only wait for evolution. Perhaps in four or five thousand years evolution may have carried men beyond this state of things."[9]

HERBERT SPENCER

Born April 27, 1820; died December 8, 1903.

The most extreme exponent of nineteenth-century laissez-faire individualism, Spencer devoted much of his literary output to describing the things governments should not do. His general social system was built around an adaptation of Darwin's theories of evolution. Spencer opposed all forms of intervention to ease poverty or suffering because such intervention was an unwarranted interference with nature's laws, which were designed to advance the species by weeding out the unfit. His most important political work is a collection of essays published under the title Man Versus the State *(1854). He also wrote extensively on sociology, psychology, and philosophy. Spencer's influence was never as great in Britain as in the United States, where his advocacy of ruthless competition and survival of the fittest by natural selection appealed enormously to the American right-wing businessmen and entrepreneurs. In this way he became the leading spirit in a school of social thought known as the Social Darwinists.*
For further reading see:
Hofstadter, Richard. Social Darwinism in American Thought. *London: Oxford University Press, 1945.*
Andreski, Stanislav. Herbert Spencer: Structure, Function and Evolution. *London: Nelson, 1971.*

In political and economic terms quietism implies that, as work is painful, people will not work unless they have to. They will not act from any inner, self-initiated impulse. People work only from the promise of reward or the fear of starvation. In practice there has developed a most peculiar double standard here. It is commonly assumed that the rich will work only if offered the incentive of even greater riches and the poor will work only under the threat of even greater poverty. This assumption seems to be an active element in the economic policies of many contemporary Western governments. Quietism assumes that the necessary spur to keep the lower classes at labour is the constant threat of starvation, as is suggested in the following:

> Hunger will tame the fiercest animals, it will teach decency and civility, obedience and subjection, to the most perverse. In general it is only hunger that can spur and goad them (the poor) on to labour; yet our laws have said they shall never hunger. The laws, it must be confessed, have likewise said they shall be compelled to work. But then legal constraint is attended with much trouble, violence and noise; creates ill will, and never can be productive of good and acceptable service; Whereas hunger is not only peaceable, silent, unremitting pressure, but, as the most natural motive to industry and labour, it calls forth the most powerful exertions; and, when satisfied by the free bounty of another, lays lasting and sure foundations for good will and gratitude.[10]

The survival of this attitude helps to explain the strong negative attitude of many people to social welfare. A great many people find themselves offended by the idea that some should benefit without having to work. It matters not that there may be no work that needs doing or no work that could not be more efficiently done with machinery, or no work that anyone is willing to pay for. But somehow, no one should be allowed to eat unless they first work. Of course, it is only the poor to whom this stricture applies. One of the persistent myths of our age is that *all* the unemployed have chosen welfare over work, that there is plenty of work available, and that if we stopped pampering the lazy and irresponsible, they would all get back to work. No amount of contrary evidence seems to have the slightest impact on these unshakable convictions.

COMPASSION

There is a considerable gulf between liberalism as understood by the laissez-faire economists and in its social and political applications. Beyond the economic sphere liberalism is much more tolerant and humane. One of its key attributes has always been its passionate defence of personal liberty, which is broadly permissive of individual eccentricity. It follows from the liberal stress on the primacy of the individual that the individual should have the maximum possible freedom of thought, speech, and behaviour. So it was through a liberal heritage that the modern world began to refine concepts of individual rights, to give juridical authority to "civil liberties"

— which in practice has come to mean an equality of individual rights enforced by law. Liberal reformers fought against slavery and also broke the power of the Lords and the established Church. To many, civil liberties were simply the enactment, the codification of the natural liberties of individuals. Despite the many problems and inconsistencies in the interpretation and application of the principles of freedom, liberalism has always embodied a deep commitment to personal liberty. A great many of the freedoms that we now take for granted are derived from liberal sources, and when, as is quite often the case, governments threaten these freedoms, we tend to resort to liberal arguments in their defence.

However, in recent years opposing tendencies have strengthened. Within the United States, in particular, those who now consider themselves the new conservatives are often allied with a narrow authoritarianism, a religious and social dogmatism alien to the spirit of free inquiry which inspired the original liberal radicalism. The machinery of representative democracy developed from the desire to institutionalize the liberal ideal of freedom. Many of the modern "radical right," while upholding the liberal economic doctrines, have grafted on to them an anti-liberal social and political philosophy. There has also been, over the years, a continuing reluctance to acknowledge the extent to which prevailing economic doctrines effectively denied real personal liberty to the great mass of the poor. Classical liberalism had been more successful in establishing the liberty of property owners to remain secure in their possessions than it had been in securing liberties for those with nothing to sell beyond their labour. This was the parting of the ways within liberalism. The reform liberals, concerned with extending the limits of social and political liberty to all, became more aware of the need to exercise some control over the effects of economic liberty. Modern liberalism approached political life as the struggle to make society rational, just, and compassionate in a way alien to the calculating doctrines of utilitarianism. The good society would afford opportunities for all to develop their own potentialities. This is the liberalism to which the new right apply the word *liberal* as a pejorative term for all that they see as unrealistic, soft, "bleeding heart," and probably socialist inspired.

ATOMISM

Finally we come to what I regard as the key concept of liberalism: an atomistic concept of society. Recalling the analogy in chapter two, this means the supremacy, the complete independence, of the marble in its bucket. In contrast to the medieval mind, which looked at the world as a natural organic unity, liberalism conceives society as an artificial construction of autonomous atom-like individuals. The individual is not part of the larger unity, but is a complete whole, joining with other complete wholes to construct a useful association. But the individuals do not create any new being, nor build anything larger than themselves. Under liberalism the individual is antecedent to, and independent of, society, creating society and government solely for the more efficient satisfaction of the needs of atomistic beings. This is the conceptual gulf between liberalism, on the one hand, and both toryism and socialism on the other. The tory and the socialist may disagree profoundly on the nature of the good society or about the proper goals of social activity, but they are at least agreed on what a society is. Their vision of a structured organic unity is at odds with the liberal interpretation of an artificial association of independent and complete individuals.

So, let us summarize liberalism under a few slogans and catch phrases. I have referred generally to "liberal individualism." Others have described it as "possessive individualism," with a greater stress on the idea of competition among individuals for the acquisition and possession of property. It is assumed that there is a limited total fund of property, of scarce resources, and selfish individuals will compete among themselves for the largest possible share of that property. And they will co-operate. They will create social institutions and form and obey laws, because they recognize that by doing so they can make their possession of property more secure. However the priorities are set, and in whatever order they are stated, it is generally accepted that liberals will be characterized by the following attributes: They will be individuals driven by an innate, unchanging human nature to be egoistic, selfish, competitive, acquisitive, and rational, and they will assume that their rational egoism will lead automatically by an unseen hand to a maximum social harmony.

Whatever party you may join and however you may vote in Canadian elections, if these labels are a more or less accurate description of your own outlook on life, you are indeed a liberal.

CHAPTER TWELVE

The Tory Tradition

Modern conservatism is in a dilemma because it is an uneasy alliance of the descendants of traditional land-owning, aristocratic, feudal conservatism — what is here being called toryism — and elements of classical laissez-faire liberalism. Conservatism also embraces those who, while not themselves being members of the land-owning nobility, have absorbed the value system of the old tories. The alliance poses a dilemma that affects individuals who think of themselves as conservatives, as well as those political parties that adopt Conservative labels. Because economic liberalism and political and philosophic toryism are drawn from incompatible roots and assumptions about the nature of human society, those who attempt to live by some blend of the two will inevitably be confronted by an inconsistency in value positions, which may lead to unrecognized tensions and stresses.

The matter now before us is to assemble some of the elements of a tory world view. It is unlikely that any one individual will hold all these positions without qualification, nor would those who consider themselves liberals or socialists necessarily reject them all. Those who find in this catalogue of attributes a number of positions with which they are generally sympathetic, or who discover here a more congenial atmosphere than with the liberal values summarized in chapter eleven, may consider themselves as being in the tory fold.

AN OBJECTIVE MORAL ORDER

Perhaps the quintessential element of toryism is the acceptance of an objective moral order, the belief in the real existence of universal, eternal principles of right and wrong. Things that are right, are right because they always have been right and always will be. The relative value system of utilitarianism in which the worth of actions is judged by their consequences in a time and space setting, or the "do-your-own-thing" attitude of many in the modern world, are both alien to toryism. Tories thus tend to believe in an objective natural law not so much in the sense of a pre-society set of natural individual rights but in the sense of universal values imposing duties. There is a moral law, superior to the shifts, fancies, or conveniences of legislators, according to which there exists an eternally valid right and wrong. The tory would fully understand and sympathize with Antigone.

At the heart of this objective moral order is the principle of prescription, the concept of custom continued until it has the force of law. There is a presumption that things that have always been, have established their own authority to continue to be. Lord Hugh Cecil saw this preference for the familiar as a natural human inclination and wrote the following:

> Natural conservatism is a tendency of the human mind. It is a disposition averse from change; and it springs partly from a distrust of the unknown and a corresponding reliance on experience rather than on theoretic reasoning; partly from a faculty of men to adapt themselves to their surroundings so that what is familiar merely because of its familiarity becomes more acceptable or more tolerable than what is unfamiliar. Distrust of the unknown, and preference for experience over theory, are deeply seated in almost all minds.[1]

This suggests that people might have different motives for their conservatism. The rich and powerful may be conservative because they desire to hold to what they have. They may fear that change will reduce their privileges. The very poor, too, may be afraid of change because their experience indicates that change usually means something worse. The desperately poor, because they cannot afford to lose what little they have, are seldom revolutionaries.

Even the most die-hard tories accept that society can, and sometimes must, change. But the burden of proof is always on the initiators and sponsors of departure from the established order. Those who would preserve things the way they are do not have to make a case. Their argument is that things are as they always have been and as they should continue to be. It is up to those who would change things to prove that there is an evil or an abuse to be corrected and that their solution will correct it. Part of the difficulty of defining a tory ideology is that it does not become a conscious manifestation until it faces some external challenge. Unless the prospect of change is seriously voiced, it is not necessary to defend the status quo. Hence, toryism is, to a large extent, identified with the innovations to which it is opposed. Change when it comes must be cautious evolutionary change, going no further than is absolutely necessary. Almost by definition, a tory must reject proposals for any radical reconstruction of society. To quote from Edmund Burke's letter to Sir Hercules Langrishe, written in 1792:

> We must all obey the great law of change. It is the most powerful law of Nature, and the means perhaps of its conservation. All we can do, and that human wisdom can do, is to provide that the change shall proceed by insensible degrees. This has all the benefits which may be in change, without any of the inconveniences of mutation. Everything is provided for as it arrives. This mode will, on the one hand, prevent the *unfixing of old interests at once*: a thing which is apt to breed a black and sullen discontent in those who are at once dispossessed of all their influence and consideration. This gradual course, on the other side, will prevent men long under depression from being intoxicated with a large draught of new power, which they always abuse with a licentious insolence. But, wishing, as I do, the change to be gradual and cautious, I would, in my first steps, lean rather to the side of enlargement than restriction.[2]

The moral force of custom is also reflected in the concept of common law, which is the foundation of the law in English Canada. The common law, the backbone of the judicial system, has its origins in the customs of the old Anglo-Saxon tribes, for whom the law was a sacred possession of the Folk—a set of eternal principles defining their rights and duties, holding them together as a people. The law was not *made*, for it existed complete from all time. At any particular instance the task was simply to discover it, to apply it in specific cases, to interpret it where there was confusion or doubt, or perhaps to write it down to avoid future ambiguity. These were the tasks of the earliest courts. Because the law existed in its entirety, the decisions the courts made as to its applicability to particular cases became part of the law, binding on future courts. In this way the law became more than the Act of Parliament, or the written code; it was also case law in which the decisions in previous cases were binding law until a higher court, or an Act of Parliament, overturned them. It was law built upon precedent, with the past continuing to guide and influence the present. This concept of the continuity and unity of past and present, of the binding impact of the past on the present, is a most tory notion.

One of the finest expositions of the importance of prescription is from the words of Edmund Burke. In party allegiance Burke was a Whig, an ardent defender of the rights of Parliament, but ideologically he represented at least some aspects of what is now called toryism. Burke's political creed was that of an economic liberal and a social conservative. In a speech in the House of Commons in 1782, he addressed the House on the nature of the British constitution:

> Our constitution is a prescriptive constitution; it is a constitution whose sole authority is that it has existed time out of mind. . . .
>
> Prescription is the most solid of all titles, not only to property, but, which is to secure that property, to government. They harmonize with each other and give mutual aid to one another. It is accompanied with another ground of authority in the constitution of the human mind, presumption. It is a presumption in favour of any settled scheme of government against any untried project, that a nation has long existed and flourished under it. It is a better presumption even of the *choice* of a nation — far better than any sudden or temporary arrangement by actual election. Because a nation is not an idea only of local extent and individual momentary aggregation, but it is an idea of continuity which extends in time as well as in numbers and in space. And this is a choice not of one day or one set of people, not a tumultary and giddy choice; it is a deliberate election of ages and of generations; it is a constitution made by what is ten thousand times better than choice; it is made by the peculiar circumstances, occasions, tempers, dispositions, and moral, civil, and social habitudes of the people, which disclose themselves only in a long space of time. It is a vestment which accommodates itself to the body. Nor is prescription of government formed upon blind unmeaning prejudices. For man is a most unwise and a most wise being. The individual is foolish; the multitude, for the moment, is foolish, when they act without deliberation; but the species is wise, and, when time is given to it, as a species, it almost always acts right.[3]

Contrast this moral certainty of Burke about the superior worth of things that have always been with the relativity of Jeremy Bentham, who accorded value to things only to the extent they had utility in promoting happiness.

EDMUND BURKE

Born in Dublin January 12, 1729; died in England July 9, 1797.

Burke was born of mixed Anglican and Catholic parentage. He was educated at Trinity College, Dublin, and for a while studied law before turning to politics. He was first elected to the House of Commons in 1765, remaining a member until 1794. As a politician he was deeply involved in the American War of Inde-

pendence, the politics of British rule in India and in Ireland, the French Revolution, and economic and parliamentary reforms in England. His most famous publication, Reflections on the Revolution in France *(1790), was one of the most significant and widely discussed books of the eighteenth century. The overriding principle of Burke's political philosophy was his recognition of a universal, eternal, natural law of reason and justice ordained by God. Burke himself summarized his position: "The principles of true politics are those of morality enlarged; and I neither now do, nor ever will, admit of any other."*

For further reading see:

Cone, C.B. Burke and the Nature of Politics. *Lexington: University of Kentucky Press, 1957.*

Stanlis, P.J., Edmund Burke and the Natural Law. *Ann Arbor: University of Michigan Press, 1958.*

Stanlis, P.J., ed. Edmund Burke: Selected Writings. *New York: Anchor, 1963.*

Wilkins, B.T. The Problem of Burke's Political Philosophy. *Oxford: Clarendon Press, 1967.*

As a corollary to this general attitude, tories *tend* to place emphasis on the social value of religion and its moral codes. Note carefully that this is stated only as a tendency, for not all tories are religious; nor are religious people all tories. Tories incline especially to long-established, formally structured ritualistic religions, that are seen as the most reliable source of prescriptive authority. Tories are, by and large, too tradition-bound to be swayed by cults and new religions. It is more than a coincidence that even in contemporary English politics, the great majority of *practising* members of the Anglican Church are also conservatives, while those members of the Labour party who are church-going at all are more likely to attend the nonconformist chapels. Religiously inclined tories take for granted the divine origin of legitimate authority.

THE ORGANIC SOCIETY

If the liberal concept of society is individualist, the tory concept is organic. Society is perceived as a unified whole that has a life and continuity of its own and individuals as part of its unity. It is a concept derived from deep within the medieval roots of toryism. Medieval philosophy visualized the entire universe, including God and the Heavens, as a unified whole within which there were the lesser wholes of the universal church and the universal state. The pattern was repeated through all the subordinate states, the separate units of the church, and all other associations. At each level there was a oneness as part of a larger oneness. The unity was not only of extent, but also of time. This is what Burke meant when he declared that the nation is "an idea of continuity which extends in time as well as in numbers and in space." Society is more than just a temporary arrangement of atomistic marbles. It is a living entity, linking past, present, and future. The society of which I am part came into existence long before I was born and will continue to exist, as the same society, long after I am dead.

Because it is an organic unity, the society must be more than a collection of parts. It must involve some structured arrangement of those parts. In social terms a structured arrangement of parts implies some idea of hierarchy, class, station in life, etc., a concept which in turn involves some perception of superior and inferior classes or, in short, the acceptance of the naturalness of inequality. In the traditional tory version of a unified society, class involved a two-way relationship in which those who enjoyed the greatest privileges also assumed the highest duties. In the late nineteenth century the English metaphysician F.H. Bradley (1846–1924) introduced the concept of "my station and its duties,"[4] which is of interest here mainly through the implications of the phrase itself. It was Bradley's argument that "the individual" of individualistic theory was a meaningless idea, for all members of any society owed their being and the meaning of their lives to their relationship with other members of that society.

> For if I am myself by sharing with others, by including in my essence my social relations, then if I wish to realize myself I must realize something which extends beyond my mere particular being and is in some way universal. I am what I am by being one of a people, by being born in a family, by living in a certain society, in a certain state; accordingly my role is determined by my function in that large social system; and so my duties are derived from reflection upon the station that I occupy within it.[5]

FRANCIS HERBERT BRADLEY

Born in London January 30, 1840; died in Oxford September 18, 1924.

Bradley was one of the dominant British metaphysicians of the nineteenth century. He spent almost his entire adult life at Oxford, where he lived largely as a recluse. Very little is published, or known, about his private life. In politics he

was conservative, to the point of being reactionary. All commentators agree that Bradley is not an easy philosopher to follow. His principal works include Ethical Studies *(1876),* Principles of Logic *(1883),* Appearance and Reality *(1893), and* Essays on Truth and Reality *(1893).*
For further reading see:
Wollheim, Richard. F.H. Bradley. *London: Penguin, 1959.*

Duty is very much a tory word. Liberals tend to focus on their *rights against* society. Tories, on the other hand, are more alert to, or conscious of, their *duties to* society. This is reflected in many ways. For example, the members of the House of Lords, once one of the great bastions of toryism (even if now infiltrated by large numbers of laissez-faire capitalists), receive no salary for their services. It is only in the last few years that they have been granted token expense allowances for the days they actually attend. Their lordships are expected to offer their time freely, to do their duty to the society that has honoured them.

THE ACCEPTANCE OF INEQUALITY

The tory world view accepts both the fact, and even the desirability, of inequality, not only of income but also of rank and power. A tory society is not an egalitarian society, for it rejects equality as a social or political goal and, going further, even denies its possibility. Accepting natural inequalities as a fact, tories find no difficulties, no attitudinal problems, in institutionalizing such inequalities. The divisions of Lords and Commoners and the preservation of aristocratic titles are accepted as part of the natural way of things, ultimately beneficial to a unified social whole. To the extent that egalitarianism is a democratic value, tories are not democrats. They take it for granted that those who have inherited superior social rank are entitled to the privileges associated with rank. Contrasting the competitive individualism of liberalism, tories offer an elitist class-structured society in which one can easily accept the fact of higher and lower social orders:

> Aye, men are created different; and a government which ignores this law becomes an unjust government, for it sacrifices nobility to mediocrity; it pulls down the aspiring natures to gratify the inferior natures.[6]

The position of socialists here is interesting. Socialists can agree with the tories of the fact: the actual present existence of a hierarchical class-based society. They agree with the tories on what society is now. They disagree with the tories, however, by denying that this structure is either desirable or permanent. They would overthrow the existing class arrangements to raise the oppressed working classes to new positions of power.

THE POSITIVE STATE

The idea of planning, of the central direction of the economy, and of the turning to the government for solutions to social and economic problems is, of course, not inconsistent with an organic world view. Tories are, therefore, much more inclined than liberals to accept a positive role for the state. A major source of conflict within Conservative parties lies here. Those conservatives who are really classical liberals, or capitalists, are committed to the economic doctrines of laissez-faire, even at high social cost. The conservatives who are really tories are more easily persuaded that moral and social obligations to the community at large must at least occasionally outweigh the economic advantages of the owners of capital.

If the society is indeed an organic unity, there should be no intrinsic antagonism between the interests of individuals and the interests of the society of which they are part. Tories are not afraid of the power of the state. They are after all, in their view, its owners. It is the instrument of the common purpose of its members, acting in their corporate capacity, under its natural leaders. Like socialists, tories will accept the state as an appropriate instrument for collective action. They will, of course, disagree about the proper direction and purpose of collective action and on the manner of organizing it. Their goals are not socialist goals. But, with their sense of unity, tories are not prepared to leave things entirely to the chance operation of the marketplace. They may prefer things to be done by private enterprise, but they will not use this as an excuse for not doing that which they consider needs to be done. If private initiative does not act, the state must. If there is a highway to be built, a new industry to be encouraged, a rising unemployment rate to be reduced, or a new natural resource to be developed, the tory will see no violation of any principle in turning to the state for action.

And it follows from the old-fashioned feudal order, out of which toryism was born, that toryism shows a much greater readiness to accept social responsibility for the well-being of all members of the society. Although, under the old feudal order the poor were very poor indeed, the community did accept responsibility for the care of the destitute as a moral obligation. The oldest of all the welfare measures, going back many centuries, made it incumbent on each parish to provide, out of its own rates, for the feeding and housing of those unable to care for themselves. The care was far from luxurious, indeed most of the time it was brutally harsh, but at least the community recognized that morally it could not let any of its members die of starvation.

Welfare to the tory mind is paternalistic welfare. It is not an egalitarian idea. There is no principle that all people are equally entitled to certain standards. The guiding principle is that the advantaged class, which intends to keep its advantages and privileges, has the responsibility of ensuring that the disadvantaged classes have certain minimum living conditions. Instead of seeking to raise the underprivileged to the point where they could control their own destiny, achieving their full economic and political security, the tory seemed prepared to say, "Be content with your pre-destined condition in life, and we, your natural superiors, will look after you." The poet Samuel Taylor Coleridge wrote extensively on what was called "tory democracy," the key principle of which was that "wisdom and ability to govern are the possessions of few; but the few must exercise their powers to mitigate the sufferings of the many."[7]

Liberalism had abandoned this ancient concept of responsibility for the well-being of all members of an organic community. Following the arguments developed by Locke, capitalist employers assumed they were buying labour freely offered by the workers. And as all they bought was labour, they had no further obligations to the workers, who were presumably still able to fend for themselves. Liberalism, by stressing the concept of bargaining among autonomous individuals, destroyed the concept of binding obligations among members of an organic community. This is another issue which, to varying degrees, divides the Conservative parties in Canada, the United Kingdom, and elsewhere. On the one hand are the laissez-faire liberals seeking to limit state intervention in economic matters, and, on the other, the paternalistic, welfare-oriented tories, who are prepared to use the power of the state to ease some of society's injustices and crueler effects. In Canada those who tend to the paternalistic attitude have been saddled with the delightful label "red tories."

CONSERVING THE HERITAGE

Because of its origins in the traditional land-owning aristocracy, toryism embodies a sense of unease about modern industrialization — a sense that perhaps society is overly preoccupied with materialistic values. Liberalism, born out of the commercial-industrial revolution, came into existence as a doctrine to rationalize the shift in power from the landed gentry to the new urban bourgeoisie. Survivors of the old aristocracy still resist that transfer. For this reason, toryism in the nineteenth century embraced the romantic movement in art and literature. Until the industrial revolution began to bury the countryside in mines, factories, and railways, no one really paid much attention to nature. But with that revolution the virtues of rural life were rediscovered. Poets such as Shelley and Wordsworth rhapsodized about skylarks, daffodils, and west winds, while painters such as Constable preserved on canvas the image of a fast-disappearing rural way of life. Most of these romantic poets and artists, who first drew attention to nature as they condemned the sordid ugliness of urban-industrial life, also expressed the most traditional of tory social and political philosophies.[8]

THOMAS JEFFERSON

Born April 13, 1743; died July 4, 1826.
Jefferson was the third President of the United States and served two consecutive terms (1801–09). Although Jefferson is remembered as an advocate of political and religious freedom, it should be noted that he inherited and continued to operate a large estate with many slaves. He holds his place in history as a principal author of the Declaration of Independence *(1776) and as a statesman, diplomat, writer, scientist, and architect.*

In the United States, Thomas Jefferson (1743–1826) expressed typically tory sentiments when he asserted:

Those who labor in the earth are the chosen people of God, if ever He had a chosen people. . . . The mobs of the great cities add just so much to the support of pure government, as sores do to the strength of the human body.[9]

Even today many true tories appear impressed by the virtues of a rural, agricultural existence, at least as something to be admired as a theoretical model, if not actually lived. There is a kind of nostalgia for a simpler life governed only by the changing seasons.

This is yet another source of the tensions within modern conservatism, for tory conservatives tend also to be conservationists. In the jargon of the present decade, they are likely to be ecologically aware preservationists anxious to protect as much of nature as possible. They are not nearly so easily convinced that industrial expansion is *always* a self-justifying benefit. This, of course, reflects back once more to the concept of an organic society. If you believe that you are one both with the past and with the future, if you believe that the generations as yet unborn will share in the same organic unity of which you are now part, you will be much more mindful of the need to preserve for those future generations some of that natural beauty that earlier generations preserved for you. Tories have, almost by definition, a broader historical sense than liberals who tend, again as a natural product of their world view, to live largely in the present. The tory character is less likely to be satisfied with immediate short-term profit and more concerned with the long-term, lasting social benefit. This almost brings us back to one of the dictionary definitions of conservatism, as distinct from its strictly political application: Conservative, one who would *conserve*; one who would change as little and as slowly as possible; one who desires to keep intact the heritage of the past; one who is reluctant to adopt new ways. There is, in the tory make-up, an ingrained reverence for the past.

One of the attributes of liberalism was the acceptance of the inevitability and desirability of progress. Tories, while not denying progress, are not as easily convinced that change is, in itself, progress. It is hard to persuade a tory that the demolition of a historic old building to make way for a highrise office block, or even for low-cost housing for the poor, has anything much to do with progress. Among many tories there is a certain scepticism about the reality of the progress that follows technological innovation. New ways, new things, are not necessarily better. The observation by Sir John Byng, who travelled in the north country of England in 1792, is typical. Looking from his coach window Sir John wrote:

> Why, here now, is a great flaring mill. . . . All the vale is disturb'd. . . . Sir Richard Arkwright may have introduced Much Wealth into his Family and into his Country, but, as a Tourist, I execrate his Schemes, which having crept into every Pastoral Vale, have destroyed the course, and the Beauty of Nature.[10]

So there is among tories a sense of historical continuity, an inclination to see the past as part of the present. This, in turn, encourages them to be preservationists, protectors of the national heritage, conscious of the need to set some limits to industrial expansion and some bounds to materialistic consumerism; especially to consumerism that relies on a built-in obsolescence to keep it thriving. Such a world view is likely to include some perceptions that there are other finer, more moral, more spiritual values than economic advancement. Tories certainly do not object to becoming rich nor are they likely to disregard casually opportunities for material benefits; they are simply more conscious that wealth is not the only object of life nor the only measure of success.

NATIONALISM AND PATRIOTISM

Because they see themselves as deriving the meaning or purpose of life from existence in an organic society, tories naturally place high value on loyalty to that society. So, they tend to set the national interest at a higher level than, say, the multinational corporate empire or the international socialist brotherhood of the working-class mythology. Here one must avoid being too dogmatic or exclusive, for one must acknowledge that the Americans, the embodiment of liberal individualism, are among the world's most fervent patriots. Nevertheless, it is still true that a high level of patriotism is consistent with other characteristics of toryism. The state, as the political organization or, more especially, the nation that invokes the concepts of a people aware of themselves as a people, is seen as the realization of a particular, unique set of values. A nation is one manifestation of an organic unity. As a tory, the mores, beliefs, and customs of my people will become part of my own being. I will describe myself in terms of my nation, so in being loyal to my nation I am loyal to myself. I will also tend to see my nation as peculiarly mine, distinct from all others. Such an identification is not, of course, unique to tories. Most of us, most of the time, are more or less chauvinistic, tending to divide the world into *us* and a somewhat undifferentiated *them*. Even the ancient Greeks believed the world to be inhabited by only two kinds of people: Greeks and Barbarians.

At the level of economic policies, the differences become sharper. Other things being equal, tories are inclined to be protectionists prepared to use tariff controls to protect home industries, even where free trade might result in lower prices. They are prepared to pay some cost for the preservation of an independent national economy. It is interesting to note that in the controversy over whether Britain should enter the European Common Market, the opposition to entry came from two major sources. On the one hand, the left wing of the Labour party saw the whole thing as a capitalist plot against the interests of the British working classes. Joining forces with them in opposition were the more traditional tories within the Conservative party who, in effect, wanted to have as little as possible to do with a lot of foreigners. They saw the European Common Market as a betrayal of the British national heritage, an assault on national sovereignty. A multinational corporation would seem to be a singularly laissez-faire capitalist invention. It would be psychologically impossible to be both a genuine national patriot and an obedient, enthusiastic servant of a multinational when the interests of the conglomerate must be set above those of any one nation or people.

Tory patriotism will often take the form of a deep affection for, and loyalty to, such national symbols as flags and anthems and a fondness for preserving historical associations. Once more our American experience demonstrates that they are not alone in this, but such feelings for the past are more appropriate to a tory world view. It is worth recalling how passions were aroused by the introduction of the new Canadian flag in 1965 when the old British ensign was dropped. Throughout the Commonwealth, tories are likely to be monarchists, their patriotism bolstered by all the trappings, rituals, and ceremonies of royalty. It is one of the problems of British politics that, while the Queen herself conscientiously tries to maintain her proper constitutional position of non-partisanship, there are elements within the Conservative party who behave and talk as though the Queen were the leader of that party. She is regarded by many as their special possession and in heart one of them. And in Canada we note how strongly a number of tories react to any attempt to diminish the role of the Queen or to eliminate royal symbols from Canadian life.

Let us now assemble a summary of the shorthand labels in the style of the last chapter to set down a capsule picture of a tory. Tories will have an organic view of the world; they will believe in objective, eternal moral values, often with a religious foundation; they will accept the ideas of hierarchy, class, and inequality; they will be prepared to use the power of the state for social purposes; being preservationists they will be distrustful of over-industrialization; and they will be nationalists and patriots.

CANADIAN AND AMERICAN CONSERVATISM

In Canada the continued existence of a traditional, but small, tory component significantly affects the character and style of Conservative parties, making them something different from their United States counterparts. A very useful explanatory theory for this separate development was put forward a few years ago by an American, Louis Hartz,[11] and further developed and modified to the Canadian condition by Gad Horowitz.[12] The essential theme of Hartz's original formulation was that in the new-world colonies founded by Europeans, the political culture of the colony took on the character of the dominant ideology in the parent nation at the time of separation. The parent societies would continue to embrace the full ideological spectrum from feudal toryism, developing gradually to modern socialism. All the elements would continue to survive, with society as a composite of their confrontation and interaction. But the colony, broken off from the parent society, would enshrine a fragment of that cultural heritage; the fragment dominant at the moment of separation. The rest would be left behind.

Hartz was concerned principally with the United States, founded and consolidated at the height of Lockean liberal individualism. The older toryism, the pre-liberal land-owning aristocracy, never gained more than an insecure footing in American society. After the War of Independence it was reduced to insignificance and impotence. The United States represents the total triumph of liberal ideology, with no countervailing force of toryism. There is no conflict between toryism and laissez-faire liberalism in American conservatism, because there is no toryism. Conservatism in the United States is nothing more than a survival of the classical liberal ideology of the nineteenth century. And because there is no toryism, there is no fertile soil for the growth, or even understanding, of the concept of an organic society. But with no understanding or tradition of the shared social obligations of an organic community, there is nothing from which socialism can grow. The limited, ineffective socialist parties in the United States, stemming mainly from European Marxists, are outside the mainstream of American political life, unsympathetically received, alien to the political culture, and largely irrelevant. The United States has thus a singularly narrow political spectrum. The range of legitimate political ideas, of acceptable political values, is contained within the bounds of liberalism. The American political culture is dominated by a "monolithic liberalism unsullied by tory or socialist deviations."[13] In the absence of toryism, the only ideology rooted in the past, committed to the conserving of old faiths, is the ideology of the once radical laissez-faire liberalism. And in the absence of any genuine socialist alternative, the burden of reform must be taken up by the "left wing" of liberalism.

In English Canada the actual timing and source of foundation was different.[14] There was, from the beginning, a small tory element, what Hartz called a "tory touch," in the Canadian experience. This "touch" was reinforced by the Empire Loyalists who fled the United States after 1776. This is not to suggest that all the Loyalists were tories, but the tory element, relatively unimportant in the larger society of the United States, became of major significance in the much smaller population of English Canada. Hartz had admitted to the "tory touch," seeing it as a minor variation in a Canadian society that remained essentially bourgeois liberal. Horowitz, in his most important paper, argued that the tory element was much more significant than Hartz had allowed, changing fundamentally the character of Canadian political culture.

In the first place it considerably modified Canadian conservatism, providing a counter to the dominance of laissez-faire capitalist ideology. Because conservatism in Canada embraces elements of a tory tradition, it is a much broader, more tolerant, more humane doctrine than its American counterpart. Not being completely swayed by the ideas of rugged anti-state individualism, Canadian conservative parties have been more socially conscious and more prepared to call upon the state for collective action than American Republicans.

The second effect is that the organic understanding of society, on which toryism is founded, has made possible the emergence of a socialist ideology. At the centre of the Hartz-Horowitz case is the proposition that without an organic view of the world, as embraced by toryism, there are no cultural roots to nourish socialism. Socialism can appear only where there has been a tradition of toryism. Thus, between toryism and socialism there is a certain empathy, a certain understanding, of the nature of the "good society."

> Another aberration which may be worthy of investigation is the Canadian phenomenon of the red tory. At its simplest level, he is a Conservative who prefers the CCF/NDP to the Liberals, or a socialist who prefers the Conservatives to the Liberals, without really knowing why. At a higher level he is a conscious ideological Conservative with some "odd" socialist notions (W.L. Morton) or a conscious ideological socialist with some "odd" tory notions (Eugene Forsey). The very suggestion that such affinities might exist between Republicans and Socialists in the United States is ludicrous enough to make some kind of a point.[15]

Canadian democratic socialists share with some Canadian tories a set of common assumptions about the need to protect the common good from the excesses of competitive capitalism. Both socialist and tory in Canada can agree that there is a role for the state in advancing the public good whenever it seems unduly threatened by private interest.

> The tory and socialist minds have some crucial assumptions, orientations, and values in common, so that from certain angles they may appear, not as enemies, but as two different expressions of the same ideological outlook. Thus, at the very highest level, the red tory is a philosopher who combines elements of socialism and toryism so thoroughly in a single integrated *Welt-*

anschauung that it is impossible to say that he is a proponent of either one as *against* the other.[16]

It is because Canadians have, as part of their political culture, some intuitive feeling for organic views that socialism becomes intelligible and respectable. Socialism in the United States is an alien thing. In Canada democratic socialist parties — the CCF (Co-operative Commonwealth Federation), and its successor the NDP, have formed provincial governments and, in large parts of the country, are a significant political force. Even the majority of those in Canada who would never, under any circumstances, vote for the NDP, nevertheless accept that it is a legitimate political movement that is entitled to seek popular support and to govern if it wins that support.

In this way the presence of the tory touch in Canadian politics extends the spectrum of legitimate political ideologies beyond the limits imposed in the United States. Mainstream Canadian political philosophies range from toryism, through competitive laissez-faire liberalism, moderated reform or welfare liberalism, to democratic socialism. And as a consequence conservatism in Canada is not the same as conservatism in the United States. The Progressive Conservative Party of Canada is not the parallel of the Republican party in the United States. Although a great many Canadians who think of themselves as conservatives think and behave like American conservatives — that is, like laissez-faire liberals — there are other Canadian conservatives who would be decidedly uncomfortable and unwelcome in American conservative circles. Their influence waxes and wanes as the party is "captured" by its left or right wings. But even when laissez-faire capitalism is most triumphant, it can never totally discount that older tory element which tries to restrain its crasser impulses.

CHAPTER THIRTEEN

The Socialist Faith

The third major ideology of the Western democracies is democratic socialism. This is the philosophy embraced, with varying levels of consistency
and intensity, by the New Democratic Party of Canada, by the Labour
parties of the United Kingdom, Australia, and New Zealand, and by the
Democratic Socialist parties of Western Europe. It is a philosophy virtually unrepresented in the United States, where the policy goals of democratic socialism must be assumed, at least in part, by the more progressive
elements of liberalism. As with other ideologies, socialist party labels and
identifications are an unsatisfactory guide to philosophies, for all parties
bend philosophic principles to political expediencies or as adjustments to
historical circumstances. Almost always, too, a party label disguises the
fact that the party includes several not always compatible wings and factions. Certainly none of the parties mentioned above are perfect examples
of democratic socialism. And here socialism concerns us more than socialist parties.

Popular definitions of socialism include public ownership of the means
of production, extensive welfare programs, the replacement of a market
economy by a planned economy, and the priority of social benefit over
private interest. Indeed, to many people, all these things or even any one
of them constitute socialism. The elderly aunt of a colleague of mine is
convinced that because her electricity is supplied by a public corporation
—Ontario Hydro—Ontario is a socialist regime not far removed from that
of the Soviet Union.

It has, however, already been demonstrated that the public ownership
of at least some elements of economic activity preceded socialist theory,

238

and that all modern governments, even those most stridently anti-socialist, are involved in a great deal of public enterprise either owned directly or controlled through publicly appointed non-profit corporations, boards, and commissions. It has also been shown how both liberal pragmatism and tory paternalism may initiate large areas of social welfare. One does not have to be a socialist to become concerned for the public relief of poverty or the provision of adequate medical care or housing. The need to conserve or allocate scarce resources, or the need to move production away from civilian luxuries to military requirements in wartime, have made clear that all regimes, whatever their ideology, must under certain circumstances resort to a centralized direction of the economy. During the great depression of the 1930s, even the liberal laissez-faire United States discovered that government had to become involved in planning the economy as an aid to recovery. And, of course, the whole structure of feudalism was predicated on the priority of the organic community over the claims of the isolated individual.

Obviously, popular assumptions about socialism are inadequate or incomplete. Public ownership, planning, welfare, redistribution of income, and so on, are clearly relevant to the discussion of socialism, for socialists will be in favour of them, but these things are not enough, of themselves, to explain what socialism is. It is necessary to look beyond the overt practices and policy proposals, to investigate more closely the conceptions of society behind them. The important point lies not so much in what is done as in the reasons for doing it. Socialism is an attitude to life, as well as a program of action. The enquirer must seek out the socialist perception of society, the vision of what the world ought to be, and of how individuals are to be related to their social setting. Policies and programs are simply a means to the end by which socialism is defined.

The problem of determining what socialism is becomes complicated by the fact that it is many different things, a genus of many species. There are Utopians, Guild Socialists, Syndicalists, Marxists, Maoists, Christian Socialists, Fabians, Anarchists, and many more, often bitterly hostile to each other.[1] The concern of this chapter, however, is with one particular brand of socialism, that which has been identified as democratic socialism, although even this is a flexible enough term to allow for considerable variation in detail and policy.

Democratic socialism has its roots in a broad socialist history going back to the radical movements of the seventeenth century, and drawing from Utopian and Marxist sources along the way. But it also owes much to Christian inspiration. In Canada, as in England, a nonconformist Christian tradition of brotherhood and social justice brought many into the socialist movement. Canadian founders of the old CCF, such as J.S. Woodsworth and T.C. Douglas, saw socialism as the political expression of their Christian social convictions. As a Methodist minister, Woodsworth's aim was a society guided by the motives of Christian charity rather than by the profit motive.

> This gentle, kindly Christian man with his message of charity and brotherhood was not the stuff of which revolutionaries, anarchists and assassins were made.[2]

Whole generations in the English-speaking Commonwealth have been raised in the tradition that a Christian society is a socialist society. In Canada, examples could be drawn not only from the earliest Christian communities, but also from the contemporary Hutterites settlements in the West. In both instances co-operative sharing is a part of life and all possessions are held in common.

J.S. WOODSWORTH

Born July 29, 1874; died March 21, 1942.
J.S. Woodsworth began his adult life as a teacher in rural schools in Manitoba in 1893. He entered the Ministry of the Methodist Church of Canada in 1896. From his earliest years he was active in the cause of working people and the poor. From 1913 to 1916 he was organizer and secretary of the Canadian Welfare League in Winnipeg. During the Winnipeg General Strike in 1919, Woodsworth was arrested on charges of treason but they were later dropped. He was first elected to the House of Commons in 1921 for the district of Winnipeg North Central (a constituency he continued to represent until his death), first as an Independent Labour Candidate and later on behalf of the Co-operative Commonwealth Federation.
For further reading see:
MacInnis, Grace. J.S. Woodsworth. Toronto: Macmillan, 1953.

FABIAN SOCIALISM

A primary model for democratic socialism is the English brand of Fabian socialism founded in the 1880s and still providing much of the intellectual base of the British Labour party.[3] The Fabian Society was an offshoot of the

Fellowship of the New Life, a religious study group established in 1882. Such a fact illustrates the major contribution of a Christian ethic to the democratic socialist ideal. Some members of that Fellowship who became more concerned with the social and economic causes of ethical problems rather than with personal morality began to drift off into new directions. In November 1883, a group of them passed a resolution:

> The members of the Society assert that the Competitive system assures the happiness and comfort of the few at the expense of the suffering of the many and that Society must be reconstituted in such a manner as to secure the general welfare and happiness.[4]

This resolution marks the birth of Fabian philosophy. The Fabian Society was dominated in its early years by some of the leading intellectuals of British life — such notables as G.B. Shaw, Sidney and Beatrice Webb, Graham Wallas, H.G. Wells, and many others.

THE FABIANS

For more information about individual Fabians, refer to the separate biographies for each of the following: Sidney Webb in chapter ten, Hubert Bland, further in this chapter, and Graham Wallas, also in this chapter.
For further reading on the Fabians, collectively, see:
Beer, Max. A History of British Socialism. *London: Allen and Unwin, 1953.*
McBriar, H.M. Fabian Socialism and English Politics 1884–1918. *Cambridge: Cambridge University Press, 1966.*
Fremantle, Anne. This Little Band of Prophets: The British Fabians. *New York: New American Library, 1955.*
Pease, Edward. The History of the Fabian Society. *London: Fifield, 1916.*

Fabianism was, and is, essentially a movement of middle-class intellectuals, driven by an unquenchable urge to expound, exhort, and preach. Their vision of what socialism might do for the working classes was inspiring:

> But in the households of the five men out of six in England who live by weekly wage, Socialism would indeed be a new birth of happiness. The long hours of work done as in a convict prison, without interest and without

242 / CONFLICTING POLITICAL IDEAS IN LIBERAL DEMOCRACIES

hope; the dreary squalor of their homes; above all that grievous uncertainty, that constant apprehension of undeserved misfortune which is the peculiar result of capitalist production: all this would be gone; and education, refinement, leisure, the very thought of which now maddens them, would be part of their daily life. Socialism hangs above them as the crown hung in Bunyan's story above the man raking the muck heap — ready for them if they will but lift their eyes. And even to the few who seem to escape and even profit by the misery of our century, Socialism offers a new and nobler life, when full sympathy with those about them, springing from full knowledge of their condition, shall be a source of happiness, and not, as now, of constant sorrow — when it shall no longer seem either folly or hypocrisy for a man to work openly for his highest ideal. To them belongs the privilege that for each one of them the revolution may begin as soon as he is ready to pay the price.[5]

GRAHAM WALLAS

Born May 31, 1858; died August 9, 1932.
Wallas was one of the key figures in the foundation of the Fabian Society and contributor to the Fabian Essays in Socialism *(1889). He was a prominent member of the London School Board 1894–1904, playing a large part in the secularization of education. He helped in the establishment of the London School of Economics in 1895 and held the first Chair of Government. Author of* Life of Francis Place 1771–1854 *(1898),* Human Nature in Politics *(1908) — his most widely known work — and several other books in the general area of political sociology.*
For further reading see:
Wiener, M.J. Between Two Worlds: The Political Thought of Graham Wallas. *Oxford: Clarendon Press, 1971.*
Qualter, T.H. Graham Wallas and the Great Society. *London: Macmillan, 1980.*
See also under the heading The Fabians *in this chapter.*

But the Fabians, not being themselves members of the working class, have had little confidence in the capacity of the workers to achieve their own destiny. In their turn, working people have never looked to the Fabians with that gratitude and admiration the Fabians seem to have expected.

> If their primary purpose was to disarm middle class suspicion and to make socialism respectable, so that even a churchwarden in his most sober moments need not be ashamed to confess a weakness for socialism, then surely they succeeded beyond their wildest dreams. They produced a form of socialism which could be eagerly embraced by the undergraduate, enabling him to give his parents (in the 'nineties) that slight shock which it is so wise to administer from time to time, while at the same time it entailed no upheaval in his present mode of life. For so far from Fabianism imposing any ascetic renunciation on its devotees, it rather implied that while it was permissible to hope that one day the evil Babylon would dissolve into the New Jerusalem, nevertheless so long as Babylon remained the old bad, capitalistic, competitive Babylon, it would be foolish not to live as did the Babylonians.[6]

These attitudes continue to bedevil democratic socialist parties. One finds in both the New Democratic Party of Canada and the various Commonwealth Labour parties, a continuing tension between a well-meaning intellectual left, drawn largely from the universities and the professions and anxious to do things for the toiling masses, and the workers who would much rather do things for themselves.[7]

The single most coherent exposition of Fabian political and economic philosophy is contained in the *Fabian Essays in Socialism*, first published in 1889 and often reprinted. Their ideas are also disseminated in hundreds of brief pamphlets collectively known as the *Fabian Tracts*. New issues of these still appear at irregular intervals.

The whole character of Fabian socialism was foreign to Marxism both in origin and philosophy. From their middle-class English intellectual background the Fabians were non-doctrinaire, persuasive, constitutional, and reformist.[8] Specifically, it appears, they rejected the concepts of dialectical materialism partly because they never really understood what Marx was saying. Although they were optimistic about the eventual victory of socialism, they were unwilling to subscribe to any overall philosophy of history to substantiate their confidence. The Fabians felt socialism would succeed not because any laws of history made this inevitable, but only because

> there were enough dedicated men and women of talent prepared to work extremely hard and efficiently to make it succeed. And it would succeed because of that skilled work, and not because of any scientific laws.[9]

SOCIALISM IN CANADA

While Fabianism has never gained much formal support in Canada, the roots of socialism in this country have been nurtured by gradualism and Christian ethics, the same concepts of British Fabianism. This makes Canadian socialism radically different from such socialism as does exist in the United States.

> Canadian socialism is un-American in two distinct ways. It is un-American in the sense that it is a significant and legitimate political force in Canada, insignificant and alien in the United States. But Canadian socialism is also un-American in the sense that it does not speak the same language as American socialism. In Canada, socialism is British, non-Marxist, and worldly; in the United States it is German, Marxist, and other-worldly. . . .
>
> Thus socialism was not alien here. But it was not alien in yet another way; it was not borne by foreigners. The personnel and ideology of the Canadian labour and socialist movements have been primarily British. Many of those who built these movements were British immigrants with past experience in the British labour movement; many others were Canadian-born children of such immigrants. And in British North America, Britons could not be treated as foreigners.[10]

According to Horowitz's argument, it is the presence of a "tory touch" that makes possible the existence of a legitimate socialism in Canada, whereas it is an unknown force in United States political life. But it is also the fact that it is only a "touch" that makes socialism in Canada weak by the standards of Europe, where toryism still has much more vitality.[11]

THE SOCIALIST WORLD VIEW: CLASS

At the very heart of any socialist world view is the conception of an organic society, a unified whole, with a life of its own, in contrast to the artificial atomistic association of individuals that is the backbone of liberalism. It is an outlook on life that socialists share with tories, so without a historical tradition of a tory organic community, socialism struggles for life in an infertile soil. Democratic socialism blends corporate, organic concepts derived from toryism with reformist, egalitarian components of a later protective liberalism. Democratic socialism tries to fit a humanitarian concern for the material well-being and social equality of all members of society into a pre-liberal vision of society as a unified organic whole. To the socialist mind there is no natural or inevitable antagonism between public and private advantage, for the best interests of individuals are served through their social membership. The selfish concerns of individuals are subordinated to the common interest of society, because the society, through the collective action of all its members, is the instrument of the individual's greatest good. Individuals work for, and within, the society, because the society exists for them.

But within this social unity, most socialists have a strong perception of class, however loosely that term might be defined.[12] There is perceived to be an identity of interest within each class, but as among the several classes, divisions are almost inevitably hostile and interests incompatible. Between the two great classes of bourgeoisie and proletariat the differences are irreconcilable. Attempts to portray the two as benefiting from some alliance for the common good are dismissed as a propagandistic device to ensure the continued dominance of the capitalists. It was central to Marx's argument that the more the proletariat produced, the greater were the profits of the bourgeoisie and the deeper the relative poverty of the workers. Marx put his point bluntly when he wrote:

> Labour certainly produces marvels for the rich but it produces privation for the worker. It produces palaces, but hovels for the worker. It produces beauty, but deformity for the worker. It replaces labour by machinery, but it casts some of the workers back into a barbarous kind of work and turns others into machines. It produces intelligence, but also stupidity and cretinism for the workers.[13]

As long as one class exploits another, social harmony is impossible.

Tories, who also acknowledge the reality of class structure, accept the existing arrangements, with all the powers and privileges conferred upon property owners, as normal and desirable. However, to the socialists, who draw most of their strength and justification from the "lower classes," particularly the urban proletariat, the unity of society and the just allocation of its resources are obstructed by the perpetuation of the existing class order. They therefore seek to eliminate the rigidities of a class structure that hinder social mobility and keep wage earners in a position of social and economic dependence. In socialist terms, equality means, above all, an equality of classes, leading to the final achievement of that socialist dream, a "classless society." There is, among socialists, a very deep sense of there being now an oppressed social class, victim of a system over which it has no control and denied an appropriate share of the wealth it creates. Note, for example, the words from that most famous of all trade union songs, *Solidarity Forever*:

They have taken untold millions that they never toiled to earn,
But without our brain and muscle not a single wheel could turn.
We can break their haughty power, gain our freedom when we learn
That the union makes us strong.[14]

Socialists do not object to differential rewards for differential services. There is nothing contrary to the doctrines or practices of socialism in proposals that some people, doing some kinds of work, should earn considerably more than other people doing other kinds of work. They take their guidance from Marx, who said, "From each according to ability, to each according to need." The fact that total equality is unobtainable does not mean that one cannot pursue a reduction in existing inequalities.

> Equality is a noble ideal. We know it will not be achieved, but that of itself
> does not invalidate an aspiration — any more than the fact that wages and
> salaries will reflect different responsibilities and opportunities means that it
> is wrong to strive for a system which endeavours to make financial rewards
> fairer. Right wing propaganda which portrays the socialist desire for a greater
> measure of equality as nothing more than pure envy of the rich, a blind
> vindictiveness and hatred of the successful is simply the weakest defence of
> vested interest and privilege.[15]

Socialists, of whatever stripe, are united in a desire to reduce those excesses of inequality which make impossible the realization of a fraternal community. The strongest objection is to the allocation of rewards based on hereditary class, status, or capital investment, but unrelated to effort. The socialist conviction is that in a capitalist society rewards are unjustly allocated.

PUBLIC OWNERSHIP

This search for equality raises once more the question of public ownership. The socialist argument is akin to the ideological argument discussed in chapters nine and ten. To the socialist the very idea that one individual should be able to make a profit from the excess value created by the labour of another is offensive. It is not the amount of money that the capitalist enjoys that is objectionable, but the way in which it is acquired. Socialists reject the key principles on which capitalism is founded: the institution of private property in industrial capacity and the treatment of labour as a saleable commodity. Capitalism necessarily and permanently denies the workers the full value of their labour.

Arguments about the cost efficiency of public versus private enterprise are not, therefore, particularly relevant. Convinced socialists are not persuaded of the virtues of private enterprise by data about the high return to investors in the private sector, nor are they persuaded by evidence of the inefficiency or waste in some public sector enterprises. They may object to those defects or seek to remedy them, but they are not at the heart of the argument. In fact, such arguments, in any context, prove very little. It is true that some public enterprises are badly managed, waste enormous sums of money, and are top-heavy with incompetent, self-serving bureaucrats. But, at the same time, other public enterprises are efficient and provide a necessary public service at low cost. In most of our cities the publicly financed and controlled firefighting services operate as well as the most up-to-date technology allows. In many parts of the world nationalized railways provide efficient, high-quality passenger transport. In Ontario, the government-operated liquor stores make a very handsome profit. On the other hand, some private enterprises are mismanaged: riddled with nepotism, or incapable of adapting to changing circumstances. Many go bankrupt, with much consequent human hardship. Others survive but at a much lower level of profit than more competent management might provide. Still others prosper despite inefficiency and waste, because they hold a monopoly over some essential service, while some manage to stay alive only because governments from time to time intervene to rescue them from their difficulties. In short, debates about efficiency or waste in this or that activity add nothing very useful to questions of public or private ownership.

But socialists advocate public ownership not on grounds of economic efficiency but because they hold that private ownership is wrong in principle. Socialists will therefore urge society to move rapidly to public ownership and control of at least the major means of production, distribution, and exchange. The stress on the *major* means is important because democratic socialists acknowledge that a democratic society must be prepared to accept some continuing level of private ownership, since not all people are persuaded of the virtues of public ownership. Democratic socialism, being pragmatic, generally is reconciled to the continued existence of a mixed economy, rejecting as both impractical and undesirable the transfer of all economic activity to social ownership. Note, for example, the wording of The Basis of the Fabian Society (1887):

> The Fabian Society consists of Socialists. It therefore aims at the reorganization of Society by the emancipation of Land and Industrial Capital from individual and class ownership, and the vesting of them in the community for the general benefit. In this way only can the natural and acquired advantages of the country be equitably shared by the whole people. . . .

The Society, further, works for the transfer to the community of the administration of *such industrial Capital as can conveniently be managed socially* [italics
added]. For, owing to the monopoly of the means of production in the past,
industrial inventions and the transformation of surplus income into Capital
have mainly enriched the proprietary class, the worker now being dependent
on that class for leave to earn a living.[16]

HUBERT BLAND

Born 1856; died April 1914.
*One of the founding members of the Fabian Society and a member of its
executive until illness forced his retirement in 1926. Bland offended many of his
fellow Fabians by what they considered his outrageous moral behaviour. One
writer described his political morality as far superior to his sexual habits. He was
one of the contributors to the* Fabian Essays in Socialism *(1889).*
For further reading see under the heading The Fabians *in this chapter.*

The route to public ownership can be followed only as fast as public
opinion is prepared to accept. By and large democratic socialists see the
nationalization of industry as a means, not an end. Its success depends
upon both the nature of the end, and the moderation or balance with which
it is pursued. Despite the sometimes strident advocacy of some socialists,
public ownership and control are not of themselves tantamount to socialism.
They are a necessary, but not a sufficient, cause of socialism. As Fabian
essayist Hubert Bland noted:

Still it must not be forgotten that although Socialism involves State control, State control does not imply Socialism — at least in any modern meaning of the term. It is not so much to the thing the State does, as to the end
for which it does it that we must look before we can decide whether it is a
Socialist State or not. Socialism is the common holding of the means of
production and exchange, and *the holding of them for the equal benefit of all.* . . . I
cannot too strongly insist upon the importance of this distinction; for the
losing sight of it by friends, and its intentional obscuration by enemies, constitute a big and immediate danger. To bring forward sixpenny telegrams as
an instance of State Socialism may be a very good method of scoring a point

off an individualist opponent in a debate before a middle-class audience; but from the standpoint of the proletariat a piece of State management which spares the pockets only of the commercial and leisured classes is no more Socialism than were the *droits de Seigneur* of the middle ages. Yet this is the sort of sham Socialism which it is as certain as death will be doled out by the popular party in the hope that mere State action will be mistaken for really Socialist legislation. And the object of these givers of Greek gifts will most infallibly be attained if those Socialists who know what they want hesitate (from fear of losing popularity, or from any more amiable weakness) to clamor their loudest against any and every proposal whose adoption would prolong the life of private Capital a single hour.[17]

In the circumstances of the late twentieth century, many democratic socialists seem to accept that further large-scale nationalization is undesirable. Much of the earlier optimistic faith in the huge social benefits that were to follow the bringing of selected industrial enterprises under public control has today faded. The original confidence has been well expressed by Professor Kelf-Cohen, writing about the attitudes of young British socialists in the first decades of this century:

There was magic in the words "Public Board" or "Public Corporation." They were to be staffed by selfless men of outstanding ability, devoted to the national interest. We assumed that such men were to be found in large numbers; naturally they had no chance to come forward in the degenerate Capitalist era in which we were living. We also assumed that the workers in the industries would be transformed by the Act of Nationalisation and devote themselves to the national interest. Thus the combination of selfless management and selfless workers would bring about the brave new world of Socialism — so utterly different from Capitalism.[18]

The disillusioning experience was that nationalization, or at least partial nationalization in a society still largely capitalist, did not bring about the anticipated change in workers or managers. Utopia did not arrive.

Not only has nationalization become politically unpopular, it has also produced a swollen unresponsive bureaucracy rather than the intended co-operative socialist society. As far as the workers were concerned, conditions in the nationalized industries did not change all that much. After the war working conditions did improve and wage earners enjoyed a higher standard of living. But conditions were better everywhere, in private as well as public enterprise. Nationalization did not generate a spirit of mutual harmony between workers and management, as evidenced by the bitter miners' strike in England in 1984–85. Managers still had to manage, behaving much as managers everywhere.

However, while nationalization did not produce the new world of industrial harmony anticipated by its advocates, the original anti-nationalization arguments have also lost much of their steam. The early prophecies of doom, the fears that nationalization would cause total social and economic disaster, have not been fulfilled. Conservative governments in Britain, at least until the government of Mrs. Margaret Thatcher, while they opposed the nationalization of the mines, the railways, and so on, were remarkably reluctant to dismantle the new public corporations, or return their activities to private enterprise. The main obstacle was that the private sector was singularly reluctant to reinvest in these activities, there being no evidence that privatization would resolve any of the problems. It is only since the 1980s that the new right-wing governments of Britain, the United States, and Canada have seriously embarked on a program of selling some of the more profitable public enterprises to the private sector. It is, as yet, far too early to assess the consequences.

Today, the "revisionists" among democratic socialists no longer see further public ownership as the key to changing the character of society. They are inclined to argue that the goals of a more democratic, more egalitarian society can be achieved within the framework of a mixed economy in which public ownership and centralized control are only two of several possible variables. In a new mood of reappraisal, many democratic socialists are inclined now to look to a model of widespread, local participatory democracy, with a decentralized socialism, putting the control of the economy in the hands of the people at a local level, rather than through a gigantic centralized bureaucracy.

In Canada, the first democratic socialist party, the Co-operative Commonwealth Federation, founded in 1933, stated its position on public ownership in its first program:

> We aim to replace the present capitalist system, with its inherent injustice and inhumanity, by a social order from which the domination and exploitation of one class by another will be eliminated, in which economic planning will supersede unregulated private enterprise and competition, and in which genuine democratic self-government, based upon economic equality will be possible. The present order is marked by glaring inequalities of wealth and opportunity, by chaotic waste and instability; and in an age of plenty it condemns the great mass of the people to poverty and insecurity. Power has become more and more concentrated into the hands of a small irresponsible

minority of financiers and industrialists and to their predatory interests the majority are habitually sacrificed. When private profit is the main stimulus to economic effort, our society oscillates between periods of feverish prosperity in which the main benefits go to speculators and profiteers, and of catastrophic depression, in which the common man's normal state of insecurity and hardship is accentuated. We believe that these evils can be removed only in a planned and socialized economy in which our natural resources and the principal means of production and distribution are owned, controlled and operated by the people.[19]

WELFARE AND LIBERTY

Similar arguments apply to questions of welfare. There are, as indicated in an earlier chapter, a large number of straightforward practical reasons why a society should move to protect itself from the worst consequence of poverty or insecurity. But socialists do not propose unemployment insurance simply to avoid the immediate political consequences of not doing so. Nor do they act only because the unemployed and their families have votes. They offer public assistance because, in a just society, no one should be forced to suffer because there is no work available. It is at the heart of the socialist ethic that society as a whole has a responsibility for the well-being of all its members. There is a willing acceptance of Lord Beveridge's principle of "a floor not a ceiling":[20] the principle that in any civilized society there is some minimum standard of living essential to any sense of human dignity and self-respect, some floor, below which no individual can be allowed to fall.

In this sense, socialists see the state not as the enemy of individual freedom, but as the instrument for achieving a social purpose, for securing the real freedoms (in the plural) of all its members. The welfare state, by liberating the many from the oppression of ignorance, poverty, and insecurity, makes freedom a universal concept. It is helpful to read again Professor Barbara Wootton's words, set out in chapter five, which are very much a democratic socialist expression of the meaning of freedom. The same argument of a freedom requiring the positive intervention of the state has been made by E.H. Carr:

Having made clear my belief that freedom in our day as a goal of political action and political endeavour must mean freedom for all, let me come to its practical applications and embarrassments. Mill's famous formula recognized liberty for all and therefore comprised equality in liberty. But Mill's liberty was limited to the political and intellectual sphere; when he wrote his famous treatise at the end of the 1850's he had not advanced, even as far as he advanced later, towards the problems of mass civilization and of economic liberty and equality. Even in the political sphere the proposition that my freedom is valid only in so far as it does not limit the freedom of others constitutes a far more serious qualification of absolute liberty than Mill himself realized. But, when we advance beyond the political sphere, the qualification becomes so far-reaching as to necessitate something almost like a re-definition of our whole conception of freedom; and it is at this point that some of those who appeared to accept the doctrine of freedom for all seem to fall by the wayside and revert to the doctrine of freedom for some. For, when we consider the paraphernalia of controls and rationing and taxation necessary to the organization of freedom from want for all, and the restrictions which these involve on the cherished liberties of some, it is not unnatural that some of these some feel that the new freedoms are not an extension of the old freedoms, but their negation. Enough volumes have been written on this theme in the last few years to fill a book-case. You can hardly pick up a newspaper today without finding an article or a letter that re-hashes the familiar argument. Nor can we escape the dilemma. The price of liberty is the restriction of liberty. The price of some liberty for all is the restriction of the greater liberty of some.[21]

Socialists, then, will be prepared to use the instrument of the state to restrict the greater liberty of some, and especially the economic liberty of the capitalist, the employer, and the wealthy, in order to produce an equality of liberty for all.

EDWARD H. CARR

Born June 28, 1892; died November 3, 1982.
  Carr began his career in the Foreign Office, serving in various posts between 1916 and 1936. He then devoted himself to academic activity, holding a number of positions at universities in Wales and England. He was the assistant editor of The Times *from 1941 to 1946. Carr is the author of more than twenty books in modern history, international politics, socialism and communism, and Soviet politics.*

DEMOCRATIC GRADUALISM

The overriding principle of Fabianism, as of all democratic socialism, is that social change must be democratic, that is, acceptable to public opinion. Democratic socialists argue that the essential precondition for effective, lasting social change is a society prepared to accept such a change. This is the critical principle that makes democratic socialism altogether different from revolutionary socialist models. It is more than a dispute about tactics. The Fabians believe that change achieved through revolution is immoral. A revolution in the name of liberty thrust upon a people unprepared to receive it is not a liberating experience, but merely an exchange of tyrants. Socialism imposed by force in an alien setting will not long remain socialism. Change comes not through some bloody holocaust, but through the slow process of education and establishing democratic institutions. The Fabians argue that radical change cannot succeed where most of those affected by it consider it immoral.

It is easier to bring about a revolution to overthrow a discredited regime than it is to build a stable new order after the revolution by totally reconstructing a society along new principles. The Fabians recognize this, preferring the hard work of practical reforms, in even such mundane matters as the provision of a municipal water supply or the working conditions in laundries, to the glamour of revolutionary heroics. Indeed, many went so far as to protest that if it could be demonstrated that socialism could not be introduced without a revolution, then socialism would have to be abandoned because the price would be too high. This is the essence, the core of democratic socialism. Change must be brought about within the existing institutional framework. Non-democratic or violent change is rejected both because it is improper and because, in the long run, it will fail.

This insistence on democratic change, moving no faster than public opinion is prepared to accept, is more than a dispute with revolutionary socialists over means. It represents a major dispute about the nature and purpose of the good society. The revolutionary socialists regard the reformers as misguided opponents, betraying the long-term interests of the workers for short-term concessions. Democratic socialists are portrayed as being unwitting tools of capitalist imperialists, perpetuating a capitalist order by easing the revolutionary stresses on the oppressed working classes. By pacifying the workers with a few concessions, such as an improvement in their standard of living or a little economic security, the reformers allegedly deny the workers their full inheritance. To the Marxists, democratic socialists are allies in the perpetuation of capitalism, and so enemies of the proletariat. By this argument, the welfare state, rather than being a stage in the development of socialism, serves principally to strengthen and sustain capitalism. Democratic socialist parties must always confront the issue of whether their goal should be a more humane capitalism in which the social good is more widely shared, or whether to press for a more radical reconstruction of society along socialist lines.

The second element of democratic socialism, which demands that change be gradual as well as democratic, widens the gulf between democratic and revolutionary socialism even further. It is axiomatic to democratic socialism that fundamental change can only be brought about by an irresistible series of minor reforms. Great change must occur slowly, for it is, said Sidney Webb, "through the slow and gradual turning of the popular mind to new principles that social reorganization bit by bit comes."[22]

If social change is to be effective in making a lasting impact on the lives and habits of the people, each stage must prepare the ground for the next, each reform provide the logic and explanation, and establish the necessity of the next. All this must proceed slowly, step by step. Societies can evolve no faster than their citizens can be persuaded to accept. Under such a concept it is the task of government to lead, to innovate, to suggest, but to go no further than public opinion will tolerate. A democratic socialist government must constantly put its record and its proposals before the electorate. Gradualism is, thus, not just tactical caution. It is a moral principle. One that concerns the relationship of change to the unity of an organic, continuing community.

Through gradualism one can adapt, learn from one's mistakes, make adjustments as circumstances require, and backtrack when necessary. Gradual change is likely to be more stable than change resulting from the violence of revolution. Sidney Webb's somewhat tongue-in-cheek doctrine was that gradual reform produces a revolution without anybody noticing it. He worked from the principle that the easiest way to change a society was to persuade the defenders of the status quo that all the innovations were really a continuation of the established order and that nothing very extraordinary was happening.

ON HUMAN NATURE

The most fundamental component of democratic socialism is the desire to replace competitive individualism by a co-operative community. Much has been made of the old inspirational cry of the French Revolution—Liberty! Equality! Fraternity!—but so far the discussion in this book has been focussed on the interplay of liberty and equality. Little has been said about fraternity, even by socialists. Yet fraternity, in the sense of a freely offered fellow-ship, or a spirit of altruism, properly belongs in the soul of socialism. It provides, or ought to provide, the inner meaning, the unifying force, to the various policy proposals of socialist movements.

The belief that competitiveness and acquisitiveness are ingrained attri-butes of an unchanging human nature is discarded. The canon of liberal-ism that claims *all* people are motivated solely by the selfish desire to ad-vance their own well-being is rejected as a class-biased over-simplification. Unquestionably, many people act selfishly and thereby profit, at least ac-cording to their own criteria of profit. But socialists do not make the jump from the observed activity of some to the inherent nature of all. The fact that large numbers of people are often selfish is not proof that all people must be selfish. Except in a strictly biological sense, socialists do not there-fore believe in a fixed human nature, especially one that limits human activity to egoistic, acquisitive behaviour. Instead of viewing the political and economic arrangements of capitalism as being peculiarly suited to meet the needs of naturally selfish beings, and therefore something to be changed only at society's peril, socialists argue that capitalist institutions are de-signed to reward competitive *behaviour* so that people are encouraged to behave in this way. Consequently, if the arrangements themselves were changed to reward a different kind of behaviour, people would learn to act in a different manner. With a change in social structures, people could gain as much satisfaction from co-operative endeavour as they do now out of competing with each other. They could learn to desire to work together and could enjoy as much social and psychological satisfaction out of shar-ing or co-operating, as our present society has led them to believe they must get from competing, achieving, winning, and so on. With good will one could create a genuine fraternal community. Liberals see social arrange-ments as responding to human *nature*, while socialists think of human *behaviour* as a reaction to social arrangements.

So, let us summarize the components of democratic socialism. First, it is democratic, committed to institutionalized, legitimized procedures, and therefore, it rejects revolution in favour of gradual change. It is egalitarian in spirit, seeing the source of genuine liberty for all in some level of eco-nomic equality. In its preference for co-operation over competition, it is committed to the replacement of the private ownership of at least the major instruments of production, distribution, and exchange by public own-ership. Because it is organic in its understanding of society, it accepts that society as a whole is responsible for the well-being of all its members. And it is optimistic about changing human behaviour.

Now, having dealt in the last three chapters with the major ideological divisions in a liberal democratic society, you should pause to reassess your own position. Ask yourself which of the three ideologies comes closest to matching your own world view. The sources that influenced the development of your set of attitudes are so varied that it is unlikely that your personal understanding of society and its purpose will fit exactly into any one of these models. But you should be more sympathetic to one over the other, so you should be able to say whether you are at heart a conservative, a liberal, or a socialist.

CHAPTER FOURTEEN

The Democratic Ideology

Liberalism, toryism, and socialism, as they have been described in the previous three chapters, are all ideologies. In some academic circles the word *ideology* has acquired a highly specialized, technical meaning. More popularly it is a derogatory expression for the ill-considered, emotion-ridden rationalizations that *other* people set up against *our* reasoned philosophies and ideas. It is fair game to dismiss contradictory arguments as "mere ideology." Neither of these interpretations is intended here. An ideology here means any broadly coherent body of cognitive and evaluative elements, accepted as facts or truths, through which the members of a group order the conduct of their public lives.

Individually, each person is guided by a set of attitudes — a complex of relatively enduring beliefs about the nature of the world and about appropriate ways of dealing with situations as they arise. These attitudes are predispositions to respond with approval or disapproval, belief or disbelief, to external events. Attitudes are the initial internal, evaluative responses to information about places, peoples, or events.[1] We hold to our attitudes because we believe them to be true, and therefore, for us our attitudes are the truth. They are the correct judgments of the world. For each individual, attitudes arise from a combination of many variables: unique personality traits, the processes of socialization, learning, and indoctrination, and the accumulated life experiences.[2] But although there is a complete attitude pattern unique to each person, those of similar backgrounds and experiences will have many attitudes in common. Members of any community or group will share some more or less structured set of beliefs, unifying the group and setting it apart from other groups. This set of shared attitudes is the basis of a group ideology through which its members define acceptable and unacceptable responses. It provides them with a shared set of beliefs, which are the assurances they need for an explanation of the world and of their own place in it. An ideology, a mixture of factual and moral beliefs, thus plays a major role in the creation of both individual and community values. It has no independent objective existence of its own, being merely an abstraction, a perception in the minds of its holders, a shared view of the world and its purpose. An ideology is neither planned nor consciously constructed; it is

> a slow emergent product rooted in social character, culture and history. . . . the enormous brain-filling, painfully learned store of principles, doctrines, dogma, premises, values, theories, prejudices, habits, codes, defenses, and the like, with which the mind is furnished.[3]

The ideology provides a mechanism for organizing the tremendous complexity of the world, reducing it to something the individual can understand and cope with.

THE IDEOLOGY OF LIBERAL DEMOCRACY

The three separate ideologies so far examined can all be fairly comfortably subsumed under the larger ideology of liberal democracy. This assumes some level of internal diversity. A liberal democracy neither achieves nor requires complete ideological conformity. A variety of individual attitude sets may coalesce under a few ideological banners. A perfect democracy might be a system in which a multitude of people, without any external pressure or compulsion, peacefully arrive at a consensus. That clearly being an impossible ideal, we accept that people will reach different conclusions about what ought to be done and how it should be done, in the absence of compulsion, or an unrelenting totalitarian indoctrination. Democracy, then, must establish some sort of machinery not for imposing unity on these differences, nor for governing without them, but for accepting their continued existence as something right and proper. It is part of the ideology of liberal democracy that people may properly disagree about certain things. Within Canada, the spectrum of legitimate political faiths encompasses everything from the remnants of a traditional pre-liberal toryism, through all the shades of liberalism, to at least the fringes of democratic socialism.

Authoritarian opponents of democracy, those who would dispense with arguing or debating to impose their own solutions, dismiss democracy as time-wasting and inefficient. But for 2,500 years wiser counsels have acknowledged that ill-considered action is more dangerous than delayed action. In 431 B.C., the first year of the Peloponnesian War, the Athenian general Pericles, in his Funeral Oration, set out one of the fundamental elements in the ideals of Athenian democracy:

> [We] Athenians are able to judge at all events if we cannot originate, and instead of looking on discussion as a stumbling-block in the way of action, we think it an indispensable preliminary to any wise action at all.[4]

PERICLES

Born c.495 B.C.; *died 429* B.C.

Athenian statesman and general. Although he became leader of the democratic movement in Athens from 461 B.C. *until his death, Pericles was the unchallenged ruler of the city. He was largely responsible for the building of the Parthenon and other great buildings. These architectural triumphs are among the reasons why the period of his rule is referred to as the golden age of Athens. His ambition to make Athens "The School of Greece" was one of the factors that aroused resistance to Athenian expansion and the war that eventually led to the defeat of Athens by Sparta. He died of the plague in the first year of the Peloponnesian war. Although his own rule was near absolute, Pericles instituted many reforms to strengthen Athenian democracy.*

But while liberal democracy implies a broad tolerance of ideological pluralism, a willingness to discuss alternatives, there are boundaries. Democracy, although many things, is not all things. No bending of the language allows for the inclusion of, say, the Republic of South Africa, Kampuchea, or Paraguay among the democracies. Neither military juntas nor hereditary autocracies belong in the democratic tradition. The Roman Catholic Church is not democratically governed, nor are most large corporations, naval vessels, or high schools. The task, therefore, is to arrive at some criteria, some defining characteristics, that would enable us to say, "These things are necessary for there to be a democracy, and those things make it impossible." It will not do, as many modern writers seem to suggest, to define democracy simply in terms of the practices of specific countries. A common proposition is that there are certain nations (Canada, the United

States, Great Britain, and so on) which are commonly called "the democracies." What they do is therefore democratic. This is an inadequate and misleading approach, offering no standard for determining which nations properly belong among those "commonly called" democracies, nor for distinguishing *commonly* called from *correctly* called. Worse, it reduces democracy to machinery, with no consideration of the ends to which that machinery is to be put. It attempts to settle the ideological differences within democracy by denying any ideological content. Yet, as has been implicit throughout this book, democracy is more than a form of government; it is an ideology, a way of looking at the world and at the goals of human endeavour. The lasting worth of democracy is in its moral objectives, not just in its decision-making machinery.

Before the nineteenth century, with only occasional exceptions, neither political theorists nor practising politicians approved of democracy. Plato included it among the corrupt forms of government, only slightly preferred to tyranny. For Plato the specific curse of democracy was the ignorance and incompetence of politicians, who elevated opinion over knowledge. To most it meant the rule of the unlettered and the unwashed, the reign of the ignorant mob, destructive of all good order and civilized living. It has been held responsible for many evils, including, even, that of taking the glamour out of war:

> War, which used to be cruel and magnificent, has now become cruel and squalid. In fact it has been completely spoilt. It is all the fault of Democracy and Science.[5]

PLATO

Born 427 B.C.; died in Athens, 347 B.C.

Plato's Republic is still one of the greatest introductions to the most basic problems that confront human beings as citizens. At the heart of all his thinking is the proposition that political and social questions can be resolved by reason and critical analysis. Plato was deeply influenced by the life, and death, of his teacher, Socrates. Much in the Republic is explicitly undemocratic, but Plato's emphasis on rationalism and the need to search for the good (i.e. the moral) life, give little comfort to modern anti-democrats. After more than two thousand years Plato's influence is undiminished. He is the most able exponent of an aristocratic intellec-

tual theory of the state. The Republic is important also for its theories of the nature and purpose of education. His Academy survived for centuries as one of the great centres of learning in the ancient world.

For further reading see:

Barker, Ernest. Greek Political Theory: Plato and his Predecessors. *London: Methuen, 1918.*

Crossman, R.H.S. Plato Today. *London: Allen and Unwin, 1937.*

Foster, M.B. The Political Philosophy of Plato and Hegel. *Oxford: Clarendon Press, 1935.*

Popper, K.R. The Open Society and its Enemies. *Part I. London: Routledge and Kegan Paul, 1945.*

Thorson, T.L. Plato: Totalitarian or Democrat? *Englewood Cliffs: Prentice-Hall, 1963.*

But since the nineteenth century, despite individual exceptions such as that just quoted, most of the world has accorded near universal approval at least to the *language* of democracy. Democracy has come to be associated with some collection of positive values, to the extent that any regime that has, claims to have, or is perceived to have some of these values is labelled a democracy. Barry Holden called it a "Hurrah" word. " 'This political system is a democracy' could be rephrased as 'Hurrah for this political system.' "[6] The primary danger in all this is the dilution of the term to the point of meaninglessness. A safer line of argument might be to agree that there are several forms of government of which we can approve because they serve their countries' needs. Yet not all of them are democracies. Therefore democracy is not the only system worthy of approval.

Once the forms of democracy were established as the major source of political legitimacy, few dared admit to being anti-democratic. But although many nations now pledge their allegiance to democracy, this does not mean they are united by a common ideal.[7] The Soviet satellites in East Europe favour the word *democratic* in their formal titles. This does not mean they, or the Soviet Union itself, are or claim to be democracies in the sense of the term in Western nations. They conceive democracy, not in terms of a free enterprise economy, a democratic franchise, and a system of competing parties, but as the abolition of an oppressive capitalist class of the owners of production. Democracy means the liberation of the proletariat from their former class dependence. Political democracy is held to be less important than, or at least dependent upon, economic democracy, which is achieved when the means of production are owned by "the people." Both the Soviet Union and the United States might agree that democracy means "government by the people." But they have markedly different conceptions of how the people might be said to govern. For one, the necessary criterion is competition among two or more political parties. For the other the primary condition is the abolition of a ruling class of bourgeois property owners.

Many of the former European colonies in Africa and elsewhere see democracy as a process for obtaining mass support for a vision of national independence, with freedom from the vestiges of a colonial mentality. The goals of modernization, increased productivity, and national self-awareness require the unifying force of a single-party rule that is, therefore, the instrument of democracy, not its antithesis.

All this, of course, complicates the task of defining democracy, the vagueness and ambiguity being exacerbated by the deep emotional connotations of the term. It is not, however, the purpose of this chapter to argue the validity or value of alternative understandings of democracy.[8] They serve simply to illustrate the point that democracy does not mean the same thing to everyone, everywhere. Two things need to be kept in mind: (1) Our interpretation of democracy is not universally shared, and (2) Others may be quite sincere when they explain democracy in different terms.

The subject matter of this book has been one particular historically-rooted form of democracy called *liberal democracy*. Unless otherwise noted, democracy here has meant *liberal* democracy, the form of democracy that prevails in Canada, the United States, the United Kingdom, Australia, New Zealand, much of Western Europe, and other places with similar arrangements. However, while the unique character of Western democracy is bedded in its liberal foundations,[9] the dominance of liberalism is, in varying degrees in different countries, modified by two countervailing forces. As has been explained in previous chapters, there survive, on the one side, the remnants of an earlier, land-owning, paternalistic toryism, whose effect in Great Britain or in Canada is to change the character of Conservative parties, softening the ruthlessness of the strict laissez-faire doctrine. On the other hand, there is in many countries a viable, legitimate democratic socialism, which further limits the hegemony of liberalism. Toryism and democratic socialism have only limited credibility in the United States, where almost the entire political spectrum is within the bounds of liberalism, ranging from a pristine competitive individualism to some far-reaching concepts of economic planning, state interventionism, and humanitarianism.

LIBERALISM AND DEMOCRACY

Liberal democracy emerged as a largely accidental combination of a set of values associated with economic liberalism and a particular set of political arrangements.[10] The accidental character of the association is stressed, for it was neither inevitable, nor originally intended. With few exceptions the early liberals were not democrats. Just as it is possible to be democratic without being liberal, so it is possible to be liberal without being democratic. Remember that slavery was legal in parts of the liberal United States until 1865. The democratization of liberalism came later in response to other demands that could no longer be ignored. Liberalism had once been a radical force directed to the destruction of outmoded, restrictive institutions. It emerged as a means of providing fresh opportunities for a new generation of inventive, ambitious, and energetic individuals. The political machinery to accomplish these ends, constitutional limits on royal absolutism, the development of representative institutions, and a limited extension of the franchise, was democratic only in comparison with what preceded it.

The major function of these new democratic institutions was to provide the maximum protection for a competitive market economy and for the capitalist class that it benefitted. The primary objective was to free the new adventurous entrepreneurs from the constraints and inhibitions of a traditional mercantilist value system. The new democracy safeguarded the rights of property owners and employers. Bentham saw it as the institutionalization of the values of an enlightened, propertied middle class whose informed, rational opinions would rescue society both from the inevitable corruption and excesses of royal absolutism, and from the irrational popular clamor and class interests of the illiterate masses. While democracy supposedly meant government by the will of the people, that is, by public opinion, public opinion was itself narrowly defined. Public opinion was not the opinion of all members of the public. According to one early nineteenth century commentator:

> Public opinion may be said to be that sentiment on any given subject which is entertained by the best informed, most intelligent, and most moral persons in the community, which is gradually spread and adopted by nearly all persons of any education or proper feeling in a civilized state.[11]

As a corollary of extending political power to the propertied middle classes, there was also a second objective, that of safeguarding the newly acquired powers of the capitalist class from further erosion by the sellers of wage labour. The vote was originally granted only to those who posed no threat to the owners of property. No thought was given to extending political, and therefore economic, power to the working classes. John Stuart Mill designed elaborate measures to ensure that, although in accordance with the logic of democracy all citizens should have a vote, the numerical superiority of the working classes would not undermine the continued rule of the rational and responsible middle classes.

So, as economic liberalism was established, a limited democratic political machinery was set up to strengthen it. In such a laissez-faire model, governments would do as little as possible. The state had only limited responsibility for housing, education, welfare, pure foods, industrial safety, town planning, or the promotion of industry. The only functions of government were the preservation of law and order, the protection of property, and the enforcement of contracts.[12]

DEVELOPMENTAL DEMOCRACY

By the late nineteenth century it had become clear to all but those who refused to look that laissez-faire liberalism was not producing the greatest happiness of the greatest number. There was obviously no "harmony of egoisms" between the rich and poor. While there were marvellous new inventions, enormous personal fortunes, and unprecedented industrial expansion, the masses of the great industrial cities lived in conditions of poverty and degradation that denied all possibility of human freedom and human dignity. The lives of the agricultural labourers were scarcely above those of the animals they tended. As a result, under pressure from many sources, including both a newly emergent social conscience and a fear of the growing strength of socialist and proletarian movements, liberalism underwent a partial transformation into what C.B. Macpherson has called "developmental democracy."[13]

The new liberalism sought ways to offset the concentration of political and economic power in too few hands. It attempted to defuse potentially dangerous opposition by some acknowledgement of the validity of the claims of the working classes for a larger share in the prosperity of the new industrial society. This new generation of liberals sought ways to ameliorate the harsher effects of capitalism through social reforms and financial and economic controls that still left the basic philosophic assumptions intact. Although the owners of capital still defined the ends and conditions of production, and set the price of labour, new regulations made some concessions to the rights of the propertyless. The democratic institutions that once protected nascent capitalism were gradually used for wider social purposes to protect the weaker from the ugliest consequences of capitalism. The new model, not content with the state as a policeman, accepted increasingly broad social and moral responsibilities. It acknowledged the obligation to protect the weak from abuse by the over-powerful. Most significantly, it recognized the exploitative and class-divisive character of the primitive laissez-faire model. The new democratic liberalism became more socially conscious, more humanitarian, more alert to the needs of the greater common good, and less trusting of an automatic good emerging from an unchecked marketplace. Since its principles were first cautiously expressed by J.S. Mill, and greatly expanded by T.H. Green, this version of democracy has contended with the older model for popular support. Within the United States the ideological battle is largely between laissez-faire economic liberals and developmental or progressive liberals.

C.B. MACPHERSON

Born in Toronto November 18, 1911.

C.B. Macpherson, one of Canada's most distinguished scholars in political theory, has been Professor of Political Science at the University of Toronto since 1956. In this period he has also held appointments as a visiting professor at several universities outside Canada and is the recipient of a number of honorary doctorates. He is a Fellow of the Royal Society of Canada and of the Royal Historical Society. His books include: Democracy in Alberta *(1953),* The Political Theory of Possessive Individualism *(1962),* The Real World of Democracy *(1965),* The Life and Times of Liberal Democracy *(1971), and* Burke *(1980).*

EQUILIBRIUM DEMOCRACY

An alternative version of liberal democracy is what Macpherson called the "equilibrium model," or the "pluralist elitist model."

> It is pluralist in that it starts from the assumption that the society which a modern democratic political system must fit is a plural society, that is, a society consisting of individuals each of whom is pulled in many directions

by his many interests, now in company with one group of his fellows, now with another. It is elitist in that it assigns the main role in the political process to a self-chosen group of leaders. It is an equilibrium model in that it presents the democratic process as a system which maintains an equilibrium between the demand and supply of political goods.[14]

This version of democracy emerged in the middle of the present century partly in response to a new mood among some political scientists who tried to avoid the debate about the ends of good government by denying that there was any issue to debate. It was part of a new enthusiasm for a purely empirical political science set apart from moral considerations.

The essential feature of this model is thus its conscious avoidance of ethical questions about the ends of government. Instead it postulates that democracy is nothing more than a machinery for deciding who the governors shall be. It asserts that, while "government by the people" has a ring to it, the people have never governed, and in fact cannot govern themselves. As governing will always be the responsibility of the few, the democratic element consists in establishing effective machinery to see to it that the people can in practice achieve the one thing still within their capacity: an effective voice in choosing their governors. It implies that the most important tasks of ordinary citizens are to express preferences among competing elites organized into parties and, through structured interest groups, to bring pressure on those parties. Primarily an American concept, it turns aside from concerns with the moral ends of society to focus on democracy as the study of voting behaviour.[15]

By reducing democracy to a market mechanism, with the politicians as entrepreneurs and the voters as consumers, it is not much more than an updated version of the older laissez-faire optimistic view, such as the view expressed by Mill that, if all opinions could be freely asserted, the "truth" and the "public good" would prevail. It departs from that original version not only by a firmer assertion of the rights of all citizens instead of just the owners of capital to participate, but also by its emphasis on democracy as machinery, not ends. It has been much more successful in democratizing the right to vote than in democratizing the process for the selection of those who may be voted for.

Equilibrium democracy accords well with other market models, which, in part, explains its ready acceptance in the United States. Opinions and ideas become part of a free market in which unregulated trade and competition ensure the public good. The device to achieve the goals of marketplace politics is a set of brokerage parties that avoid any solid ideological commitment, existing simply to offer consumers (voters) the best deal.[16]

The competing parties seek power by offering platforms and policies instead of goods, while the people pick their preferred policy, buying it with their vote. Under such a conception there seems no fundamental objection to turning over an election campaign to an advertising agency as just another marketing problem. Current Canadian political practice is fully in accord with this model.

PARTICIPATORY DEMOCRACY

Critics of democracy as a marketplace of ideas countered with the objection that the opinion market was as restricted in practice as its economic variant and, further, that the elite who controlled the economic marketplace also controlled the opinion market. One solution to these obvious inadequacies and anti-democratic tendencies, was an innovation called "participatory democracy," a widely trumpeted concept during the 1960s and 1970s. Democracy, it was argued, can be a reality only when citizens become more deeply involved in government policy and decision-making; when they collectively act to initiate policies rather than merely to approve or disapprove those offered by competing elites. Public opinion, previously discounted as nothing more than a legitimizing force in democracy, was to be elevated to a more regular, structured interventionist role. People would participate not only occasionally by the brief act of marking a ballot, but also through continuous involvement in parties and in the organized articulation of their group interests. Political participation may be defined as those voluntary activities through which citizens attempt to influence the selection of their political leaders or the decisions taken by those leaders.[17] The people would, for the first time, genuinely govern themselves. In many ways this was a return to nineteenth-century ideals of a well-informed, concerned citizenry, alert to its power to influence events. The difference is that the nineteenth-century writers restricted "public opinion" to that small segment of the middle classes who might actually share these characteristics; whereas the modern advocates of participatory democracy claimed they wanted to extend it to the entire population.

This is, perhaps, where a certain lack of realism crept in. In a liberal democratic society, where people are free to pursue their own interests, one cannot easily persuade the uninvolved and the uninterested to become model democratic citizens. There is an unfortunate tendency among some intellectuals and political enthusiasts to assume that they are interested in public affairs because they are civic-minded people aware of the importance of public duty. The world, they argue, would be a better place if everyone modelled their lives after theirs and joined in their concerns. They do not easily accept the idea that they are interested in these things simply because they find them interesting in the same way as other people are interested in soap operas, making money, automobiles, or ballet.

Despite the best efforts of the democratic-process activists, there is little evidence of any strongly held, inherent inclination for most people to become regularly involved in politics. In practice, participation has seldom matched the criteria of informed, rational, tolerant political activity required by traditional democratic theory. The consequences of an enforced participation by those who do not really care, and who make no effort to inform themselves, could well be disastrous. There is, for example, no evidence to suggest that Australia, where voting is compulsory, is any more democratically governed than is Canada, or that there is any more widespread political awareness. Worse still is the prospect that the fact of participation might be artificially inflated to give the appearances of a greater public demand than might really be the case. "Write-in" campaigns and referenda can exaggerate the capacity of a small, well-organized segment of society to impose its image of the world on an indifferent, apathetic, or otherwise preoccupied majority. Extreme involvement, high pressure participation, can result in a rigid fanaticism or unyielding partisanship.

On the other hand, of course, too little involvement, a silence or apathy too widely spread, is easily interpreted as acquiescence. It is common for those in power to assume that the absence of publicly voiced objection is the same as consent or approval. Citizen withdrawal from the political process works almost exclusively to the advantage of the status quo, and to the preservation of the power of entrenched elites. There is a fine balance to be drawn between active participatory involvement, which holds political leaders accountable, and an artificial, formal participation, which could weaken the effectiveness of the genuinely concerned.

Some have asserted that while the idealism behind more democratic participation was praiseworthy, the model in its more uncritical forms placed the demands on democratic citizenship unreasonably high.[18] It ignored the complexity of political affairs, discounting the other demands on the time and energy of individuals. Above all it ignored the real problem that, if citizens are to participate intelligently they must have a readily available, easily intelligible source of more or less complete and objective information. This is so far from the reality of any advanced society that it nullifies whatever merit the idea might have in principle. All governments systematically withhold from their people the information essential for the genuinely intelligent participation of the electorate. The most carefully guarded secret of all is the extent of official secrecy.[19] Even members of opposition parties who devote their entire energy to the heart of the political process cannot get adequate information from the government or the bureaucracy. It might be true in theory that democratic governments ought to respond more directly to public opinion. In practice this would not be easy to achieve.

Most of the real issues governments have to deal with are of such complexity that it would be almost impossible to frame questions in a form that could be intelligently or usefully answered by the general public. Even such an apparently straightforward issue as capital punishment would not be readily resolved by a direct appeal to the "will of the people." Beyond a simple, and rather meaningless, "yes" or "no" to the question "Do you favour capital punishment?" innumerable qualifications would have to be dealt with. For precisely what crimes, in what circumstances, subject to what level of discretion by judges or juries, under what extenuating circumstances, and with what rights of appeal would the death penalty apply? Would there be categories of murder to be treated differently: murder of police officers or prison guards, murder in the commission of another crime, terrorist murder, and so on? Would it apply only to murder, or to other crimes as well, or instead? So many answers could be given to these, and many other possible questions, that the public voice would be more likely to confuse rather than resolve the question.

An objective appraisal of how people behave demonstrates that constructive proposals come rarely from the people as a whole. The "will of the people" is not an initiating will of some organic being, but rather the generally passive agreement by some large number to what is put before them, or what is expressed in their name, by some single individual or by a very small group. Collectively the people do not govern, although in the best of circumstances they may freely and genuinely approve of what their governments are doing.

THE UNIFYING ELEMENTS

If they have done nothing else, these several versions of what liberal democracy might involve illustrate the inadequacy of dictionary definitions. Whatever else it might be, democracy is not "government of the people, by the people, for the people." But behind all the variations, there is a faith, an ideology that sustains and unifies liberal democracy, distinguishing it from alternative meanings of democracy, from the non-democratic aspects of liberalism, as well as from other overtly anti-democratic ideologies. For democracy is an ideology, a normative faith in some meaning and purpose of life. It is not just a neutral machinery for processing whatever is fed into it, although the nature of that machinery may be critical to the achievement of the goal.

Although in their pure form they are too simplistic, the etymological roots of the word do indicate a starting point: *demos*, the people, and *kratos*, rule. However it may be refined or qualified, democracy must have something to do with "the people" (however they may be identified) having some determining role in how they are governed. In the liberal version of democracy this has been taken to imply some notion of majority rule as a machinery for decision-making, together with some arrangements for the protection of minorities. As explained in chapter seven, both elements are essential. Since unanimity on most issues is impossible, a decision-making machinery is essential, for governments must govern with, or without, the consent of all the governed. But liberal democracy also recognizes that the will of the people as expressed in the ballot box is no more than the dominant view among those who actually vote. It is usually something far short of the will of *the people* in any organic or corporate sense, or even in the sense of the combined will of *all* the people. The verdict of a plurality of voters, who may have made their decisions on the basis of a variety of inconsistent or contradictory reasons, is not a valid expression of Rousseau's General Will. Recognizing that the majority vote is only a temporary and accidental aggregation, democracy will make concessions to the minority, whose members are, nevertheless, full members of the community. For, despite the assertions of the victors, it cannot be claimed that those who voted a party into office thereby gave their unanimous approval to every single policy of that party.

Democracy also involves some notion of representation. Beyond the smallest communities and certain private associations, direct democracy, government of the people by themselves, is impossible. Once the community becomes too large for all to meet together in one assembly, democracy must become a representative system. Representation, however, is a complex idea which, in the English language, has two distinct meanings. In one sense a representative means a "spokesperson for," such as a lawyer representing me in court or an ambassador representing my country abroad. The representative is an advocate, a qualified person, speaking on our behalf to protect our interest. This is what representation originally meant in the gradual evolution of parliament. When the people were represented by their "natural superiors," only a few were expected to have any say in the selection of those representatives. But representative also means "sample of" or "typical", as in "she represents the new generation of women" or "he represents the sports fan at his most boorish." Under the influence of democratic ideology these two principles became confused, so there emerged an expectation that parliaments, as assemblies of spokesmen, ought also to be assemblies of typical voters. Many today express regret that Parliament is not "representative" enough because it contains too few women, or ethnic minorities, or trade unionists, or too many lawyers, or whatever. Parliament, by this reasoning, ought to be a cross section of the nation. Yet in a system where each party, in each constituency, is free to select the candidate of its choice without any reference to what is being done by other parties, or in other constituencies, only the most wildly improbable set of coincidences could produce such a result.

Accepting the goal of representation of the people is thus only the beginning of the problem. One must consider not only what is to be meant by representation, but also the machinery for achieving its ends. Consideration must be given to such questions as the eligibility of individuals to be candidates or voters. Voting rights may be restricted to those holding formal citizenship, by some arbitrarily defined age limit, or by length of residence in the district, or it may be denied, as in the United Kingdom, to criminals, the insane, and members of the House of Lords. Until fairly recently only males could vote (as late as 1940 for Quebec provincial elections); and generally only men owning certain minimum amounts of property. One must determine if the qualifications for candidates are to be the same as, or more restrictive than, those for voters. Limits may be imposed upon the amount of money candidates may raise or spend on their campaigns. In an open democracy all candidates should be assured reasonably equal facilities for presenting their programs to the electorate. Voting hours and the accessibility of polling places should be such that all have a reasonable opportunity to cast their ballots. If all votes are to have an approximately equal weight, the disparity in the populations of electoral districts must not be so great as to give some electors far greater representation than others. It is necessary to demonstrate that all votes are fairly counted. The voting system itself ought to produce results reasonably reflecting the wishes of the electorate, not being so designed as to give permanent advantages or disadvantages to one or more parties. The boundaries of electoral districts must be impartially drawn so as not to bias the results too heavily. The way in which these practical questions are resolved will determine, in large part, the kind of objectives the system can be expected to pursue.

Democracy needs also to be concerned with the relationships between the people and their elected representatives. It is part of the democratic ideal that representatives should be accountable to the represented. But how accountable?

But it is now, I think, recognized that if you set up a government in which men will immediately be hauled up if they do wrong, they may very easily be hauled up if they do right and you will not get a government capable of doing anything at all.[20]

With too little accountability there may be an abuse of power, and with too much there may be stagnation. All this points to some very significant differences between elitist and participatory theories of democracy. In the United States, traditional notions of democracy, well-rooted in populist history, accord tremendous authority and prestige to the ballot box. As well as representatives in Congress, state legislatures, and local government, Americans elect their chief executive, state governors, a wide range of officials, even sometimes to the level of chiefs of police, judges, sheriffs, county auditors, attorneys-general, coroners, and so on. The more elitist British confine the electoral process to the selection of representatives at either the national or the local government level. This is also a guiding principle in Canada, although here the process may be broadened to include school boards and various public utilities commissions. Outside the United States it is more widely accepted that popular election is not a reliable instrument for the selection of the experts responsible for much of the day-to-day business of government. The same desire to limit popular control over the activities of representatives led to the abandonment of early proposals for annual parliaments.[21] Too frequent elections make it extremely difficult for a government to get on with the task of governing. Governments must, from time to time, do unpopular things, and must compel all people some of the time to do, or refrain from doing, something against their will. Given a reasonably long interval between elections, governments have an opportunity to do as they feel they must and then let time determine the wisdom or otherwise of their actions.

The idea of democracy also involves some consideration of the ends to which the machinery is directed. Here the principle of equality, especially political and legal equality, must be accorded high priority. Democracy began as a doctrine of equality, a radical assault on the ancient privileges of hierarchy and rank. At least in theory it meant an equality before the law. To de Tocqueville, for example, democracy and egalitarianism were almost synonymous. But his was a social and political equality, which was optimistically assumed to give all an equal chance to improve their economic well-being. It took time for some to accept that the consequent economic inequalities negated the possibility of that social and political equality, which was supposed to be its foundation. Because extreme economic inequality appears incompatible with other equalities, democracy cannot survive without some moderation of at least the worst excesses of economic inequality. This, in turn, would seem to be best achieved not by the imposition of upper limits but by the guaranteeing of some minimum level of economic security commensurate with the full life of a citizen. As the complex issues of equality of opportunity and the equality of condition were discussed in chapter six, they do not need to be repeated here.

The liberal element of liberal democracy implies some component of private property, especially the private ownership of productive capacity and the private purchase of labour. However, as demonstrated in chapter ten, private ownership is in practice today everywhere qualified by extensive public ownership, regulation, and control. The original concept of the private ownership of capital is also severely modified by the overgrowth of large corporations, both national and multinational. Individual capitalists, in the sense of those who invest their own money in some enterprise that they personally operate for their own advantage, now make a relatively minor contribution to the national economy. Their role has been taken over by giant enterprises, often employing tens of thousands managed by professional, salaried experts, under the control of Boards of Directors who need pay little heed to the hundreds of anonymous shareholders. Despite government intervention, social programs, and the occasional victories of the trade unions, capitalism still flourishes in Canada. The curbing of its excesses have, if anything, strengthened it. Ours is still a liberal society, even if the earliest entrepreneurial adventurers might not now recognize their creation.

Finally, liberal democracy must embrace some idea of personal freedom. Without liberty, liberal democracy has no meaning. This, of itself, is far too simple an assertion to be of much use, for, as indicated in chapter five, liberty is another ambiguous concept that can mean several quite different things. But whether liberty be a singular concept, an absence of legal restraint, especially in economic affairs, or whether it be a plural concept, implying a range of specific liberties that might be secured only through limiting economic liberty in some instances, liberty carries the assumption of self-willed choice of action. In a narrowly political sense related to the mechanics of democratic government it implies a freedom of association, a freedom to participate, or not participate, in political movements: parties seeking public office or groups advocating some special cause or interest. It implies the freedom of speech to propose or oppose various principles, to canvass for voter support, and to ask questions and demand answers. Democracy, as a system of ends, exists to promote the maximum possible human freedom compatible with the other objectives of a good society. For, as has already been demonstrated, there are bounds and limits in all issues of freedom. Liberty is circumscribed to the extent that it invades the equal liberties of others, or to the extent that it violates other rights, or causes unwarranted harm to some wider public good. It is a right, but not an absolute right.

CONCLUSION

If this book has had a unifying theme it is that in a liberal democracy people can and do disagree. As Canadian society has many roots, we should not be too surprised or discouraged to discover that friends and associates, otherwise apparently quite normal, persist in holding what to us are very peculiar political ideas. Even our most firmly held, most cherished beliefs, are disputed by others who are neither fools nor rogues. We also discover that political arguments are not only about policies and parties, nor simply about what governments should or should not do, nor just about the honesty or competence of this or that political leader. They are also about some quite fundamental philosophic assumptions on which policies are based. There cannot, for example, really be any very sensible argument about welfare payments to the unemployed unless there is first a settling of the question of the purpose of welfare, which in turn requires some understanding of the perceived purpose of any social activity.

The second theme is that this diversity of view is healthy. A liberal democratic society is not one in which all people must think alike. If everyone you meet is in very solid agreement on almost everything, there may be something seriously wrong. It may be because you live in a closed society where only one point of view is being disseminated. You and everyone else may be in agreement because none are given the opportunity or information to form independent judgments. It is only in dictatorships—whether formalized government dictatorships or the dictatorship of an intolerant public opinion—that all think alike. It is not a natural state of affairs. In a truly democratic society where there is no official truth, one must expect to find one's most fundamental beliefs questioned. A liberal democratic society is one that legitimizes, permits, and encourages a wide diversity of political philosophy and behaviour. It is a society in which people can agree to disagree.

In a liberal democratic society, sincerity of faith, conviction of being the possessor of ultimate truth, belief in having some dispensation from God, or being simply a member of a numerical majority do not confer absolute authority. No members of a democratic community believing in that democracy are entitled to deny to any other group in the society the same freedom of thought, expression, or behaviour they claim for them-

selves. No one in a democracy is infallible. This does not preclude some constraints on free speech. In Canada, for example, one may not legally advocate or preach race hatred nor incite people to the violent overthrow of government. These are outlawed not because they are "wrong" or unpopular but because their expression causes intolerable harm to other Canadians or to society at large. The ultimate goal of democracy is, surely, some version of what Bentham once called "the greatest happiness of the greatest number." In other words, it is an idea that the purpose of political activity is to liberate the human spirit, enabling the greatest possible number of people to pursue their own version of the good life, to the extent that it does not impede the exercise of the same freedom by others.

Even in the most non-democratic, illiberal society, in the most rigid autocracy, or the most absolute despotism, some argument has to be tolerated, if only because the machinery does not exist to prevent it. And even the most rigid ideological movements tend to break into warring factions. But in the dictatorships the limits of permissible dissent are very narrow. Outside those limits, dissent, disagreement, debate, become illegal, punishable offences. On the other hand, in even the most liberal of liberal democracies there are limits beyond which one may not legitimately wander. One can generalize by saying that the wider the limits, the more democratic the society is. The principle has elsewhere been expressed:

> Liberal democracies define political crimes narrowly as the use of force, or the advocacy of such use, against the state. Totalitarian or authoritarian regimes extend the definition to include peaceful opposition to or criticism of the government. The definition of a political crime is an almost infallible test of the genuineness of liberal democracy.[22]

Here it is not being chauvinistic or ultra-patriotic to suggest that by these criteria Canada is a more democratic society than is, say, the United States. Within the United States the bounds of legitimate political positions, the views one may hold without losing public respect or being subject to public abuse, go no further than the outer limits of liberalism. The mainstream of American political controversy ranges from a far-right laissez-faire liberalism to a humanitarian, interventionist liberalism. Within Canada these boundaries are extended to include, on the one hand, some traces of a genuine tory conservatism and, on the other, a legitimate democratic socialism capable of winning respectable public support. This being so, Canada can properly claim to be a more tolerant society, and, therefore, a more democratic society.

Notes

CHAPTER ONE: POLITICS AND POLITICAL SCIENCE

1. The form of democracy we are familiar with in Canada, the United States, the United Kingdom, and other countries of a similar character should properly be referred to as "liberal democracy." The significance of the qualification and the distinction between liberal democracy and other possible democratic forms will become clearer as we proceed. In the meantime it is useful to become accustomed to the label, for this book is concerned almost exclusively with *liberal* democracy. For a useful account of the variations of democracy, see C.B. Macpherson, *The Real World of Democracy* (Toronto: Canadian Broadcasting Corp., 1965).
2. J.D.B. Miller, *The Nature of Politics* (Harmondsworth: Penguin Books, 1965), 54–55.
3. W.J.M. Mackenzie, *Politics and Social Science* (Harmondsworth: Penguin Books, 1967), 17.
4. Two books among many that attempt a review of the various theoretical approaches to politics are: Alan C. Isaak, *Scope and Methods of Political Science* (Homewood, Ill.: Dorsey Press, 1965) and J.C. Charlesworth, ed., *Contemporary Political Analysis* (New York: Free Press, 1967).
5. For a valuable account of some modern members of the Machiavellian school, see James Burnham, *The Machiavellians: Defenders of Freedom* (New York: John Day, 1943).
6. Niccolo Machiavelli, *The Prince* (New York: Modern Library, 1940), 56.
7. Niccolo Machiavelli, *The Discourses* (New York: Modern Library, 1940), 150.
8. Herman Finer, *Mussolini's Italy* (London: Gollancz, 1935), 218.
9. Allan R. Ball, *Modern Politics and Government* (London: Macmillan, 1979), 242.

10. Michael Oakeshott, "Political Education" (1951), reprinted in his *Rationalism in Politics, and Other Essays* (London: Methuen, 1962), 127.
11. See the quotation from St. Paul in chapter eight.
12. Jeremy Bentham, "The Principles of Morals and Legislation." In Bhikhu Parekh, ed., *Bentham's Political Thought* (London: Croom Helm, 1973), 66.
13. Karl Marx and Friedrich Engels, "Manifesto of the Communist Party (1848)." In Harold J. Laski, ed., *Communist Manifesto: Socialist Landmark* (London: George Allen and Unwin, 1967), 135. This edition of the *Manifesto*, with its lengthy Introduction by Laski, is probably the best available single-volume summary of the ideas of Marx.
14. Karl Marx, "The Eighteenth Brumaire of Louis Bonaparte (1852)." In R.C. Tucker, ed., *The Marx-Engels Reader*, 2nd ed. (New York: Norton, 1978), 595.

CHAPTER TWO: THE CONCEPT OF THE STATE

1. R.M. MacIver, *The Modern State* (Oxford: Oxford University Press, 1926), 22.
2. John Austin, *The Province of Jurisprudence Determined* (London: Murray, 1832), lect. 6.
3. Jacques Maritain, *Man and the State* (Chicago: Phoenix Books, 1951), 5.
4. Two excellent brief accounts of this changing society can be obtained from H.J. Laski, *The Rise of European Liberalism* (London: Unwin, 1936) and H.K. Girvetz, *The Evolution of Liberalism* (New York: Collier, 1963).
5. The concept of social contract does appear in both Greek and medieval political theory, but these earlier manifestations do not concern us here.
6. Thomas Hobbes, *Leviathan* (1651), ed. C.B. Macpherson (Harmondsworth: Penguin Books, 1972), 161.
7. Ibid., 186.
8. John Stuart Mill, *Principles of Political Economy* (1848; reprint London: Longmans, Green, 1904), 570.
9. Ibid., 572.
10. See Robert E. Lane, *Political Ideology* (New York: The Free Press, 1962).
11. The medieval concept of corporation is excellently treated in Otto Gierke, *Political Theories of the Middle Age* (Cambridge: Cambridge University Press, 1951), 22–30.
12. From Ernest Barker, *Greek Political Theory* (London: Methuen, 1960), 7.
13. F.C. Copleston, *Aquinas* (Harmondsworth: Penguin Books, 1955), 230.
14. T.H. Green, *Lectures on the Principles of Political Obligation* (London: Longmans, Green, 1927), sec. 18. These were delivered in 1879–90 and originally published posthumously in 1895.

CHAPTER THREE: THE NATURE OF RIGHTS

1. Sophocles, *The Theban Plays*, trans. E.F. Watling (Harmondsworth: Penguin Books, 1962), 138–39.
2. Cicero, *The Republic*, III, 22, as quoted by T.L. Thorson and G.H. Sabine, *A History of Political Theory*, 4th ed. (Hinsdale: Dryden Press, 1973), 161–62.
3. See John Locke, *Second Treatise on Civil Government* (1690), available in many editions, and for an excellent commentary, C.B. Macpherson, *The Political Theory of Possessive Individualism* (Oxford: Clarendon Press, 1962).
4. *The Charter of Rights and Freedoms: A Guide for Canadians* (Ottawa, 1982).
5. J.S. Murphy, *Political Theory: A Conceptual Analysis* (Homewood, Ill.: The Dorsey Press, 1968), 53.
6. A.P. d'Entreves, *Natural Law: An Introduction to Legal Philosophy* (London: Hutchinson, 1951), 13.
7. Bhikhu Parekh, *Bentham's Political Thought* (London: Croom Helm, 1973), 262.
8. Ernest Barker, *Political Thought in England, 1848–1914* (London: Oxford University Press, 1928), 32–37, for an excellent brief summary of the argument.

CHAPTER FOUR: FREEDOM OF EXPRESSION

1. C.J. Brown, et al., *The Media and the People* (New York: Holt, Rinehart and Winston, 1978), 152.
2. Schenck v. United States, 249 U.S. 47 (1919), at 52.
3. Niccolo Machiavelli, *The Discourses* (New York: Modern Library, 1940), 528.
4. *Reports of the Commission of Inquiry Concerning Certain Activities of the Royal Canadian Mounted Police*, vols. 1–3 (1979–81).
5. Brian Bunting, *The Rise of the South African Reich* (Harmondsworth: Penguin Books, 1964), 165, provides more details.
6. 341 U.S. 494 (1951), at 497.
7. Ibid., at 509.
8. Ibid., at 516–17.
9. Ibid., at 581–84.
10. John Stuart Mill, *Essay on Liberty* (1859) (New York: New American Library, 1962), 180–81.
11. A valuable explanatory tool for this strong psychological motivation to keep intact any related set of attitudes is what is called "cognitive dissonance." There is a large literature on this subject, beginning with Leon Festinger, *A Theory of Cognitive Dissonance* (London: Tavistock, 1959).

12. One of the worst offenders here, enforcing strictly the most rigid of Official Secrets Acts, and taking harshly punitive action against any offenders, is the government of the United Kingdom.
13. E.F. Williams, *Press, Parliament and People* (London: Heinemann, 1946), 64.
14. See, for example, R.D. Altick, *The English Common Reader: A Social History of the Mass Reading Public, 1800–1900* (Chicago: University of Chicago Press, 1957).
15. Ralph Miliband, *The State in Capitalist Society* (London: Quartet Books, 1973), 205.
16. Ibid., 213.
17. See, for example, J.J. Mathews, *Reporting the Wars* (Minneapolis: University of Minnesota Press, 1957) or Phillip Knightly, *The First Casualty* (New York: Harcourt Brace Jovanovich, 1975).
18. Williams, *Press, Parliament and People*, 66.

CHAPTER FIVE: THE MEANING OF LIBERTY

1. Isaiah Berlin, *Two Concepts of Freedom* (Oxford: Clarendon Press, 1958), 7.
2. The distinction between positive and negative freedom is well brought out in Isaiah Berlin, op. cit.
3. There are two excellent brief books that explore, from different perspectives, the relationship between these forces, especially as between capitalism and Protestantism. They are R.H. Tawney, *Religion and the Rise of Capitalism* (1926) and Max Weber, *The Protestant Ethic and the Spirit of Capitalism* (1930). Both have been reprinted several times.
4. See, for example, J.J. Ashton, *The Industrial Revolution 1760–1830* (London: Oxford University Press, revised 1969), 88–91.
5. Adam Smith, *Wealth of Nations* (New York: Modern Library, 1937), 324.
6. Ibid., 13.
7. Ibid., 14.
8. Ibid., 421.
9. Lionel Robbins, *The Theory of Economic Policy* (London: Macmillan, 1952), provides an excellent account of the economic functions of the state.
10. F.W. Coker, *Recent Political Thought* (New York: Appleton-Century, 1934), 394.
11. F.A. Hayek, *The Road to Serfdom* (Chicago: University of Chicago Press, 1944), and since reprinted many times.
12. Ibid., 41–42.
13. Ibid., 102.
14. E.S. Turner, *Roads to Ruin: The Shocking History of Social Reform* (Harmondsworth: Penguin Books, 1966), 238.
15. As quoted by John W. Dodds, *The Age of Paradox* (London: Gollancz, 1953), 158.
16. Henry Mayhew, *London Labour and the London Poor* (New York: Dover Publications, 1968). There are numerous works describing the appalling condi-

tions of the poor in the great industrial cities of the nineteenth century, but none can be more impressive than Mayhew's monumental study, first published in 1861.

17. T.H. Green, "Liberal Legislation and Freedom of Contract," a lecture delivered in 1881, and reprinted in J.R. Rodman, ed., *T.H. Green: Political Theory* (New York: Crofts Classics, 1964), 51.
18. Ibid., 52.
19. Ibid., 55.
20. Barbara Wootton, *Freedom Under Planning* (London: George Allen and Unwin, 1945), 9.
21. R.H. Tawney, *Equality*, 4th ed. (London: Unwin Books, 1952), 228.
22. Hayek, *Road to Serfdom*, 25–27.

CHAPTER SIX: QUESTIONS OF EQUALITY

1. Thomas Hobbes, *Leviathan*, ed. C.B. Macpherson (Harmondsworth: Penguin Books, 1972).
2. Canada, House of Commons, *Debates*, 1918, I, 643.
3. R.H. Tawney, *Equality*, 4th ed. (London: Unwin Books, 1952), 57.
4. Ibid., 228.
5. Oddly enough, in practice diamonds are one of the most rigidly price controlled and monopolized commodities on the market.
6. In practice, many with access to the black market were able to obtain much more than their "fair share."
7. Ralph Miliband, *The State in Capitalist Society* (London: Quartet Books, 1973), 237.
8. John Stuart Mill, *Essay on Liberty* (New York: New American Library, 1962) 196–97.
9. This is distinct from the privately funded great "public" schools, which are actually private schools for the privileged.
10. This has been only the sketchiest of outlines of the English education system. There are innumerable variations in detail both in the original scheme and in the changes in recent years. But none of these concern us here.
11. Alexis de Tocqueville, *Democracy in America* (1840), vol. 2, trans. Henry Reeve (London: World Classics, 1953), 594–96.

CHAPTER SEVEN: DEMOCRACIES AND MAJORITIES

1. Niccolo Machiavelli, *The Discourses* (New York: Modern Library, 1940), 263.
2. John Locke, *Second Treatise on Civil Government* (1690) (London: Dent, Everyman Edition, 1943), secs. 95 and 96.

3. It could be made true *by definition*; that is, we could define democracy as meaning simply majority rule. But we have in mind here something deeper than that, some concept of democracy as being concerned also with liberty, equality, the protection of rights, and so on.
4. Alexis de Tocqueville, *Democracy in America* (1835), vol. I, trans. Henry Reeve (London: Worlds Classics, 1953), 192–93.
5. Ibid., 193–94.
6. Ibid., 188.
7. See John Stuart Mill, Review of the two volumes of *Democracy in America*, by Alexis de Tocqueville, *Edinburgh Review* (October 1840): 1–47.
8. John Stuart Mill, *Essay on Liberty* (1859) (New York: New American Library, 1962), 142.
9. Ibid., 135.
10. Changed to direct popular election by the 17th Amendment in 1913.
11. The "People's Charter" in England proposed, in 1838, a six-point Charter that included annual parliamentary elections. It was rejected precisely because it would have been an instrument of direct popular democracy.
12. The development of party discipline has undermined this independence, but that is a matter beyond the immediate concern.
13. P.J. Stanlis, ed., *Edmund Burke: Selected Writings and Speeches* (New York: Anchor Books, 1963), 186–87. Burke lost this particular election.
14. G.H. Sabine, *A History of Political Theory*, 4th ed., T.L. Thorson, ed. (Hinsdale: Dryden Press, 1973), 492.
15. R.A. Dahl, *A Preface to Democratic Theory* (Chicago: University of Chicago Press, 1956), 36.

CHAPTER EIGHT: THE RIGHT TO DISSENT

1. A.D. Lindsay, *The Essentials of Democracy* (London: Oxford University Press, 1929), 29.
2. Ibid., 12. For a somewhat fuller summary.
3. Ibid., 12.
4. Ibid., 12–13.
5. John Locke, *Second Treatise on Civil Government* (1690) (London: Dent, Everyman edition, 1943), sec. 97.
6. C.W. Cassinelli, *The Politics of Freedom* (Seattle: University of Washington Press, 1961), 86–89.
7. Rom. 13:1–7.
8. Martin Luther, "On Good Works," trans. W.A. Lambert, *Werke*, vol. 6, 250.
9. John Knox, "Appellation." In G.H. Sabine, *A History of Political Theory*, 4th ed. (Hinsdale: Dryden Press, 1973), 345.
10. *Hansard*, vol. 9 (July 1807), 798.
11. For a brief but bitter account of the brutal and degrading punishments inflicted on those workers who tried to improve their lot, see Joyce Marlow, *The Tolpuddle*

Martyrs (London: Andre Deutsch, 1971). For a more thoroughly documented and more extensive account see the two excellent volumes by J.L. and Barbara Hammond: *The Village Labourer, 1760–1832* (London: Longmans, Green, 1913); and *The Town Labourer, 1760–1832* (London: Longmans, Green, 1917).

12. Ernest Barker, *Church, State and Education* (Ann Arbor: University of Michigan Press, 1957), 72–108. Read this essay, "A Huguenot Theory of Politics (1930)," for a brief but valuable account of the *Vindiciae* and its later significance.
13. Locke, *Second Treatise on Civil Government*, sec. 222.
14. See chapters three and five.
15. T.H. Green, *Lectures on the Principles of Political Obligation* (1882) (London: Longmans, Green, 1927), 117.
16. P.E. Trudeau, *Approaches to Politics* (Toronto: Oxford University Press, 1970), 35–37.
17. This happened in Hungary in 1956 when the Voice of America encouraged the uprising with promises of aid that the United States was in no way equipped to deliver.
18. Thomas Hobbes, *Leviathan*. ed. C.B. Macpherson (Harmondsworth: Penguin Books, 1972), chap. 21.

CHAPTER NINE: THE RIGHT OF PROPERTY

1. T.H. Green, *Lectures on the Principles of Political Obligation* (London: Longmans, Green, 1927), sec. 214.
2. Karl Marx and Friedrich Engels, "Manifesto of the Communist Party." In H.J. Laski, *Communist Manifesto: Socialist Landmark* (London: Allen and Unwin, 1967), 137–39.
3. There is a *First Treatise on Civil Government*, also published in 1690, but it is largely concerned with some obscure theological problems of no interest to the modern reader.
4. John Locke, *Second Treatise on Civil Government* (London: J.M. Dent, Everyman edition, 1943), sec. 25.
5. Ibid., sec. 26.
6. Ibid.
7. Ibid., sec. 27.
8. Ibid., sec. 30.
9. Ibid., secs. 47–48.
10. Ibid., sec. 50.
11. Ibid., sec. 36.
12. C.B. Macpherson, *The Political Theory of Possessive Individualism* (Oxford: The Clarendon Press, 1962), 215.
13. Locke, *Second Treatise on Civil Government*, sec. 33.
14. Asa Briggs, *Victorian Cities* (Harmondsworth: Penguin Books, 1971), 64.
15. Marx and Engels, "Manifesto," 145.

CHAPTER TEN: LIMITS ON PROPERTY

1. Walter Lippmann, *The Public Philosophy* (New York: Atlantic-Little, Brown & Co., 1955), 109.
2. J.L. and Barbara Hammond, *The Village Labourer, 1760–1832* (London: Longmans, Green, 1913).
3. Two of these have been summarized and paraphrased in J.W. Dodds, *The Age of Paradox* (London: Golancz, 1953), 161–64. The first, dated 1840, is entitled "A Report on the Sanitary State of the Labouring Classes, as Affected Chiefly by the Situation and Construction of their Dwellings, in and about the Metropolis." The second, dated 1842, is entitled "The Report of an Inquiry into the Sanitary Conditions of the Labouring Population of Great Britain."
4. G.M. Trevelyan, *Illustrated English Social History*, vol. 4 (London: Longmans, Green, 1952), 1.
5. *John Donne: Complete Poetry and Selected Prose*, ed. John Hayward (London: Nonesuch Press, 1945), 538.
6. Trevor Lloyd, "State Capitalism and Socialism: the Problem of Government Handouts." In Laurier LaPierre et al., eds., *Essays on the Left* (Toronto: McClelland and Stewart, 1971), 161–73.
7. The criteria for socialism, or for a socialist interpretation of the world, are more fully developed in chapter thirteen.
8. Sidney Webb, "The Basis of Socialism: Historic." In Bernard Shaw et al., *Fabian Essays in Socialism* (London: Allen and Unwin, Jubilee Edition, 1948), 43–54.
9. Ibid., 43–45.
10. Ibid., 45–46.

CHAPTER ELEVEN: THE LIBERAL MIND

1. The word "tory" provides a fascinating example of etymological evolution. Derived from an Irish word it was applied in the seventeenth century to the dispossessed Irish who were plundering the English settlers. From this it came to be applied to Irish Catholics in general. This was the excuse to use it as a label for those who opposed the exclusion of the Catholic James, Duke of York, from the succession to the Crown. Hence, when the major English parliamentary parties began to emerge, the descendants of the "anti-exclusionists" — the Cavaliers and Royalists — were called "Tories," by which route it came to be a label for royalist, monarchical, traditional parties in general. In the United States, those in the British party in the War of Independence were also called tories.
2. Elie Halévy, *The Growth of Philosophic Radicalism* (1928; reprint Boston: The Beacon Press, 1955).
3. H.K. Girvetz, *The Evolution of Liberalism* (New York: Collier Books, 1963), 23.

4. H.J. Laski, *The Rise of European Liberalism* (London: Allen and Unwin, 1936), 11. This book is highly recommended to the student wanting to know more of the origins of a liberal ideology. Note also C.B. Macpherson, *The Political Theory of Possessive Individualism* (Oxford: Clarendon Press, 1962).
5. Adam Smith, *Wealth of Nations* (Chicago: University of Chicago Press, 1976), 478.
6. H.J. Laski, *Rise of European Liberalism*, 15.
7. Ibid., 20.
8. Kenneth Minogue, *The Liberal Mind* (London: Methuen, 1962), 22.
9. Richard Hofstadter, *Social Darwinism in American Thought*, rev. ed. (Boston: The Beacon Press, 1955), 47–48.
10. William Townsend, "Dissertation on the Poor Laws, 1785." In E.H. Carr, *The New Society* (Boston: Beacon Hill, 1957), 42.

CHAPTER TWELVE: THE TORY TRADITION

1. Lord Hugh Cecil, *Conservatism* (London: Williams and Norgate, 1912), 9.
2. *Edmund Burke: Selected Writings and Speeches*, ed. Peter J. Stanlis (New York: Doubleday-Anchor Books, 1963), 263.
3. Ibid., 330–31.
4. As those without specialized training in philosophy will not find Bradley easy to follow, they should refer to Richard Wollheim, *F.H. Bradley* (Harmondsworth: Penguin Books, 1959).
5. Ibid., 247.
6. Russell Kirk, "Prescription, Authority, and Ordered Freedom." In Frank S. Meyer, ed., *What is Conservatism?* (New York: Holt, Rinehart, and Winston, 1964), 24.
7. Crane Brinton, *The Political Ideas of the English Romanticists* (Oxford: Oxford University Press, 1926; reprint Ann Arbor: University of Michigan Press, 1966), 73.
8. Ibid.
9. Thomas Jefferson, *Works*. vol. 4, 85–86.
10. Quoted by Robert L. Heilbroner, *The Worldly Philosophers* (New York: Simon and Schuster, 1972), 57–58.
11. Louis Hartz, *The Liberal Tradition in America* (New York, Harcourt, Brace, 1955); and *The Founding of New Societies* (New York: Harcourt, Brace, and World, 1966).
12. Gad Horowitz, "Conservatism, Liberalism, and Socialism in Canada: An Interpretation," *Canadian Journal of Economics and Political Science*, 32(2): (1966) 143–71.
13. Ibid., 148.
14. It is important to stress that this argument applies only to English Canada, for

in the Hartz-Horowitz thesis, Quebec, representing a different moment of departure, enshrines a pre-liberal political culture.

15. Horowitz, "Conservatism, Liberalism, and Socialism," 158.
16. Ibid., 158–59. For a brief commentary, and summary of criticisms of Hartz-Horowitz, see David Bell, "Political Culture in Canada." In M.S. Whittington and Glen Williams eds., *Canadian Politics in the 1980s* (Toronto: Methuen, 1981), 108–25.

CHAPTER THIRTEEN: THE SOCIALIST FAITH

1. Two useful introductory outlines to the varieties of socialist philosophies and movements are, Edmund Wilson, *To the Finland Station* (London: Secker and Warburg, 1941) and Alexander Gray, *The Socialist Tradition* (London: Longmans, 1946).
2. H. Blair Neatby, *The Politics of Chaos* (Toronto: Macmillan, 1972), 99.
3. Under other names, and with variations in detail, the Fabian conception of socialism is reflected in other democratic socialist movements, particularly those in the English-speaking world. In continental Europe the primary exponent of evolutionary socialism was Eduard Bernstein (1850–1932), who shared with the Fabians a disbelief in the effectiveness of revolution as an instrument of social progress. The name *Fabian* was adopted from an obscure and rather far-fetched allusion to a Roman general, Fabius Cunctatus.
4. Edward Pease, *The History of the Fabian Society* (London: Fifield, 1916), 32.
5. Graham Wallas, "Property Under Socialism," *Fabian Essays in Socialism* (London: Allen and Unwin, 1889), 139.
6. Alexander Gray, *The Socialist Tradition* (London: Longmans, 1946), 400.
7. It is ironic that when, in 1981, a group of disillusioned members broke away from the British Labour party to form the new Social Democratic party, they were formally expelled from the Fabian Society. Although in attitudes and values the most Fabian of British politicians, they could not remain in a society that specified "eligible to be a member of the Labour Party" as a condition of membership.
8. T.H. Qualter, *Graham Wallas and the Great Society* (London: Macmillan, 1980), 31–35.
9. Ibid., 34.
10. Gad Horowitz, "Conservatism, Liberalism, and Socialism in Canada: An Interpretation," *Canadian Journal of Economics and Political Science*, 32(2): (1966) 159.
11. Ivan Avakumovic, *Socialism in Canada* (Toronto: McClelland and Stewart, 1978).
12. "Class" is variously defined, but common to all definitions are some notions of large, more or less permanent groups, identified by the social relationships involved in the means of producing a livelihood. Classes reflect arrangements

of producers, owners, and consumers. Necessary to any class analysis is the idea that one class will be in a position to appropriate the labour of another.

13. Karl Marx, "Economic and Philosophic Manuscripts." In T.D. Bottomore ed., *Karl Marx: Early Writings* (New York: McGraw-Hill, 1964), 124.
14. Composed in 1915 by Ralph Chaplin, poet, writer, and organizer for the Industrial Workers of the World. It is unfortunate that most of those who attempt this song in some labour demonstration can manage no more than a few ragged words from the chorus.
15. David Owen, *Face the Future* (Oxford: Oxford University Press, 1981), 4.
16. *The Basis of Fabian Socialism* in Pease, *History of the Fabian Society*, 269.
17. Hubert Bland, "The Outlook." In G.B. Shaw et al., *Fabian Essays in Socialism* (London: Allen and Unwin, 1889 — and since reissued many times), 198.
18. R. Kelf-Cohen, *Nationalisation in Britain* (London: Macmillan, 1961), x.
19. *Co-operative Commonwealth Federation Programme*, adopted at the first National Convention, held at Regina, Saskatchewan, July 1933. This is what later came to be known as the *Regina Manifesto*.
20. See chapter six.
21. E.H. Carr, *The New Society* (London: Macmillan, 1951; reprint Boston: Beacon Press, 1957), 109.
22. Sidney Webb, "The Basis of Socialism — Historic." In G.B. Shaw et. al., *Fabian Essays in Socialism* (London: Allen and Unwin, 1889), 32.

CHAPTER FOURTEEN: THE DEMOCRATIC IDEOLOGY

1. "Attitude" is a more useful word than "opinion," for opinion carries the notion of expression. Our attitudes are what we "really" think or feel. Our opinions are what we say we think or feel, which may not always be the same thing.
2. There is an enormous literature on the nature of attitudes, but as an excellent introduction see Milton Rokeach, *Beliefs, Attitudes, and Values* (San Francisco: Jossey-Bass, 1968).
3. R.E. Lane, *Political Ideology* (New York: Free Press, 1962), 425–26. Note also L.P. Baradat, *Political Ideologies: Their Origins and Impact* (Englewood Cliffs: Prentice-Hall, 1979).
4. Thucydides, *The History of the Peloponnesian War*, trans. R. Crawley (London: Everyman Edition, 1945), 94.
5. Winston Churchill, *A Roving Commission: My Early Life* (New York: Scribner, 1935), 65.
6. Barry Holden, *The Nature of Democracy* (London: Nelson, 1974), 2.
7. Giovanni Sartori, *Democratic Theory* (New York: Praeger, 1965), 9.
8. C.B. Macpherson, *The Real World of Democracy* (Toronto: Canadian Broadcasting Corporation, 1965), for a detailed expansion on these alternative versions.

288 / NOTES

9. H.J. Laski, *The Rise of European Liberalism* (London: Unwin, 1936), for an excellent description of the character of liberalism.
10. The following paragraphs are freely adapted from T.H. Qualter, *Opinion Control in the Democracies* (London: Macmillan, 1985), chap. 10.
11. William A. Mackinnon, *On the Rise, Progress, and Present State of Public Opinion in Great Britain and Other Parts of the World* (London: Saunders and Otley, 1828), 15.
12. As Locke expressed it in the formative years of liberalism: "Political power, then, I take to be the right of making laws . . . for the regulating and preserving of property," *Second Treatise on Civil Government* (London: Dent, Everyman Edition, 1943), sec. 3.
13. C.B. Macpherson, *The Life and Times of Liberal Democracy* (Oxford: Oxford University Press, 1977), 44–76.
14. Ibid., 77.
15. See, as typical of this approach, B.R. Berelson et al., *Voting* (Chicago: University of Chicago Press, 1954).
16. See R.A. Dahl, *Preface to Democratic Theory* (Chicago: University of Chicago Press, 1956) for an analysis of this conception of democracy, not only as a description of how the American political system works, but as a justification of it as a successful system.
17. Adapted from Sidney Verba and N.H. Nie, *Participation in America* (New York: Harper and Row, 1972), 2.
18. G.A. Almond and Sidney Verba, *The Civic Culture* (Boston: Little, Brown, 1965). Almond and Verba refer to the participatory model as the "rational-activist" model.
19. David Leigh, *Frontiers of Secrecy* (London: Junction Books, 1980).
20. A.D. Lindsay, *The Essentials of Democracy* (London: Oxford University Press, 1945), 59.
21. This had been a key element in the program of the Chartist Movement in mid-nineteenth century England.
22. M.O. Dickerson and Thomas Flanagan, *An Introduction to Government and Politics* (Toronto: Methuen, 1982), 54.

Index